The Pictorial History of
WORLD
WAR I

The Pictorial History of
WORLD WAR I

G D Sheffield

Bison Books

Published by
Bison Books Ltd
176 Old Brompton Road
London SW5 0BA

ISBN 0 86124 386 2

Printed in Hong Kong

To My Parents

PAGE 1: *Armed with grenade
launchers, US troops look over toward
German positions near Mulhouse,
June 1918.*

PAGES 2-3: *Entitled* The Last Flight
of Captain Ball, *this painting by
Norman Arnold depicts the British
ace's SE5 engaged in fatal combat
with German Albatros fighters.*

PAGES 4-5: *German troops establish a
defensive position in a newly formed
mine crater.*

Contents

Introduction

Leon Trotsky once wrote that 'war is the locomotive of history,' and World War I bears witness to the truth of this statement. Consider the world on the eve of war in 1914. Europe was the undisputed political center of the world; the USA was a peripheral state with little influence among the Great Powers. Much of Europe was dominated by empires ruled over by hereditary monarchs. Ireland, Poland and Czechoslovakia did not exist as even nominally independent states. Millions of Africans and Asians were ruled from Paris and London; and Britain could automatically assume that Australia, Canada and New Zealand would follow any lead that the 'Old Country' gave. No state was ruled by a government claiming to derive its philosophy from Karl Marx; Lenin was an obscure revolutionary in exile from his homeland. In Britain, the average weekly wage of the agricultural laborer was a mere 17s. 6d. (87½p, then equivalent to $3.50); women, and part of the working classes, were excluded from the franchise. Blériot had flown a primitive aircraft across the English Channel just four years previously.

Four short years later, much had changed. The Austro-Hungarian Empire had collapsed, to be replaced by a series of successor states, including Czechoslovakia. Imperial Germany was wracked by revolution and emerged as an unstable democratic republic. The Ottoman Empire spawned modern Turkey and fresh territories for the British and French empires. Czarist Russia became the Union of Soviet Socialist Republics, the world's first 'workers and peasants' state ruled by the erstwhile refugee Lenin. Britain's white Dominions had grown to nationhood during the war; they were shortly to be joined by an independent Ireland. The USA had flexed its muscles on the world stage and could never again be ignored. Economically and strategically, France and Britain had been fatally undermined and within a generation their colonial empires would begin to crumble. In Britain, the working man was, in real terms, better off than ever before, and the franchise now included all adults. The motor vehicle was firmly established and in 1919, Alcock and Brown were to fly across the Atlantic in a Vickers Vimy bomber.

Seventy years on, World War I is still a living issue. Pétain and Haig are still controversial figures, to some heroes, to others villains. A British television series about the Etaples mutiny of 1917 caused a heated political debate 69 years after the events it portrayed. The Western Front still casts its shadow across the collective folk memory of nations. The name 'Verdun' causes the Frenchman mentally to shudder; the names 'Passchendaele' and 'Argonne' have the same effect on the Briton and American respectively. For a German or a Russian the case is a little different, for their huge casualties of 1914-18 were exceeded by their casualties in 1941-45, but that war was the direct product of its terrible ancestor fought just two decades previously.

World War I was the first 'total' war, and a total war deserves total history. However, in a book of this length, to attempt to cover every topic in depth is impossible. Thus this book makes no apology for concentrating on the military history of the war; too often, discussion of history deals with the 'causes' and 'consequences' of wars, ignoring the course of conflicts. This history highlights certain themes within the war. Tactical developments on the Western Front were crucial, but little mentioned in most popular histories. Also, armies are not monolithic organizations, but collections of individuals and units. The character of armies can have an important influence on combat, and so a recurring theme in this book is the evolving nature of the armies of 1914-18. Equally, the importance of morale is stressed, for it was the collapse of the German will to resist that ended the war.

Inevitably, a book of this kind is in large part a synthesis of the work of others. Some of the most important recent works in the field, and a few older ones, are mentioned in the select bibliography.

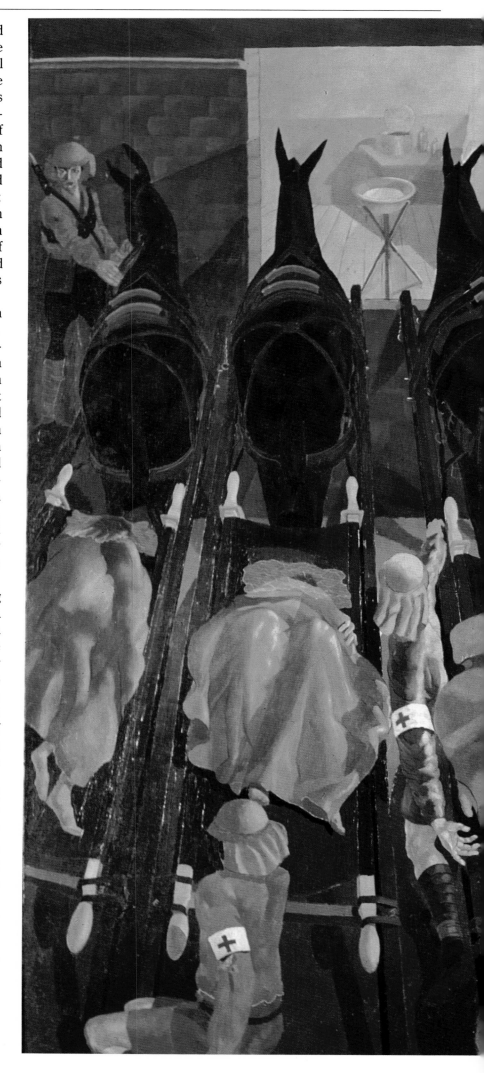

BELOW: *Sir Stanley Spencer's painting entitled* Wounded at a Dressing-Station at Smol, Macedonia, September 1916. *During September 1916 British troops were involved in an unsuccessful Allied offensive against the Bulgarian Army, as part of an attempt to break out from the bridgehead around Salonika. Spencer shows the steady stream of wounded passing through the dressing station on the Doiran-Vardar sector of the front line.*

1914

The Guns of August

Chronology 1871-1914

1871	Franco-Prussian War ends with the defeat of France
	German Empire proclaimed
1882	Triple Alliance signed between Austria-Hungary, Germany and Italy
1888	Wilhelm II ascends German throne
1892	Franco-Russian alliance
1904	*Entente Cordiale* between Britain and France
1914	
June 28	Archduke Franz Ferdinand assassinated at Sarajevo
July 5	Germany gives Austria a 'blank check' of unqualified support
July 28	Austria declares war on Serbia
July 30	Austria and Russia order mobilization
August 1	Germany declares war on Russia Germany and France begin to mobilize
August 3	Germany violates Belgian neutrality and declares war on France
August 4	Britain declares war on Germany
August 14	The Battle of the Frontiers begins
August 23	Mons
August 26	Le Cateau
August 29	Guise
August 30	Tannenberg
September 3	Lemberg
September 6-11	Marne
September 13-25	Aisne
September 19	First battle of Ypres begins
November 1	Turkey enters the war. Battle of Coronel
November 18-25	Lodz
December 6	Austrians defeated in Serbia
December 8	Battle of the Falkland Islands

The armored cruiser Scharnhorst *of Vice-Admiral von Spee's crack East Asiatic Squadron at Cape Coronel, 1 November 1914. Hopelessly outclassed, the elderly British cruisers* Good Hope *and* Monmouth *were quickly sunk. The German success was short-lived, however, for a British force of battlecruisers trapped von Spee's Squadron off the Falkland Islands on 8 December. The British battlecruisers sent all the German vessels to the bottom, with the exception of one light cruiser which was caught and sunk a few months later.*

The Origins of the War

The first shots of World War I were fired in the Bosnian town of Sarajevo on 28 June 1914. Archduke Franz Ferdinand, the heir to the thrones of the Dual Monarchy of Austria-Hungary, was murdered along with his wife by Gavrilo Princip, a young Serb nationalist. These deaths led to the first general European war since 1815. In 1914, Austria-Hungary was in decline as a Great Power. In the previous 60 years, she had been excluded from her traditional spheres of influence in Germany and Italy by the rise of the new nation states. Consequently, by the turn of the twentieth century, Austrian attention was focused on the Balkans. There, the small state of Serbia, had, under Russian protection, increased in size and power as a result of the Balkan Wars of 1912-13, and acted as a stimulus for the growth of nationalism among the ethnic Serbs within the heterogeneous Hapsburg empire – a tendency which Vienna feared could ultimately lead to the disintegration of Emperor Franz Josef's domains. The assassinations in Bosnia – which had only been formally annexed to Austria-Hungary in 1908 – were seen as an insolent Serbian challenge which could not go unanswered. Assured of German support on 5 July, Austria issued an ultimatum on 23 July, which would have virtually reduced Serbia to a satellite state. When the Serbians demurred, the Austrians declared war on 28 July.

Russia watched the developing crisis with concern. She regarded herself as the patron of Slavic peoples in the Balkans; any extension of Austrian influence in the region threatened her southern trade route via the Dardanelles. On 30 July, Russia mobilized. This the Germans could not ignore.

Bismarck, the German Chancellor from 1873 to 1890, had succeeded in maintaining a diplomatic balancing act, concluding the Triple Alliance with Austria and Italy but also (unbeknown to the Austrians) signing the 'Reinsurance Treaty' with Russia, and avoiding antagonizing Britain. Only France, whom Germany had stripped of the

provinces of Alsace and Lorraine in the wake of the 1870-71 war, remained an unreconcilable enemy. The accession of Kaiser Wilhelm II in 1888 was followed by a marked deterioration in Germany's diplomatic position. Wilhelm's bellicose *Weltpolitik* (World Policy) replaced the subtle and devious *Realpolitik* of Bismarck, who was sacked in 1890. The Reinsurance Treaty was not renewed, and in 1892, Bismarck's nightmare became cold reality. France and Russia signed an alliance, and Germany faced a future war on two fronts.

Wilhelm also effectively alienated Britain, who had previously been well disposed toward Germany. Growing economic and colonial rivalry clouded this relationship, but the biggest single factor was the rapid growth of the German navy. British policy was based on avoiding entangling alliances, and relying on the Royal Navy for its defense. Indeed, the Royal Navy was maintained at twice the combined strength of the two next largest navies (the so-called doctrine of the Two Power Standard). Wilhelm, and von Tirpitz, the Secretary of the Navy, determined to challenge British naval superiority; the German Navy Laws of 1898 and 1900 set in motion a dangerous arms race between the two powers. In 1906 the British made a bold move which rendered the bulk of its capital ships obsolete at a stroke: HMS *Dreadnought* was launched, the first 'all-big-gun' battleship, armed with ten 12-inch guns, heavily armored and some 4 knots faster than earlier ships. The spiral of the arms race continued upward, but, largely thanks to Sir John 'Jacky' Fisher (First Sea Lord from 1904 to 1910, and again from 1914 to 1915) and Winston Churchill (First Lord of the Admiralty from 1911 to 1915), the Royal Navy retained its lead. Largely as a result of this naval rivalry, a diplomatic revolution took place. In 1904, Britain and France, enemies for most of the nineteenth century, signed the *Entente Cordiale*, which was less than a treaty of alliance but which signified the abandonment of 'Splendid Isolation.' Three years later, Britain reached a similar agreement with another traditional foe, Russia. The division of Europe into two armed camps appeared complete.

Article 231 of the Treaty of Versailles of 1919 placed responsibility for the war firmly at the door of Germany. This view became discredited in the 1930s, when it was generally believed that the Great Powers, armed to the teeth, had slid into war through statesmen's blunders and miscalculations. Certainly, domestic politics, armaments and economic rivalry all played a part in creating the preconditions of

BELOW: *A French poster ordering general mobilization. Unlike the mobilization at the beginning of the Franco-Prussian War, 40 years previously, the French army mobilized* *relatively swiftly in 1914. Large numbers of native colonial troops were raised and brought to fight in Europe alongside the conscripts from the mother country.*

ABOVE LEFT: *The arrest of Gavrilo Princip, 28 June 1914, after the murder of Archduke Franz Ferdinand and his wife. These assassinations provided the catalyst which sparked off World War I.*
LEFT: *Mobilization in France. The outbreak of war brought a temporary truce between political and social factions in France, with men of all shades of opinion uniting against the common enemy, Imperial Germany, who had defeated and humiliated France in 1871.*
RIGHT: *Mobilization is announced in a German city. As in France and Britain, the outbreak of war was greeted with joy by huge crowds in the cities of Germany and Austria-Hungary. This phenomenon has been described by one historian as the 'community of August.'*

war, as did the general acceptance of 'Social Darwinism,' a bastardized form of the theory of the 'survival of the fittest' applied to international relations. Moreover, militarism, in the sense of excessive civilian enthusiasm for the military values and ideas was, in varying degrees, rife throughout Europe. Even liberal Britain was not exempt; the outbreak of war was greeted with outbursts of popular enthusiasm in all the European capitals. This was more than satisfaction at the prospect of conflict with a hated enemy; it was a celebration of war itself. Europe was perhaps ready for war – any war – in August 1914; the murders at Sarajevo merely provided the opportunity.

The cozy consensus of the interwar years was shattered in the 1960s. The German historian Fritz Fischer claimed that in 1914 Germany was prepared to go to war to achieve the status of a *Weltmacht,* or World Power. If they did not 'plan' the war, by issuing the 'blank check' of 5 July they encouraged the Austrians to move against Serbia even after it became clear that Russia would become involved. Fischer further suggested that, once at war, Germany rapidly developed war aims which reflected the prewar aspirations of some industrialists and extreme Pan-Germans for an economic zone

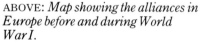

ABOVE: *Map showing the alliances in Europe before and during World War I.*

TOP LEFT: *Dreadnoughts and their escorting destroyers of the German Navy. The naval arms race between Germany and Britain drove Britain in to the arms of the Entente.*

LEFT: *A naval review for Wilhelm II of Germany. The German Navy League spread enthusiasm for a navy among the German population.*

RIGHT: *A rather flattering portrait of Kaiser Wilhelm II, which disguises his withered arm. Wilhelm's mother was English, and throughout his life he regarded the British with a curious mixture of admiration, envy and scorn. He was particularly jealous of his uncle, King Edward VII.*

dominated by Germany. *Mitteleuropa* would have included Belgium, parts of France and Russia and, ultimately, Austro-Hungarian territories. The implied continuity between Imperial foreign policy and that of Hitler's Third Reich caused a storm of controversy in Germany, and there are other objections to Fischer's thesis: the British Colonial Office, for example, began to think about the postwar distribution of a defeated Germany's colonies as early as 6 August 1914, and yet it would be unwise to suggest that Britain went to war primarily to enlarge her empire. Likewise, it could be argued, the outbreak of war suddenly presented the Germans with an opportunity of realizing plans that had previously been little more than pipe-dreams. However, Germany does appear to have welcomed the war in September 1914.

One person who bears a large measure of responsibility for the events of that month had died several years before. General Alfred Graf von Schlieffen, German Chief of Staff from 1891 to 1906, had formulated a plan to fight a war on two fronts. A token force would face the Russians, while the bulk of the German Army would crush the French before the slow-moving 'Russian Steamroller' could become effective. Schlieffen's Plan bequeathed two legacies to his successor, Moltke. Firstly, in order to outflank the French, neutral Belgium was invaded. This brought Britain into the war, not merely out of moral outrage (Britain had guaranteed Belgium neutrality in a treaty of 1839) but also because she could not allow the Belgian ports to fall into the hands of the German navy, or allow German ships into the English Channel. Secondly, speed was essential to the Schlieffen Plan. Germany had to respond rapidly to Russian mobilization because the only plan they had was Schlieffen's, and that also meant an attack on France. Germany inevitably faced a war on two fronts.

BUCKINGHAM PALACE

My message to the Troops of the Expeditionary Force. Aug. 12th 1914.

You are leaving home to fight for the safety and honour of my Empire.

Belgium, whose country we are pledged to defend, has been attacked and France is about to be invaded by the same powerful foe.

I have implicit confidence in you my soldiers. Duty is your watchword, and I know your duty will be nobly done.

I shall follow your every movement with deepest interest and mark with eager satisfaction your daily progress, indeed your welfare will never be absent from my thoughts.

I pray God to bless you and guard you and bring you back victorious.

LEFT: *King George V's message to the troops of the British Expeditionary Force, dated 12 August 1914. The BEF was described by the British Official Historian as being in every respect the finest army that Britain ever sent abroad. It was largely destroyed in the series of battles culminating in the First Battle of Ypres.*

BELOW LEFT: *German troops are given parcels of comforts before departing for the Front. The uniforms of the German soldier of 1914 were fairly elaborately decorated with braid and other distinguishing marks. They were to be greatly simplified in the course of the war.*

ABOVE: *Crowds celebrate the outbreak of war in the Odeonplatz, Munich, 2 August 1914. Circled is Adolf Hitler, then an obscure failed artist. He enlisted in a Bavarian unit and fought bravely, being awarded the Iron Cross twice. Technically he was an Austrian subject, but had moved to Germany to avoid being conscripted by the Hapsburg army.*

LEFT: *A crowd in Trafalgar Square cheering the Union Flag, August 1914. The outbreak of war was greeted with popular enthusiasm, and men of all classes enlisted as ordinary privates.*

The Armies of the Powers

For millions of reservists, the war began with an urgent summons to the regimental depot. In the years following the Franco-Prussian War, all the continental powers had adopted a form of universal conscription, whereby men served for two or three years with the Colors before returning to civilian life. Germany's field army included 82 infantry divisions; 31 of these were reserve formations. The French, despite a smaller population, were dubious about divisions composed entirely of reservists – only 25 were included in a field army of 73 divisions.

The French army of 1914 wore flamboyant uniforms (red trousers, blue coats, white gloves), apparently reflecting an outdated, Napoleonic addiction to the 'spirit of the bayonet.' Their gray-clad adversaries have been characterized as a ruthlessly efficient force, led by a thoroughly professional General Staff. In reality, the situation was more complex. Certainly, French military thought stressed the utmost importance of offensive action at both strategic and tactical levels, but in this, they were not unique. The British and the Germans both emphasized the offensive, and also the inculcation of moral qualities in the soldier to help him overcome the disadvantages of operating on the defensive. However, in its relative neglect of firepower, the French army, influenced by the teachings of Colonel Grandmaison, had adopted the doctrine of the all-out offensive in its most extreme form. Similarly, while it is true that the Germans had the best-trained and best-led continental army, its much-vaunted General Staff produced and presided over the Schlieffen Plan – a plan that failed as dismally as the oft-derided French Plan XVII. In the event, the phlegmatic French commander, Joffre, was to prove a greater asset than his neurotic German rival, Moltke.

BELOW LEFT: *Alfred Leete's famous recruiting poster. Lord Kitchener was appointed as Secretary of State for War in August 1914 and set out to raise a mass army of volunteers. Although a national hero, he did not fit easily into Asquith's Liberal government, being the only soldier in the cabinet.*
BELOW: *Generaloberst Helmuth von Moltke. From 1906 to November 1914, Moltke was the Chief of the German General Staff and de facto Commander in Chief. He was the nephew of the victor of 1866 and 1871, but lacked his uncle's drive and ruthlessness.*

BELOW LEFT: *The author of the Schlieffen Plan. According to legend, on his deathbed Alfred Graf von Schlieffen stressed the importance of keeping the right of the immense wheel strong. In fact, Moltke deviated from* the original plan. Hitler's original plan for the invasion of 1940 was largely based on Schlieffen's original but was modified to include a Blitzkrieg attack through the Ardennes.

BELOW: *A painting of a mock attack by mounted German cuirassiers and dragoons on peacetime maneuvers in 1913. The German cavalry stressed shock action over dismounted action, and proved inferior to the cavalry of the* BEF in both respects. Unlike the British, the Germans made little use of horsed cavalry in the West after 1914, although they were used on the Eastern Front.

LEFT: *A stylized depiction of German infantry on exercises. In 1914, Germany's army was probably the finest on the European mainland. The standard German infantry weapon was the bolt-action Mauser rifle. Here the infantrymen are deployed in skirmish order. Unlike the French, the Germans had abandoned brightly colored uniforms except for use on the parade ground. The German field gray uniforms served the same purpose as the British drab, or khaki, equivalent.*

ABOVE: *German infantry and cavalry on maneuvers in Silesia in 1913. Note the close formed lines and the troops entrenched in the foreground.*
RIGHT: *Volunteers waiting to enlist outside Whitehall Recruiting Office, London, in 1914. The numbers of men prepared to enlist dwindled in late 1914, and the British were forced to introduce conscription in 1916.*

Austria-Hungary contributed 74 infantry divisions to the Central Powers' order of battle. Only one-quarter of the army's personnel were ethnic Hungarians, and even fewer were Germans; the majority were Czechs, Slavs and Italians, including, for example, the future leader of Yugoslavia, Josip Broz (Tito). This lack of homogeneity – compounded by the division of the reserve forces into the Hungarian *Honved* and the German *Landwehr* – posed a question about the political reliability of the army. The Russians also had their problems. The Russian Army (of 85 infantry and cavalry divisions, 35 reserve divisions and a large militia) was numerous but badly organized. Like the rest of Europe, the Russians had planned for a short war, and this belief led to the chronic shortage of munitions and weapons at the end of 1914, when the initial stockpile had been exhausted. Czarist Russia was a backward state, but was rapidly modernizing; had the war begun even five years later, the army would have been a very different force.

The British army of 1914 differed in two essentials from its continental counterparts. It was small, being primarily intended to police the Empire; and it was raised from volunteers, not conscripts. The four (later six) divisions of the British Expeditionary Force (BEF), relied heavily on individual reservists to bring them up to war establishment; up to 60 percent in some battalions were time-expired men. While there were no reserve units on the European model, by November 1914 units of the Territorial Force – battalions of part-time volunteers, originally recruited for Home Defense duties – were reaching the front. The Boer War had had a salutary effect. By 1914 the marksmanship of the infantry had reached an extremely high standard, and the cavalry proved themselves to be more effective than either the French or the Germans. The 'Contemptible Little Army' (as the Kaiser is alleged to have called it) was, man for man, the most efficient in Europe.

LEFT: *General Sukhomlinov, the Russian Minister of War. France and Britain had great expectations of the 'Russian Steamroller,' but the army's performance was hampered by a chaotic supply system, and the Russian invasion of East Prussia was defeated.*
RIGHT: *'Papa' Joffre, the French Commander in Chief, photographed at GQG in May 1916.*

The Battle of the Frontiers

The French and German armies marched in accordance with rigid plans, both of which ended in failure. Plan XVII reflected the French obsession with the offensive and involved a lunge into Alsace-Lorraine with two armies. The Schlieffen Plan was also the consequence of an obsession: the German obsession with the Carthaginian victory of Cannae, in 216 BC. Some 1½ million men were to attempt to repeat this battle of envelopment on a grand scale. Five armies were to skirt around the French frontier defenses, by wheeling through Belgium, and then pass to the west of Paris and encircle the French forces. Two armies would remain on the defensive, acting as a pivot for the other five. The problems of supplying the wheeling forces were enormous; indeed, had not Moltke significantly modified it, the Schlieffen Plan would probably have proved unworkable on logistic grounds alone.

The war began with a German attack on the fortress of Liège. The Belgian fortresses had to be taken, or at least masked, without delay, in order to allow the main force to advance unmolested. The first assault, on 5 August, failed, but a Major General Erich Ludendorff established his reputation by rallying the broken troops and capturing the town on the following day. The fortress held out for a further 10 days. The staunch defense of Liège and other Belgian fortresses delayed the beginning of the great wheel until 18 August.

After some preliminary skirmishing, Plan XVII had begun in earnest on 12 August. Dubail's First Army and de Castelnau's Second Army advanced into Lorraine, where they encountered the German Sixth and Seventh Armies (under Kronprinz Rupprecht of Bavaria and von Heeringen); with Moltke's tacit approval, their defensive role – one of

the fundamental tenets of the original Schlieffen Plan – was abandoned. The French were defeated at the battles of Morhange and Sarrebourg on 20 August, and the Germans advanced toward the frontier. Belatedly, the French discovered that *élan* was less effective than carefully sited machine guns and well-co-ordinated artillery support. Their battles also brought some problems to OHL (Oberste Heeresleitung, or German Supreme Headquarters). Rupprecht's armies were too small to defeat the French right decisively, especially as the French were falling back on their frontier defenses (which the Schlieffen Plan had been designed to avoid). Worse, Moltke's attention was deflected from Belgium at the very moment that the decisive battle on the right was developing.

The small Belgian field army had fallen back into the fortress of Antwerp after fighting on the River Gette on 20 August; the Germans were forced to weaken their right wing by detaching two corps to guard the flank of von Kluck's First Army against a possible sally. On the same day Brussels fell; a trail of burned villages and executed civilians marked the advance of the German army. *Schrecklichkeit* (translated by the British as 'Frightfulness') was to characterize the German counterinsurgency technique down to 1945.

Joffre was unperturbed by the defeats of Morhange and Sarrebourg. On 21 August he ordered Third and Fourth Armies to attack into the Ardennes. GQG (Grand Quartier Général, or French General Headquarters) had attributed to the Germans their own disdain for reservists, and thus underestimated enemy strength by one-third. With minimal reconnaissance, the French attacked this supposedly weak spot in the German line, and were beaten in a series of confused

PREVIOUS PAGES: *Belgian troops at the defense of Liège. This picture typifies the romantic view commonly held in Britain of 'gallant little Belgium.' The Belgian army acquitted itself well in the early stages of the Battle of the Frontiers, and again in 1918.*

BELOW LEFT: *The German advance: artillery moving through a French village, 35 miles from Paris, watched by sullen French civilians.*
RIGHT: *Three French generals: Joffre (left), Langle de Cary (center, Fourth Army) and Guillaumat. The latter was proposed as a successor to Pétain during the crisis caused by the German Spring Offensive of 1918.*
BELOW: *Belgian infantry during the Battle of Halsine, August 1914, armed with the Belgian 7.65mm Mauser M1889 rifle. In 1915 they adopted a khaki uniform.*

LEFT: *French dead lie slumped in a hastily prepared position. The rigid adherence to Plan XVII in August sentenced the French army to heavy casualties. When war once again broke out in 1939, however, the French were wedded to a defensive outlook – in part, a direct consequence of the offensive disasters of World War I. The uniforms shown here were later changed to 'horizon blue.'*

BELOW RIGHT: *German medical orderlies collect wounded men at night. Alongside them are dead French zouves, distinctive in their 'Turkish'-style uniforms.*
BELOW: *A French village is burned and its inhabitants massacred. Civilian guerrillas, or 'Francs Tireurs,' were dealt with harshly by the advancing Germans. The Belgian city of Louvain was sacked, a callous act not calculated to win over neutral opinion.*

encounter battles on the 21st and 22nd. The terrain in the Ardennes is in some places broken (if not quite the 'trackless waste' it has sometimes been portrayed) and communications between French columns proved difficult to maintain. Individual units fought well but the French were soundly defeated and suffered heavy casualties; 3rd Colonial Division, for example, sustained 11,000 casualties out of 17,000. GQG had no alternative after the battles of Virton and Semois but to permit Third and Fourth Armies to retire behind the Meuse.

As the First, Second and Third Armies crossed into France on 20 August the Germans were presented with the opportunity of inflicting a decisive defeat on Lanrezac's French Fifth Army. Lanrezac's flank was exposed by the retreat of the Third and Fourth Armies, leaving him open to an eastward attack by von Hausen's Third (Saxon) Army, while von Bülow's Second Army pinned him with a frontier assault and von Kluck marched around his flank. Unfortunately, there was no one to co-ordinate these attacks. Almost 200 miles away in Coblenz, Moltke's attention was fixed on Alsace. Had an Army Group commander been appointed, these problems could have been overcome. As a poor compromise, Kluck was placed under Bülow's command; the latter cautiously refused to allow Kluck to execute a wide turning movement and the First Army was allotted a mere supporting role.

The resulting battle of the Sambre (21-23 August) was a German victory, but far from the decisive one that could have been obtained. French attacks were beaten off, with heavy casualties, but German assaults were badly co-ordinated. Bülow attacked a full day earlier than Hausen; when the Third Army began to cross the Meuse on the 23rd, Lanrezac had already been pushed to the south, and the flank attack was wasted. On the same day, to the west, Kluck had blundered into the BEF, much to Kluck's surprise, as he had only the vaguest idea as to the whereabouts of the British. In fact, Smith-Dorrien's II Corps (3rd and 5th Divisions, with Cavalry Division in reserve) were positioned along the Mons-Condé Canal, deployed in shallow trenches. The Germans, advancing in close columns, were shattered by the accurate and rapid British rifle fire. According to venerable tradition, the Germans believed each British battalion was equipped with 28 machine guns; in fact, they possessed two. The British

casualties – 1600 – were comparatively small, and certainly Mons only briefly checked Kluck's advance; yet it made a tremendous impact in Britain. For the first time since Waterloo, British blood had been shed in Europe and recruits for the New Armies began to pour in.

In the north, as Lanrezac and Sir John French (the British Commander in Chief) retreated, the Germans appeared poised for victory, but in the south, the attempt to envelop the French right by the Sixth and Seventh Armies failed. After a costly attack on Nancy, on 9 September, Moltke ordered a retreat to the starting lines of 17 August. Kronprinz Wilhelm (Fifth Army) was also forced to retire after he was counterattacked by the French Third Army. Moreover, the German right wing armies were approaching exhaustion; Kluck's men had marched 340 kilometers by 23 August. The BEF and Lanrezac's men were also suffering, covering 30 miles a day in retreat, but they were falling back on their bases, while the Germans were advancing away from theirs. Contrary to expectation, the Allied armies were still intact. At Le Cateau on 26 August, Smith-Dorrien again stopped Kluck in his tracks long enough to allow II Corps to escape; and in the battle of Guise on 29 August Lanrezac attacked Bülow in the flank and then retired. Bülow stopped to lick his wounds for two days.

For both the defenders and the invaders, it was a time of crisis. Only the personal intervention of Lord Kitchener, the British Secretary of State for War, dissuaded Sir John French from pulling the BEF back to St Nazaire to recuperate. Joffre replaced Lanrezac with Franchet d'Esperey, one of the Fifth Army's Corps commanders; Anglo-French relations improved as a result. On 25 August, Joffre effectively abandoned Plan XVII, pulling back the French center and right, and forming a new Sixth Army on the BEF's left. The Germans too, made drastic alterations to their plan. Two Corps were sent to East Prussia in the wake of the early German setback at Gumbinnen; and Kluck, believing the French Fifth Army and BEF were defeated, decided to wheel and pass to the east rather than to the west of Paris in order to harry the 'broken' Allied forces. In doing so, Kluck exposed his flank to a counterstroke from Paris. On 3 September, Allied aircraft spotted this maneuver. Orders were issued and what the British called the 'Retreat from Mons' came to an end.

The Battle of the Marne

The first man to perceive the tremendous opportunity presented to the Allies by Kluck's inward wheel was Galliéni, the Military Governor of Paris. Galliéni ordered Maunoury's Sixth Army forward on 4 September, thus anticipating Joffre's orders for a general advance on the 6th. The French generals were thinking along approximately the same lines. On the German side, all was confusion. Moltke had finally abandoned the Schlieffen Plan, and was, instead, seeking to achieve a small double envelopment in Lorraine. The three westernmost armies were strung out in echelon, marching southeast, but Kluck at first ignored his designated role as flankguard. Even after further sharp instructions arrived from OHL, he was tardy in obeying his orders; the First Army was still redeploying when the French attack began.

For the ordinary *poilu* and 'Tommy,' the first news of the Battle of the Marne came simply as an order to halt – and then to advance back along the road they had been retreating along. The battle began on 5 September, ahead of schedule, when Maunoury brushed against IV Reserve Corps, Kluck's flankguard. On the following day the French Fifth and Sixth Armies and the BEF advanced to envelop Kluck and Bülow. Foch's newly created Ninth Army guarded d'Esperey's flank, and the Fourth and Third Armies were to attack at Verdun.

Kluck soon found himself under severe pressure. Finding himself attacked from both the west and the south he attempted to crush Maunoury by transferring corps to his right wing. In doing so, he was operating within his orders to act as a flankguard, and was also meting out fearful punishment to Maunoury – on the 7th, reinforcements were dispatched from Paris in a fleet of taxicabs – but Kluck also opened up a gap between his First Army and Bülow's Second, which was filled only by four cavalry divisions and some Jäger (Rifle) battalions. Into this gap advanced the French Fifth Army and the BEF.

The sudden reappearance of the BEF – which had been assumed by the Germans to have been routed – came as a profound shock to Moltke. In spite of the success of the Third Army in defeating a foolish attack by Foch in the marshes of St Gond, and Kluck's unrelenting pressure on Maunoury, Bülow's position appeared to be critical. There was nothing available to plug the gap and prevent the BEF from separating the two armies. Moltke's control over the battle was now slight, and he was beginning to panic. On 8 September, Colonel Hentsch, his Intelligence Officer, was sent out from OHL to visit Bülow. Hentsch found him in a poor state of morale. It was agreed that the Second Army should fall back to the northeast if the Allies managed to cross the Marne.

The BEF had continued to retreat for 24 hours after the general halt order was issued, thanks to confusion between GQG and GHQ (General Headquarters). Its advance was perhaps the most important action on the Marne, although not because of the speed of the BEF's march, which was conducted at a snail's pace: about eight miles a day, as opposed to the 30 miles achieved on the retreat. Rather, it was the impact on Moltke's morale that led him to send out Hentsch with wide discretionary powers to order a retreat if he thought fit. When the BEF crossed the Marne at La Ferté sous Jouarre on the 9th, it was enough to trigger off Bülow's retreat, which began at midday; Kluck was forced to fall back in step with Bülow. Moltke, overwhelmed by a sense of responsibility and guilt, suffered something approaching a nervous breakdown. He was replaced on 13 September by General Erich von Falkenhayn, the Minister of War. By that date the Germans had fallen back to the River Aisne. The Allies had achieved a strategic victory, but, as the fighting on the Aisne was to show, the Germans were far from beaten. The Battle of the Marne had been lost in the mind of Moltke, not in fighting on the ground. Nonetheless, it was a turning point in the war. The attempt to defeat France by a knock-out blow had failed. the entire basis of prewar German strategy had crumbled; Germany was now committed to a two-front war.

ABOVE: *General Galliéni, the Military Governor of Paris, who urged Maunoury's Sixth Army forward to protect Paris. He had served in the war of 1870 and rose to become Governor of Madagascar in 1896, and at one stage had been Joffre's superior. He became Minister of War in 1915, but resigned in 1916 because of a dispute with his civilian colleagues.*

RIGHT: Les Invalides, *Paris. Civilian cars were requisitioned to take reinforcements to the Front during the Battle of the Marne.*
BELOW RIGHT: *Belgian carabiniers with dogs drawing machine guns retreating to Antwerp, 8 August 1914.*
BELOW: *German 7.7cm field gun, model 96N/A, of 5th Field Artillery Regiment. A fine study of men on campaign.*

The Battle of the Aisne saw the embryonic beginnings of trench warfare. The Germans held a ridge, rising above the river; it was impossible to outflank, except by a wide turning movement, for which the Allies had no troops available. Nevertheless, the Allies almost punched through this position. The British, who crossed the river at Venizel on 13 September, were marching straight into a 10-mile gap between Kluck and Bülow. Only the fortuitous arrival on the Chemin des Dames of VII Reserve Corps, which had force-marched 40 miles in the previous 24 hours, prevented the British from breaking through: VII Reserve Corps had only been released by the fall of Maubeuge on 8 September. Both sides began to fight from holes in the ground – a far cry from the developed trench systems of 12 months later – but it was enough to reduce the battle to stalemate.

Falkenhayn attempted to regain the initiative with a suitably modified version of the Schlieffen Plan, moving troops to his right wing and attempting to outflank the Allies. Joffre responded in kind, thus was born what became known as the 'Race to the Sea,' which was in reality a mutual attempt at outflanking by extending northward – a race which was continued until both sides reached the sea. Ferdinand Foch, who had begun the war as a corps commander, was appointed as a *de facto* Army Group commander in the north to co-ordinate the Allied forces in the area, which included the BEF (which had begun transferring from the Aisne on 1 October) and the Belgian Field Army. The latter force, personnally commanded by King Albert, had made a notable contribution to the Allied effort in tying down a force of six divisions in besieging Antwerp and then breaking out. The hastily formed Royal Naval Division (RND), which included two brigades of raw recruits, had been landed to defend Antwerp, which fell on 10 October. Some 1600 men were captured, and 1500 interned in neutral Holland. The RND, which was at one stage accompanied by Winston Churchill, First Lord of the Admiralty, delayed the fall of Antwerp for perhaps five days. As Liddell Hart argued, the defense of Antwerp placed a brake on the German advance at a crucial moment; and the Allies were given time to regroup in Flanders. The Germans had had their share of good fortune on the Aisne; if Ypres was to be held the Allies were to need rather more than mere luck.

RIGHT: *A German cartoon depicting the Kaiser ('Kaiser Bill' to the British) speeding toward Paris in his motor car, with the winged figure of victory perched alongside. Although in theory Germany's supreme warlord, Wilhelm had little influence on the 1914 campaign, and in later years was pushed aside by Ludendorff and Hindenburg. His son, Kronprinz Wilhelm (Little Willie) commanded an army, and later an army group in the West.*

ABOVE: *General von Kluck, who led the German First Army at the Battle of the Marne. Kluck saw the possibility of being cut off from Bülow's Second Army and turned east to regain contact with the outer flank of Bülow's army.*

BELOW: *An idealized painting of German infantry storming an enemy position, 1914.*

Zeichnung von F. Jüttner

Victoria!!

The First Battle of Ypres

The first Battle of Ypres (or 'Ee-pris' to the British regulars) was the consequence of the last spasm of the Race to the Sea. The BEF arrived in Flanders during 10-13 October, and immediately advanced to outflank the advancing Germans. The appearance of Rupprecht's Sixth Army from Lorraine by 19 October forced the BEF back, and the struggle for Ypres began. Ypres was the key to the Western Front; if the Germans could occupy it, they could cut off the BEF from the Channel ports and roll up the Allied line. Thus it was as important for the British to hold Ypres as it was for the Germans to take it. The ensuing struggle was to be bitter in the extreme.

The offensive began on 17 October with an attempt to break through on a wide front from the sea to the La Bassée Canal. The Germans deployed eight divisions of fresh troops, 75 percent of which were enthusiastic, but poorly trained volunteers, mostly university students under the age of 20. The BEF, defending the Ypres sector, succeeded in repulsing the German assaults, aided by the arrival of Haig's Corps from the Aisne on 20 October. Further north, the Belgians only managed to hold their line by flooding the coastal sector at Nieuport. The enthusiastic young volunteers sustained heavy losses; the Germans called this battle the *Kindermord von Ypres*, the Massacre of the Innocents at Ypres. Germany could ill-afford the wastage of such prime officer material.

The fighting at Ypres was a mixture of the old and the new, of open warfare and trench fighting. The future Field-Marshal Montgomery, then a subaltern in the Royal Warwicks, even led an attack on 13 October with a drawn sword. Another reminder of an older style of warfare came with the arrival in Flanders of the Kaiser, who intended to make a triumphal entry into Ypres. The BEF was to deny him his ambition – but only just. Seven German divisions, supported by heavy artillery, attacked on a narrow front between Messines and Gheluvelt on 31 October. At the latter place the British line gave way and the road to Ypres appeared to be open. There was a delay in bringing up reserves to exploit the gap, and a hastily mounted counterattack by 360 men of 2nd Worcestershires (all that remained of a battalion with a nominal roll of 1100) pushed the enemy back and halted the German attack. Further south, Allenby's dismounted cavalrymen were forced off Messines Ridge in a battle in which a Territorial infantry battalion, 1/14th Londons (London Scottish), first saw action. The 'ridges' of Flanders were not physically impressive; none was more than 180 feet high, but in a war dominated by artillery, the slightest rise was invaluable for observation. The British did not recapture Messines Ridge until 1917.

ABOVE: *German machine gunners in a trench near Antwerp. The machine gun is a 7.92mm caliber MG08, which could fire 300 rounds per minute.*
BELOW LEFT: *Men of 1st Cameronians, Houplines, 19 December 1914. The soldiers are wearing cap comforters in place of the usual cap.*
RIGHT: *Congestion in Thielt marketplace, 12/13 October 1914. The transport of 2nd Scots Guards, 7th Division, is passing through the square. This division was formed from regular battalions withdrawn from garrison duty in the Empire.*

LEFT: *German volunteer troops at Langemarck during the First Battle of Ypres. In prewar Germany, students were allowed to defer their military service. When war broke out, large numbers of students volunteered and, despite their lack of training, were sent into battle at the end of 1914.*

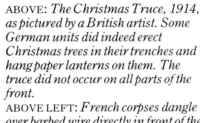

ABOVE: *The Christmas Truce, 1914, as pictured by a British artist. Some German units did indeed erect Christmas trees in their trenches and hang paper lanterns on them. The truce did not occur on all parts of the front.*
ABOVE LEFT: *French corpses dangle over barbed wire directly in front of the German trench line, complete with rifle embrasures. The Christmas decorations indicate the time of year. In the winter of 1914, barbed wire defenses were usually much less elaborate than this, consisting of perhaps a few strands of wire.*
FAR LEFT: *German Guard infantry advancing under heavy shellfire. They wear the standard M.1910 uniform, with the addition of red piping on the cuffs and the collar. Prussian Guard units attacking along the Menin Road on 11 November were described as looking like 'grey ghosts coming down out of the clouds.'*
LEFT: *British and German soldiers fraternizing at Ploegsteert (Plugstreet) on Christmas Day 1914. The truce was not repeated in 1915, although informal truces for the collection of wounded were common.*

The final German attack was launched on 11 November. Despite being reinforced by the Indian Corps (of two divisions), the British line was pierced by a Prussian Guard division north of the Menin Road. Ahead of the Prussians were the British guns and Divisional Head-quarters; nothing else. Having lost heavily in the advance, the attackers lost cohesion and halted. This allowed the British to impro-vise a makeshift counterattack, launched by cooks, batmen, and anyone else who could carry a rifle. The *coup de grâce* was delivered by 2nd Oxfordshire Light Infantry.

By 22 November the battle was over. The Allied line (by the end of the battle, more French than British were fighting in Flanders) was unbroken. The German plan had failed; they were faced with the prospect of fighting a war on two fronts. Indeed, Falkenhayn withdrew nine divisions and sent them to the East in November. The Schlieffen Plan had failed partly because it was too ambitious, and partly because its execution had been mishandled. However, it left Germany with the strategic advantage: their army was sitting on enemy soil. Behind their lines were some of the richest industrial regions of France and Belgium. The German army could afford to sit on the defensive in the West, and defy the Allies to expel them. Plan XVII had failed dismally, but the French had to continue to attack to throw the Germans off their territory. The first Battle of Artois began on 14 December; this and the Winter Offensive in Champagne were the first of many offensives that were to last until the French army mutinied in 1917.

Ypres had destroyed the old BEF. Fifty thousand men became casualties, and those that survived were exhausted by their troglodyte existence. Their German enemies were in the same situation; and on Christmas Day, an entirely unofficial truce spontaneously occurred on some, but by no means all, parts of the Ypres sector, when British and German soldiers fraternized in No Man's Land. To the fury of their High Commands, they played football, swapped cap badges and cigarettes, and even had their photographs taken. The Christmas Truce was an oasis of sanity in a deadlocked war where the trenches stretched from the Swiss border to the English Channel.

Tannenberg

In response to France's urgent pleas for help, the Russians instigated a campaign that led to one of the most crushing German victories of the war. On 17 August, the Russian First Army invaded East Prussia from Poland – a Russian possession which formed a salient, sandwiched between German territory and the Austrian province of Galicia. The communications in the salient were poor, even by Russian standards; they had been deliberately left under-developed in order to hinder any attack by the Central Powers. Ironically, in 1914 this prudent measure was to impair the forward movement of Russian, not German, armies; and these logistical problems were compounded by the offensive beginning more than a week earlier than had originally been intended.

The Russian plan was suggested by the geography of East Prussia, where invading armies were forced to move either south or north of the Masurian Lakes. Their First Army (under Rennenkampf) was to move north of the Lakes, while their Second Army (under Samsonov) was to strike from the south, from Poland, enveloping von Prittwitz's Eighth German Army. As the First Army moved cautiously forward, Prittwitz advanced to meet Rennenkampf with three of his four corps, then began to conduct a fighting retreat. The two forces met in action at Stallupönen on 17 August. Three days later, Prittwitz was defeated at Gumbinnen, a defeat that led to Moltke's decision to dispatch troops from the West on 25 August. Prittwitz decided to abandon most of the province and retreated west 100 miles to the Vistula. He had been

ABOVE: *Russian infantry in a Polish town. The Russian army was poorly supplied and its communications were weak.*
LEFT: *General Rennenkampf, commander of the Russian First Army, seen in August 1914. Unfortunately for the Russian war effort, Rennenkampf had poor relations with his own chief of staff as well as with Samsonov.*
RIGHT: *The reality of the 'Russian Steamroller' – Russian prisoners walk away into captivity.*

RIGHT: *German reservists depart for the Eastern Front. Railways played a crucial role in the Schlieffen Plan. The original intention was to defeat France quickly, then transfer men by rail to defeat the Russians. In the event, the Germans were able to halt the Russians in East Prussia without sizeable transfers of men from the West.*

badly shaken by reports that Samsonov and a mythical third Russian force were threatening his rear. Prittwitz soon recovered his nerve, and even approved a plan devised by his Operations Officer, Colonel Max von Hoffmann, to attack Samsonov, but he had lost the confidence of OHL and was replaced by Hindenburg, who brought Ludendorff – the hero of Liège – as his Chief of Staff. The aged Hindenburg was perfectly complemented by the dynamic Ludendorff, and they adopted Hoffmann's plan. A cavalry division was to watch the First Army, while three corps were to be rapidly moved south to join XX Corps (under Scholtz) in crushing the Second Army. The Germans knew that Rennenkampf had halted and would be unlikely to interfere because the Russians habitually sent radio messages 'in clear,' although contrary to popular belief all armies were guilty of this on occasion in 1914.

Stavka (Russian High Command) erroneously believed that the Germans were retreating and thus ordered Samsonov to interpose the Second Army between the enemy and the Vistula, overrunning Scholtz en route. Samsonov entered East Prussia on 23 August, and began to gain the upper hand in the battle with the badly outnumbered German XX Corps, even after the arrival of François' German I Corps by rail. However, when von Bülow's I Reserve Corps and, later, von Mackensen's XVII Corps appeared, having marched 90 miles, two of the Russian Corps found themselves surrounded on three sides. Samsonov attempted to extract his head from the noose, but François, disobeying orders, pushed out a cordon of men across the enemy's line of retreat, and captured 60,000 prisoners. A further 32,000 others were taken by the other German formations. Samsonov, with half of his army destroyed and the other half falling back in disorder, met a lonely death by his own hand. The Battle of Tannenberg was over. Hindenburg then moved against Rennenkampf, who in his haste to avoid the fate of his rival, Samsonov (with whom he had once brawled in public), lost 125,000 men and 200 guns in his retreat. Compared to Tannenberg, the Battle of the Masurian Lakes was a disappointment to the Germans; but East Prussia had been cleared of the enemy, and, in Hindenburg and Ludendorff, the Germans had discovered a formidable military team.

ABOVE: *An idealized German illustration of Russian gunners surrendering, 10 September 1914. The battle of Gumbinnen on 20 August had been a Russian victory, but the Russians suffered heavily at the same place on the retreat after Tannenberg.*

LEFT: *The victors in the East – Ludendorff (second from the left), Hindenburg (center) and Hoffmann (right). Although the least-known of the three, Hoffman was the architect of Germany's successes on the Eastern Front.*

ABOVE RIGHT: *General Alexander Samsonov, commander of Russian Second Army, in full dress. The Czar lost confidence in the Russian military leadership after their failures in the East, and he personally assumed command of the army.*

TOP RIGHT: *A map of the Russian advance into East Prussia. Although in theory strategically sound, the inept handling of this offensive led to disaster.*

TOP, FAR RIGHT: *The second stage of the Battle of Tannenberg, showing the Russian attacks and German counterattacks.*

RIGHT: *Russian cavalry attack German infantry. The Russians employed large numbers of cavalry, both regular and Cossack, but both were largely ineffective in the Tannenberg campaign.*

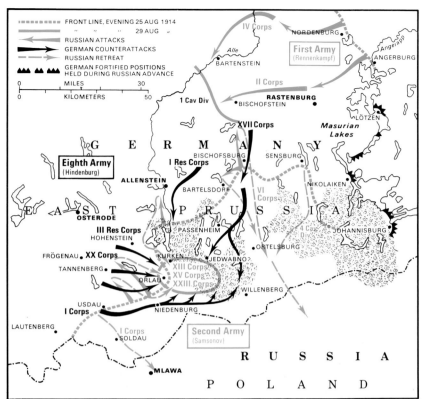

Lemberg

The Austrian Chief of Staff, Conrad von Hötzendorf, was perhaps Austria-Hungary's greatest military asset. His plan for a campaign against the Russians in 1914 was sound; but his army was not. Conrad wanted a double attack to be launched, with the Austrians striking north from Galicia, and the Germans moving south from East Prussia to pinch off the Polish salient. However, the campaign ended in disaster, not triumph. The Germans were unable to fulfill their prewar promises; indeed, they would have preferred the Austrians to remain on the defensive. Worse still, at the same time as Conrad was planning an offensive out of Galicia, the Russians were planning to thrust into it. Galicia offered a very desirable strategic prize to the Russians: it offered an invasion route into Hungary, and perhaps even Silesia. The Russian Third and Eighth Armies would remain on the defensive on the left, while the Fourth and Fifth Armies would attack to the south, and attempt to encircle the Austrian left, cutting them off from their base at Cracow.

The Galician campaign began as a series of encounter battles along the frontier. Three Austrian armies advanced from northeast Galicia, aiming to sever the railway lines running to Warsaw and Brest-Litovsk, from Lublin and Cholm. Neither Austrian nor Russian reconnaissance was very effective. The Austrian First Army smashed into the Russian Fourth Army at Krasnik and took 6000 prisoners. The Fourth Army nearly pulled off a spectacular victory at Komarov over the Russian Fifth Army (26 August), but bad news from the east caused the Fourth's commander, Auffenberg, to break off the battle.

LEFT: *The Austrian Chief of Staff, Conrad von Hötzendorf. He fell out of favor when Franz Josef was succeeded by Emperor Karl in 1916 and demoted to a command on the Italian Front.*
RIGHT: *An Austrian heavy howitzer. The war on the Eastern Front, no less than that in the West, was an artillery war. The gunner is armed with the Austrian 8mm Mannlicher M.1895 rifle.*
BELOW: *Russian infantry prepare a counterattack at Lemberg. They are armed with the Russian 7.62mm M.1891 rifle. Generally speaking, Russian equipment was of good quality, although often in short supply. At Lemberg, the Russian armies delivered a smashing blow against the weaker of the Central Powers.*

ABOVE: *General Alexeiev, commander of the Russian army group facing the Austrians at Lemberg.*
LEFT: *A column of Austrian infantry. Ironically, Austria, which had precipitated the war in order to retain its status as a great power, was to collapse as a result of it.*
RIGHT: *Russians and Austrians in hand-to-hand combat. Note the figure of the Virgin on the Austrian standard.*

The Russian Third and Eighth Armies (under Ruszki and Brusilov) had switched from a defensive to an offensive posture and had rolled forward into the Austrian right flank, defeating the Austrian Third Army at Zlotchow on 25 August. The advancing Russians now threatened the extended lines of communication of the Austrian left, who, ironically, were in danger of becoming victims of their own success. The ever-optimistic Conrad attempted to launch a counter-offensive against Plehve's Russian Fifth Army and Brusilov's Eighth, by redeploying the Third and Fourth Armies and using the Second, which had recently arrived from Serbia. The Russians forestalled this attempt. On 30 August they attacked near Lemberg. On the following day, a Hungarian division and some of the Third Army's cavalry were routed and the Russians were able to move through the gap in the Austrian line and outflank the Lemberg position.

The last hope the Austrians had of salvaging anything from the campaign vanished when their Third Army and Plehve clashed at Rawa-Russka. Both sides attempted to turn the other's flank, but by

11 September Conrad had to admit defeat, and ordered a general retreat to the River San, 140 miles away. The Austrians were able to fall back intact, thanks to Russian messages being transmitted 'in clear,' leaving nearly all of Galicia in the hands of the Russians, who were able to begin reducing the province's fortresses at their leisure. The Germans, victorious in the north, began to refer to the Hapsburg alliance as being 'fettered to a corpse.'

The cadaver had had no better luck in its campaign against its *bête noir*, Serbia. Three small armies, under Field Marshal Potiorek, crossed the Serbian frontier on 12 August, but on the 15th, half of the Second Army was ordered to Galicia, to be followed by the other half four days later. The Serbs, skillfully led by General Putnik, absorbed three Austrian offensives and then launched one of their own. By 15 December, not a single soldier of the Austrian Imperial and Royal Army remained on Serbian soil. The Austrians had lost 227,000 casualties out of 450,000 men involved; they had achieved nothing, except a weakening of the effort against the Russians in Galicia.

The Struggle for Lodz

The Galician disaster forced an urgent reorganization upon the armies of the Central Powers. François was left in command of a much-truncated Eighth Army in East Prussia, while four corps were moved by rail south to take up a position on the Austrian left flank in southwest Poland. This new Ninth Army was commanded by Hindenburg, with Ludendorff as his Chief of Staff and the 'power behind the throne.'

After a preliminary skirmish, Hindenburg launched his offensive into Poland on 8 October. One corps remained to guard the line of the Vistula; another set out for Ivangorod, to the southeast of Warsaw; two others, commanded by Mackensen, advanced on Warsaw itself. Simultaneously, the Austrians, having regrouped, re-entered Galicia, reaching the besieged fortress of Przemysl on 9 October.

The Russians met this blow with one of their own. The Front Commander, Grand Duke Nicholas, redeployed northward to meet the threat to Central Poland. The Tenth Army reinvaded East Prussia; the Fourth, Fifth and Ninth pushed toward Silesia; their flanks were protected by a further four armies, two on each side. In the face of this formidable force, Mackensen halted short of Warsaw, and on 19 October he began to retreat, systematically wrecking the communications – tearing up railway lines and cratering roads – as he did so. The Russians halted to repair the railway. Hindenburg, who was appointed Commander in Chief of German troops in the east on 1 November, discovered this from an intercepted wireless message sent 'in clear.'

LEFT: *Serbs test captured Austrian 8mm Mannlicher M1895 rifles Belgrade, 1915. The Serbian army outfought the Austrians in 1914. Their standard infantry weapon was the 7.65mm Mauser M1893 rifle.*
TOP LEFT: *Austrian Uhlans (lancers) advance through a Polish village. Under their overcoats, Uhlans wore red breeches and blue tunics.*

ABOVE: *Russian soldiers with a portable Marconi radio station. Wireless communications were in their infancy in 1914. The Russians were not the only army to make the mistake of broadcasting in clear in the early part of the war, but they paid most dearly for the lapse.*
TOP: *A 7.62mm PM1910 Russian machine gun, mounted on a motorcycle combination in an anti-aircraft role.*

Hindenburg and Ludendorff asked OHL for more troops with which to inflict a decisive blow on Russia. At the time, Falkenhayn still hoped to break through the British positions at Ypres and refused the request, but even with only locally available troops, which now included the Austrian First Army, the Germans forced the 'Russian Steamroller' to grind to a halt short of its objective of Silesia. Ludendorff and Hoffmann attempted to repeat the strategy of Tannenberg. This plan sent the Ninth Army (now commanded by Mackensen) north by rail to Thorn. On 11 November, it attacked southeast and hit the junction between the Russian First and Second Armies. The attempt to achieve a second Tannenberg narrowly failed. The Russian Second Army was trapped at Lodz and had to be relieved by the Fifth Army, but in turn this threatened the 50,000 Germans of XXV Reserve Corps with envelopment. The Russians even brought up extra trains to take away the prisoners, but the Germans succeeded in cutting their way out.

The Lodz campaign was indecisive, in that neither side succeeded in destroying the other, but in strategic terms it was a victory for the Germans. The end of December found the Central Powers, reinforced by corps sent from Ypres, holding a line in front of Warsaw. Although in East Prussia the Eighth Army was struggling to hold the line of the Masurian Lakes, and, to the south, the Austrians had again been pushed back to the crest of the Carpathian Mountains, the immediate threat to Silesia had been averted.

The casualties on the Eastern Front during 1914 had been enormous. An intense debate was opened between the 'Easterners,' Hindenburg and Ludendorff, who believed that the main effort in 1915 ought to be devoted to knocking Russia out of the war, and the 'Westerners,' led by Falkenhayn. The evident weakness of Russia, and the urgent need to prop up Austria-Hungary led to Falkenhayn reluctantly adopting an 'Eastern' strategy in 1915. This decision gave the *Entente* an unexpected respite, and valuable time for its reserves – the vast armies being raised by the British Empire – to be trained and equipped before further offensives on the Western front.

The Struggle for Germany's Colonies, 1914-18

Germany had been a comparative latecomer to the nineteenth-century scramble for colonies, but by 1914 she had possessions scattered across the globe. Her Pacific colonies were captured without bloodshed by Australian and New Zealand troops by the end of August, but the German naval base of Tsingtao, on mainland China, only capitulated after a protracted siege by a force which mainly consisted of troops of Britain's ally, Japan. The Japanese, having achieved their aim of expansion in China, then sat back and made a healthy profit from the war, mainly at the expense of their allies.

An Anglo-French force swiftly overran German possessions in Togoland in August. Further along the West African coast, in the Cameroons, the Germans, under Major Zimmermann, resisted the Allies until February 1916. About 64,000 men, drawn from the British, Belgian and French Empires, were needed to take the colony. The German force never numbered more than 1500 European and 6500 African soldiers.

The Union of South Africa had only been created in 1910; the outbreak of war was greeted by a rebellion of 11,300 Afrikaaners – successors to the 'Bitter-Enders' of the Boer War – against the pro-British stance of the government of Generals Botha and Smuts, who were regarded as traitors. The rebellion was not suppressed until February 1915, after which 60,000 men, divided in four columns, invaded German South West Africa (now called Namibia). Six thousand Germans waged a guerrilla campaign which lasted until July.

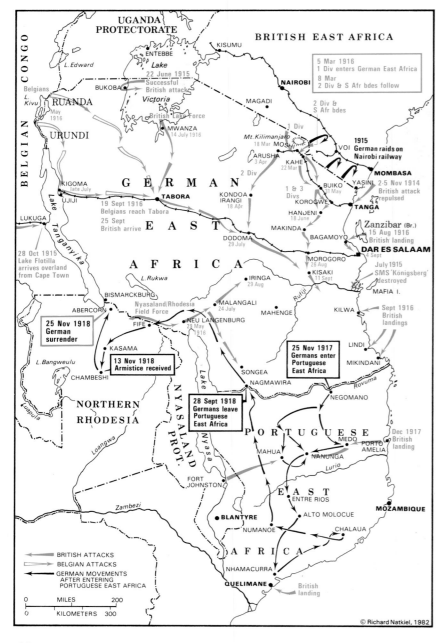

BELOW LEFT: *The campaigns in East Africa. British troops were tied down by a small German force using guerrilla tactics. Unlike the Germans, the British were slow to use African troops and relied on Indians and* *Europeans, although eventually the King's African Rifles was expanded as a result of the East African campaign. British generalship was also poor and the British found it difficult to adapt to the terrain.*

BELOW: *German Schutztruppe (colonial troops) and Askaris with an obsolete light artillery piece. Like all guerrilla armies, the Germans in East Africa relied heavily on captured enemy equipment. By 1918, most* *Germans were armed with British or Portuguese weapons, and a principal aim of battle was the capture of ammunition. Other items were made locally, including artificial gasoline.*

ABOVE: *Natives being trained by German reservists in New Guinea, 1914. Too far from Germany to receive help, the German colonies in the Pacific soon fell to a Commonwealth expeditionary force sent out from Australia and New Zealand.*

RIGHT: *German Askaris mounting guard over an aircraft, German East Africa, 1914. An attempt was made to fly a Zeppelin airship out to Lettow-Vorbeck in 1917, but for the most part he received little help from the Fatherland.*

BOTTOM: *Lettow-Vorbeck, the German commander in East Africa (second from right). An authoritarian leader, Lettow-Vorbeck was an unlikely guerrilla general; he was a Prussian Junker by background and staunchly conservative in his views. His achievement was to inspire his native soldiers to outmarch the British; they remained undefeated until 1918.*

BELOW: *Japan seized the major port of Tsingtao from the Germans in 1914. Here a British officer poses alongside two Japanese soldiers (one a medical orderly). Although a British ally, Japan refused to send troops to the West, and made significant strides as an industrial and commercial power during the war years.*

On the other side of the continent, from a similar irregular campaign, emerged one of the greatest guerrilla leaders in history: Lieutenant Colonel Paul von Lettow-Vorbeck, a 44-year-old regular soldier. Lettow-Vorbeck could never deploy more than 15,000 men, 12,000 of whom were African 'Askaris,' yet he tied down no less than 372,950 troops of the British Empire. The Germans successfully beat off an amphibious assault on the port of Tanga in December 1914, and then ranged far and wide over German East Africa, striking hard at the pursuing British columns and then escaping. This remarkable campaign only came to an end 12 days after hostilities ended in Europe, on 23 November 1918, when Lettow-Vorbeck surrendered to the British in their colony of Northern Rhodesia (now Zambia).

The East African campaign was the most extreme example of a tendency noticeable in all of the African campaigns: the disproportionately large numbers of troops needed to defeat far smaller numbers. Casualties were also huge: in East Africa, the British suffered losses of 347,000 men, 336,500 of whom were due to sickness, not bullets and shells. In retrospect, it is extremely doubtful that the capture of the German colonies was worth this huge investment of blood and treasure. By capturing the sea ports, German commerce raiders were deprived of their bases; but it was perhaps unnecessary to campaign in the hinterland. Cut off from their homeland by the British naval blockade, these colonies could have made only minimal contributions to the German war effort. Potentially, the German colonies could have been useful 'bargaining chips' after a compromise peace, but the British government never seriously contemplated such a peace. The campaigns against the colonies can perhaps be seen as a reflex action of an Imperial power – they were there, so they were attacked. A sober judgment might say that these campaigns made little contribution to the eventual Allied victory, and absorbed many troops that could have been more profitably employed elsewhere.

The Evolution of Trench Warfare, 1914-18

Trench warfare was not unique to World War I. Trenches had been a feature of siege warfare for many centuries. What was unusual about the situation that arose in the fall of 1914 was that two opposing lines of trenches covered the entire front, reducing a previously mobile campaign to a static siege. These trench systems had humble beginnings; often they were merely individual 'scrapes,' enlarged and connected together, with perhaps a single strand of wire in front. By late 1915 they were relatively sophisticated, consisting of three or more parallel trenches, connected by lateral communication trenches. All were dug on a zigzag pattern, with 'traverses' designed to minimize blast. The front trench had a 'firestep,' from which men could fire over the parapet. At first, this forward trench was heavily defended. Later, fewer men were situated in the front line, as the emphasis on 'defense in depth' developed. Out into No Man's Land belts of barbed wire provided the first line of defense, sometimes festooned with tin cans which provided a rudimentary early-warning system. The width of No Man's land varied according to the terrain. At the beginning of 1917, the trenches on Vimy Ridge were barely 30 yards apart; opposite Montauban before July 1916 it was about 250 yards wide; on other sectors, wider still. In some places, there were no continuous trenchworks. At Festubert in January 1916, a British battalion found solid breastworks, while the front line was held by a series of 'grouse butts,' or outposts, which had to be relieved at night. In the extreme south, in the Vosges Mountains, both sides used a similar system of outposts. On the Eastern Front, No Man's Land was often wide, sometimes as much as three miles, and generally the trenches were less well developed, reflecting the greater fluidity of warfare in that theater.

LEFT: *Men of the York and Lancaster Regiment (62nd Division) in the Oppy-Gavrelle area, in 1916. Repairing the wire that formed an integral part of trench positions was a never-ending task for infantry on the Western Front.*
BELOW LEFT: *German troops relaxing in a shallow dugout in a quiet sector. Note the trench cooker. The men are wearing a soft peakless cap rather than the* Pickelhaube *or spiked helmet.*

ABOVE: *In the mountainous Argonne, conventional trenches were sometimes replaced by barricades, such as these loop-holed plates.*
LEFT: *The weapons of trench warfare: men of the East Yorks with artillery signal rockets mounted on a rack. This photograph, taken in the Arleux sector on 2 January 1918, demonstrates the relative sophistication of the equipment available by the end of the war. In 1914 only the German army had sizable stocks of weapons useful for trench warfare.*

Behind the lines developed a complex infrastructure of dumps, headquarters, casualty clearing stations, roads, light railways, estaminets (a cross between a café and a bar), brothels, and many other components of the logistic 'tail.' When in the trenches, troops lived in dugouts. The officers' dugout was more elaborate and comfortable than that of the Other Ranks. Captured German dugouts amazed the British by their luxury. They were deep, had electric light, bunk beds and other refinements. This reflected the different philosophies of the two armies. The Germans intended to stay in the area, the British were determined to advance. French trenches often came under criticism by British soldiers for their unsanitary conditions. In 1918 American troops sometimes voiced the same complaint. Another reason for the comfort of German trenches was that their units tended to remain in the same sector for months at a time. By contrast, when not engaged in a major battle, the British regularly rotated their troops up and down the line: the 2nd Division were unusual in remaining in the La Bassée sector for 4 months after receiving a mauling at Arras in May 1917.

Some parts of the Front were notorious for being active sectors, where trench raids, shelling, and sniping were frequent, and battalions could expect to lose numbers of men. One such was the Ypres salient. Other sectors were relatively quiet, where the troops could have a 'cushy' existence: the Somme before July 1916 was such a quiet sector. The main armies had differing attitudes toward trench life. The French, by and large, adopted a policy of live and let live. When not actively engaged in a major battle, they sought to minimize casualties. The British High Command, however, insisted on a policy of the 'domination of No Man's Land' – raiding, bombing, patrolling, taking part in local offensives – in order to keep the men on their toes and to increase morale. This led to a steady attrition of men and probably had the opposite effect to that intended on morale. The British sustained 107,776 casualties in minor actions and normal trench warfare from January to June 1916. This policy reached its full flowering during 1916, when trench warfare had become more sophisticated, with increased bureaucratic control by High Command over front-line soldiers during the previous year. However, even before that, certain 'elite' units had carried on active warfare, such as 2 Royal Welsh Fusiliers, where Siegfried Sassoon earned the nickname of 'Mad Jack' for his outrageous bravery. The Germans tended to follow the lead of the army they were facing, but Allied troops differentiated between 'Saxon' troops, who were supposed to be lazy and easy-going, and 'Prussians' who were not. The trench raid was a reversion to a more primitive type of warfare; in sharp contrast to the highly mechanized killing of the shell and machine gun, raiding parties wielded coshes or sharpened entrenching tools, or threw 'bombs' (grenades). The objective was usually to gather intelligence, or to gain a local ascendency.

ABOVE: *Foot inspection by the Medical Officer of the 12th East Yorks at Reclincourt, 9 January 1918. 'Trenchfoot' was a common complaint and many precautions were taken against it, including the rubbing of foul-smelling whale oil into the feet.*
TOP: *On quiet sectors a semblance of normality could be achieved. This Australian is haymaking within 2000 yards of the front line, near Hamel, 6 August 1918.*
RIGHT: *The results of one night's ratting, March 1916.*

Truces, of varying types, were not uncommon; the truce of Christmas 1914 was far from unique. They occasionally took the form of fraternization, but more often simple inertia. Refraining from shelling at mealtimes, for fear of retaliation, and firing deliberately inaccurately, or at certain well-defined times was not unknown. These practices made trench life that little bit more bearable. These actions were usually sanctioned at the very lowest level, but occasionally higher authorities would approve, for example in January 1916 the British 2nd Division at Souchez refrained from offensive action in order to put their trenches in a state of repair, having recently been flooded.

The day of the average soldier began before dawn, with what the British called 'Stand-to,' manning the parapet to repel any possible dawn attack. There was the constant threat of sudden death arriving in the form of a shell or bullet. Much of the day was involved in a running battle with other enemies – the cold, the wet, lice, rats and mud. Sleeping rough could be bearable, even pleasant, in the summer; in winter, it was trying in the extreme. Lice were something that soldiers learned to live with; the phrase 'to chat' was coined, killing 'chats' or lice being a sociable activity. Food was for the most part monotonous, although for the Allied soldiers it was generally plentiful. A typical meal would consist of hardtack biscuits, bully beef and, in the BEF, such delicacies as Maconochie Stew or Tickler's Plum and Apple Jam. The Germans had a more meager diet; the Allied naval blockade began to bite early on in the war. Perhaps the worst feature of trench life was the constant weariness experienced by everyone. Merely moving up a crowded trench, heavily laden, was exhausting. The British soldier generally served for 4 days in the front line, followed by 12 in support and reserve, and then went back to what the army quaintly termed 'rest.' This period frequently involved arduous manual labor; the novelist Saki (H H Munro) serving as an NCO in the Royal Fusiliers, commented that, on hearing that heaven was a place of eternal rest, many men renounced their religion.

In the face of these appalling conditions, how was morale maintained? Alcohol (wine for the French, rum for the British, beer for the Germans), frequent reliefs, occasional leave, paternal officers, mail from home, patriotism, regimental pride – all these factors played an invaluable role, but ultimately it was a matter of small group loyalty: one 'stuck it' so as not to let one's pals down. This *Grabenkameradschaft*, the comradeship of the trenches, united officers and men and different nationalities, and divided mankind into those who had served in the subterranean world, and those who had not.

ABOVE: *An evening's entertainment in a comfortably equipped German dugout, 1915. Note hanging decorations, accordion and improvised percussion from the soldier with bayonet and shell casing.*
RIGHT: *Behind the lines: an Australian receives his issue of clean underwear after a bath, Ypres, 31 October 1917. The clothes would have been deloused, but the soldier would pick up a fresh lot of 'chats' before long.*

The War at Sea: Opening Moves, 1914

In August 1914 both the British public and the Royal Navy anticipated that a cataclysmic battle would occur between the British Grand Fleet and the German High Seas Fleet in the North Sea. Once command of the sea had been safely won, the Royal Navy would, according to the contemporary interpretation of the theories of the influential American naval historian Alfred T Mahan, destroy the German merchant fleet and starve the Germans into submission by blockading their homeland. Both the Royal Navy and the British public were to be disappointed. The strategies of the rival fleets ensured that a new Trafalgar never came to pass. The Kriegsmarine was numerically inferior, possessing in August 1914 19 modern capital ships to the Royal Navy's 29. Thus the Germans sought to avoid major fleet actions in which they would be outnumbered. Instead, they aimed to lure isolated squadrons out into the North Sea which could be destroyed in detail. In pursuance of this strategy, a number of 'pinprick' raids were launched on the east coast of England. Lowestoft was bombarded on 3 November, Scarborough, Hartlepool and Whitby on 15 December. This strategy failed, largely because the British had obtained German Naval code books early in the war, which allowed the High Seas Fleet's signal traffic to be read by the Admiralty, giving the Royal Navy a priceless advantage.

RIGHT: *Admiral Sir Christopher Cradock, commander of the ill-fated British squadron defeated at the Battle of Coronel. He had only one modern ship, the light cruiser HMS Glasgow, and was outgunned by the newer German vessels. The defeat of Cradock was a serious blow to the prestige of a navy unchallenged since 1805, and caused much unjustified anger in Britain.*

RIGHT: *The German cruiser* Scharnhorst. *The flagship of von Spee's East Asiatic Squadron,* Scharnhorst *was sunk off the Falkland Islands on 8 December 1914.*

BELOW: *HMS* Audacious *sinking.* Audacious *was exercising with 2nd Battle Squadron off the Irish coast when it struck a mine. The news of the loss of this superdreadnought was suppressed for fear of its impact on civilian morale.*

LEFT: *Australian infantry embark at Melbourne, 18 October 1914. Control of the sea allowed the mobilization of the British Empire to proceed unhindered.*
BELOW: *The remains of the German commerce raider* Emden *on the rocks at North Keeling, November 1914.*

Churchill wrote of Jellicoe, the Commander in Chief of the Grand Fleet, that he was 'the only man on either side who could lose the war in an afternoon.' The British war effort and, indeed, the survival of the British Empire, ultimately rested on British naval supremacy. Jellicoe was not prepared to risk this on a single action; he had the awful precedent of Tsushima in 1905, when a Russian squadron had been destroyed in one day by the Japanese. Furthermore, since that date the Royal Navy had been re-equipped with new, unproven technology, the Dreadnought. So Jellicoe avoided a head-on clash, and instead pursued a strategy of distant blockade; a strategy that was cautious, unglamorous and frustrating, and yet absolutely correct.

The naval war opened with minor victories for both sides. The BEF was transported to France unmolested; and the severing of the German trans-Atlantic telegraph cable by a British ship proved to be an inestimable advantage to the Allies. However, the dramatic arrival of the German battlecruiser Goeben and light cruiser Breslau in Constantinople, having eluded their British 'shadows' in the Mediterranean, received more public attention than these undoubted victories. These German vessels helped to push Turkey into the war on the side of the Central Powers. Although denied a Trafalgar, the British were heartened by the action in the Heligoland Bight on 28 August. The Harwich Flotilla, a force of light ships commanded by Commodore Tyrwhitt, was supported by Sir David Beatty's battlecruisers in an attack which succeeded in sinking or crippling 6 German light cruisers. The façade of a glorious victory concealed grossly deficient Staff work and poor communications. The Germans, however, knew nothing of this and were impressed and alarmed by the boldness of the British.

Other events foreshadowed the course the naval war was to take. The sinking of three old British cruisers, Aboukir, Cressy and Hogue on 22 September, and that of the Dreadnought Audacious in October, was achieved not by a capital ship, but by undersea weapons; a U-Boat and a mine. The chasing of German merchant shipping and commerce raiders from the oceans was equally significant. The light cruiser Emden preyed on Allied shipping in the Indian Ocean with great success – until it was sunk by the Australian cruiser Sydney on 16 November. The Emden's parent body, the East Asiatic Squadron, also had a brief period of success in the Pacific, destroying a British squadron of outdated cruisers at Coronel on 1 November. The Royal Navy's revenge was swift and decisive. A superior fleet, which included the battlecruisers Inflexible and Invincible, was dispatched south under the command of Vice-Admiral Sturdee, who surprised the German commander von Spee off the Falkland Islands. The Scharnhorst, Gneisenau, Nürnberg and Leipzig were sunk; only Dresden escaped – for the moment. This was the true measure of British naval superiority. German overseas squadrons would inevitably wither on the vine, for, with the bases of the Grand Fleet lying squarely across the German egress to the world's sealanes, they could neither be reinforced nor return home. The Royal Navy merely had to avoid defeat in order to retain its command of the sea. In this situation, the idea of a 'new Trafalgar' was a dangerous irrelevance. The same description could be applied to the German High Seas Fleet. It was too small to break British domination of the seas; but it was large enough to appear threatening to the British. It is difficult to avoid the conclusion that it should never have been built.

LEFT: *The commander of the* Emden, *Captain Müller.* Emden *sank 17 merchantmen in just three months. Another German commerce raider, the* Karlsruhe, *had a similar career in the West Indies. The surface raider's role was soon to be assumed by the submarine.*

BELOW: Inflexible *at the Battle of the Falkland Islands, 8 December 1914. This photograph, taken from* Invincible, *shows survivors from* Gneisenau *in the sea. Most of the survivors were picked up by the British battlecruisers, who lowered cutters and steamed slowly over the spot where* Gneisenau *sunk.*

1915
The Expanding War

Chronology 1915

February 9	Beginning of winter battle in Masuria
March 10	Neuve Chapelle
March 18	Naval attempt to force Dardanelles
April 22	Second Ypres begins
April 25	Gallipoli landings
May 1	Gorlice-Tarnow begins
May 9	Franco-British spring offensive begins
May 23	Italy declares war on Austria-Hungary
May 26	Asquith forms Liberal-Unionist coalition in Britain
June 22	Lemberg recaptured by Austrians
August 4	Capture of Warsaw by Germans
August 6	Second wave of landings at Gallipoli (Suvla Bay)
September 25	Champagne, Artois and Loos offensives begin
September 28	Battle of Kut
October 2	Russian retreat ends
October 5	Franco-British landings at Salonika
October 7	Austrians invade Serbia
November 24	Battle of Ctesiphon
December 19	French replaced by Haig as British Commander in Chief

LEFT: *A sniper of the Australian Expeditionary Force looks across No Man's Land in search of a target on 'Dead Man's Ridge' some 100 yards away. Australian soldiers gained a reputation as aggressive fighting troops during the Gallipoli Campaign, although their informal approach to discipline was disapproved of by many senior officers in the British Army.*

Deadlock in the West, 1915-18

Joffre's strategy for 1915 was straightforward. The French commander in chief's aim was to drive the Germans from French soil, by pinching off the Noyon salient. It was to be attacked from two sides; from Artois and from Champagne. Joffre did not necessarily expect to break through immediately. By 'nibbling' at the German line he hoped to wear the enemy down until their line collapsed. This was the meaning of 'attrition' in 1915; later it came to mean something rather different. The BEF was more or less forced to conform to French strategy as it was the smaller army, although growing in size. Thus, with the exception of the German offensive at Ypres in April, the war in the West in 1915 was to consist of a series of these attritional battles designed to weaken the German line.

On paper, Joffre's strategy was sound; he had every reason to believe that trench warfare would prove to be a short-lived phenomenon. The offensive was renewed in Champagne in February 1915. Gains were measured in yards and the French casualties were about 240,000. This was to be the pattern of the year: costly battles, few gains, and little sign of a breakthrough. Why did the battles of 1915 – and all offensives until March 1918 – fail so completely to unlock the front and allow a return to open warfare?

The answer often given is that it was the fault of the generals; that the armies consisted of 'lions led by donkeys.' Before coming to a judgment about the competence or otherwise of High Command in 1914-18, there are a number of points to consider. It has been argued that warfare consists of technological 'cycles.' In 1914, the defense had a temporary ascendency over the offensive, just as in 1939-41 the situation was reversed. This was mainly because of technological developments. The Anglo-American view of the war is colored by an inaccurate folk memory of 1 July 1916, the 'First Day on the Somme,' when 60,000 losses were incurred by the British Fourth Army for little gain. From this, one might deduce that machine guns and artillery were, by themselves, the technological 'cause' of the impasse. The truth is rather different.

Throughout the war, armies had relatively little difficulty in breaking into the enemy positions, using artillery and infantry. Even on the notorious (and atypical) 1 July 1916, 18th (Eastern) and 30th Divisions, and neighboring French formations managed to take all their objectives. The difficulty was not in the 'breaking in,' but the 'breaking out,' or exploitation. Generally speaking, it was easier for a defender to bring up reserves to plug the gap in the line than it was for the attacker to bring forward his reserves to take over from the assault troops, whose attack had usually lost impetus, and often had suffered heavy casualties.

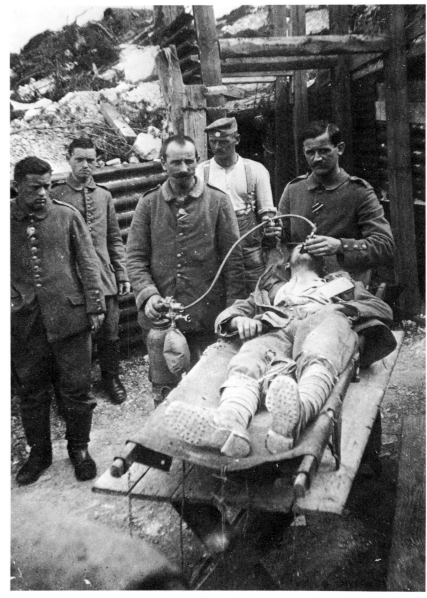

World War I was a modern war being fought without the benefit of modern communications. Lacking the portable 'walkie-talkie' radio (although primitive radios were becoming more widespread by 1918), troops were dependent on visual signals, which were usually ineffective, or field telephones, which were reliant on all-too easily cut wires. Thus situation reports had to be sent back by word of mouth, by runner. Hours might pass before reserves could be sent forward, and then they faced a difficult journey over No Man's Land; if they were kept too far forward, they were vulnerable to hostile artillery fire. Conversely, it was much quicker for the defender's reserves to arrive by rail and join the battle. Thus, attackers would often create a salient in the enemy line which they were unable to break out of; instead they would find themselves attacked on three sides. Worse, the principal instrument of exploitation, horsed cavalry, had been rendered obsolete by the tremendous firepower of modern weaponry. It was retained by the British in the absence of anything else, and it had occasional successes even after 1914. Its natural successor, the tank, was then a slow, cumbersome and, above all, unreliable beast, which was not available in large numbers until late 1917.

ABOVE: *An ANZAC road-repairing gang taking their midday meal. Although the Allies imported large numbers of Chinese coolies to provide labor, the infantry were also called on for this task.*

ABOVE LEFT: *Two Germans operate a 'man-power-station.' This machine inflated a balloon.*

LEFT: *Medical care in the trenches: a gas casualty is treated. The introduction of gas in 1915 necessitated the development of new medical techniques to care for the wounded.*

RIGHT: *A British signal exchange in a captured German dugout on the Somme, 1916.*

ABOVE: *Men of the First Canadian Expeditionary Force in England, 1914. They were soon to see action at Second Ypres in May 1915.*
LEFT: *A French officers' mess in the field, August 1916.*
ABOVE RIGHT: The Kensingtons at Laventie *by Eric Kennington. The 1/13th Londons were a Territorial battalion in 56th Division.*

Contrary to the public image of World War I commanders as un-imaginative 'donkeys,' a tactical revolution took place from 1914 to 1918. The warfare of 1914 was quasi-Napoleonic, but that of 1918 had more in common with the *blitzkrieg* of 1940. Infiltration tactics, chemical warfare, ground-attack aircraft, combined infantry/armor actions, scientifically planned artillery barrages – all these were commonplace in 1918. Strangely, while the new 'gimmick' weapons (such as gas and tanks) are remembered, these tactical innovations are not. Broadly speaking, all armies had employed linear infantry tactics in 1914, but as early as May 1915 Captain André Laffargue, a French officer, was beginning to think along the lines of training 'storm-troopers,' who could fight their way forward in small groups. It was the Germans who developed this idea, by which picked men, heavily armed, would infiltrate the enemy positions, bypassing obstacles and pushing on into the rear to cause maximum disruption to the enemy, leaving the second wave to mop up pockets of resistance. This technique was used at Cambrai and Caporetto in 1917, and when used against the British on the Somme in March 1918 broke the deadlock, leading to the resumption of open warfare. It is possible that the stalemate could have been ended earlier, had these tactics been developed in 1915 or 1916, but it is likely the experience of three years of war was needed to develop them. Independently of the Germans, both the French and British had by 1918 abandoned the linear advance and adopted more flexible small-group tactics – in the words of Major-General Sir Ivor Maxse, the 'line' was replaced by the 'worm.'

Similarly, rigid defensive tactics, based on holding three lines of trenches, were replaced by 'defense in depth,' largely as a result of the German experience on the Somme in 1916. Advancing troops were firstly met by a series of outposts, and then by a 'battlezone' of mutually supporting strongpoints, which would split up the assaulting troops, making it easier for them to be counterattacked. The rear lines consisted of machine-gun pits and field artillery, where reserves waited to launch their counterattacks. Artillery tactics also underwent a profound change. Simple attempts to destroy enemy positions by sheer weight of shell, moving from target to target with ponderous 'lifts,' were replaced by the 'creeping' barrage and the 'hurricane' bombardment, both of which are explained within the context of the campaign studies below.

The Eastern Front was characterized by a more mobile type of warfare. This simply reflected the vastness of the Eastern theater, where, despite the huge size of the armies involved, it was impossible to hold everywhere with great strength. Certainly, warfare in the East was just as costly as in the West; the Austro-Hungarians suffered 1,200,000 dead from 1914 to 1918, the French (who began the war with a larger army) 1,385,000. But modern warfare *is* costly. The proportion of casualties in Montgomery's nine divisions at Second Alamein in 1942 was similar to that of many actions in the earlier war, and the casualties on the Eastern Front in World War II – which was the main theater of war – matched Verdun or the Somme. As French General Mangin said in World War I, 'Whatever you do, you lose a lot of men.' Thus the generalship of the Great War should be set into the general context of twentieth-century warfare, and viewed against a background of bitterly gained experience and development of tactics. To view the generals of 1914-18 collectively as bone-headed 'donkeys' is a gross oversimplification, but it is a prejudice which is difficult to eradicate.

Neuve Chapelle

Neuve Chapelle was the BEF's first independent offensive, although it had originally been planned as a joint operation with the French. Although they withdrew their promise of support, Sir John French decided to go ahead with the plan, largely to impress his ally with his willingness to bear his share of the fighting. The attack began on 10 March, by which time the BEF had grown to 13 infantry and five cavalry divisions. The order of battle included Territorial battalions (later formed into divisions), Indian divisions (which included British units) and Regular battalions which had returned from garrison duty abroad. The latter were the final, undiluted reservoirs of prewar soldiers, and were among the best troops on either side of the Western Front at that time.

The attack was made by Haig's First Army, and was a model of meticulous staffwork. Even historian Liddell Hart, no admirer of Haig, conceded that the plan was 'original and well thought out.' The First Army was to attack on a narrow front of 2000 yards and pinch off the Neuve Chapelle salient, followed by an advance onto the southern end of Aubers Ridge. A second offensive would then break out into the open country beyond. The Royal Flying Corps (the RFC) provided photographic reconnaissance, which was used to print accurate trench maps that were widely issued, even to junior officers. The attacking battalions practiced the assault on mock-ups in the rear of the British positions until they were thoroughly familiar with the role they were to be called upon to fulfill. The artillery was to deliver a sudden, sharp blow. Lacking shells and heavy guns to destroy the German dugouts

BELOW: *A group of recruits for 10th Lincolns (Grimsby Chums). Like many newly raised Kitchener units, this battalion was issued with blue uniforms before khaki was available.*

The core of this battalion was a company raised by the headmaster of a school. Most units were raised by the Government.

and trenches, the British gunners were to fire a 35-minute bombardment, which was to disrupt and disorientate the defenders, cut the enemy wire and then lay down a curtain of fire to prevent reinforcements reaching the front. The artillery was allocated 100,000 shells, one-sixth of the BEF's entire stock.

Promptly at 0730 hours on 10 March, the bombardment began. At 0805 hours it lifted and the assault battalions of three brigades attacked across the 200 yards of No Man's Land. The Germans could deploy only six companies on this front. On the extreme right, a battalion of the Garhwal Brigade lost its way and ran into a position untouched by the British shelling, but in the center the Garhwalis and 25th Brigade (8th Division) encountered little opposition; the bombardment had done its work well. By 0900 hours the Garhwalis were established in the Smith-Dorrien trench, to the east of Neuve Chapelle village, having taken 200 prisoners, and 2nd Rifle Brigade and 1st Royal Irish Rifles had leap-frogged through the first wave of 25th Brigade and passed through the damaged village. Only on the left, where the shelling had been ineffective, was there a setback. A single company of II Jäger Battalion had caused heavy losses among 2nd Scottish Rifles and 2nd Middlesex of 23rd Brigade.

Once they had broken in, the British were unable to break out. At one point, 25th Brigade was held up by the Royal Artillery's bombardment, which had to adhere to a rigid timetable. By the time the reserves were ordered up to exploit the gap at 1730 hours, the Germans had had five hours in which to scrape together reinforcements; and the attack failed. The battle continued until 13 March, but by then the decisive moment had long passed. The British had lost 12,000 men. Neuve Chapelle was, in retrospect an important battle. It demonstrated what could be achieved by a 'hurricane' bombardment. The events of May, and the gradual overcoming of the shell shortage, caused this lesson to be forgotten. The lessons of Neuve Chapelle were shelved until November 1917, when they were taken down and dusted off, with startling results.

ABOVE LEFT: *A German 25cm trench mortar in an artillery park at Etray, March 1915. The* minenwerfer *was much feared by Allied troops.*
LEFT: *Winston Churchill (center), wearing a French 'Adrian' pattern helmet, at French XXXIII Corps HQ, 1915.*
RIGHT: *Men of 2nd Argyll and Sutherland Highlanders, Bois Grenier, spring 1915. Note the government-issue goat-skin jackets.*

The Second Battle of Ypres

At about 1700 hours on 22 April 1915, a British officer saw a 'panic-stricken rabble' of French colonial troops running away from the front line 'with grey faces and protruding eyeballs, clutching their throats and choking as they ran.' They were the victims of the first use of chlorine gas on the Western Front. The attack had been preceded by a brief, but ferocious bombardment. Then the greenish-yellow gas had been released from cylinders in the German front line; it turned into a bluish-white mist and drifted across the front of the 45th Algerian and 87th Territorial Divisions, who simply ran, leaving a gaping hole, four miles wide, in the French line.

The gas had been developed by Professor Fritz Haber, a German chemist. Tear gas had been employed unsuccessfully on the Western Front, and at Bomlimov, in the East, when over 18,000 shells containing Xylyl bromide had been fired at the Russians but the extreme cold had prevented the gas from vaporizing. One consequence was that OHL had little faith in the Ypres attack, and had provided few reserves to exploit the complete surprise that could have been achieved by this weapon. In the event, the Germans advanced rather cautiously for two miles until they reached their own gas and then stopped altogether, fearful of advancing into the poisonous cloud of their own making. The British were able to cobble together a defensive force, in which the 1st Canadian Division played a prominent role, and establish a new line.

LEFT: *Germans lay out pipelines before conducting a gas attack. Although gas shells were widely used as a delivery system, the older method was not entirely abandoned.*

BELOW: *German artillerymen and horses in gas masks. The Second Battle of Ypres witnessed the first successful gas attack. By 1916, chemical warfare was accepted as yet another hazard of life at the front.*

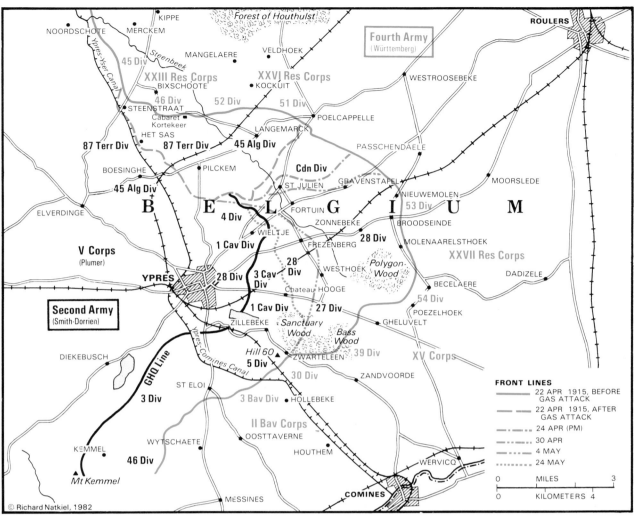

© Richard Natkiel, 1982

FRONT LINES
22 APR 1915, BEFORE GAS ATTACK
22 APR 1915, AFTER GAS ATTACK
24 APR (PM)
30 APR
4 MAY
24 MAY

ABOVE: *The poisonous cloud: a cylinder for projecting gas is tested. The psychological damage wreaked by chemical warfare was probably greater than the physical damage inflicted. Neither side employed gas in Europe during World War II for fear of retaliation; a classic example of successful deterrence.*

TOP: *The Second Battle of Ypres. Ypres took on an almost mystical significance for the British. Perhaps it would have been wise in strategic terms to shorten the line by abandoning the salient altogether, but to do so would have been unacceptable to the British public. The British lost 90,000 killed, 70,500 missing and 410,000 wounded defending the Ypres salient from 1914 to 1918.*

On 23 April local British counterattacks kept the Germans occupied, but on the following day the Canadians, who were holding the tip of the salient, were subjected to another gas attack. Unlike the French, the Canadians stood firm, wearing handkerchiefs soaked in water or urine as primitive gas masks. In doing so, they laid the basis of their reputation as some of the finest troops in the British Empire; in four days fighting, they lost 7000 casualties. The stubborn resistance of the Canadians and other British units prevented the line from collapsing, but Smith-Dorrien, the commander of the Second Army, recognized that he could not hold the present positions indefinitely. On the morning of 22 April, the Ypres salient had been 10 miles wide, but by the evening of the 25th its width had been reduced to a mere three miles, while it remained about five miles deep, and was dominated on three sides by German artillery. On 27 April Smith-Dorrien recommended a withdrawal of some 2½ miles. French then sacked his rival. Legend has it that the Chief of the General Staff, 'Wullie' Robertson, broke the news to Smith-Dorrien with the words ''orace, you're for 'ome.' The new commander of the Second Army, Plumer, endorsed Smith-Dorrien's proposal. This time, French accepted it. Given his promise to aid Joffre in the imminent Artois offensive, there was little else that he could do. During 1-3 May, the BEF pulled back to its new position. After some further heavy fighting, notably for Frenzenberg Ridge (8-14 May), the battle came to an end.

Although the Allies self-righteously denounced the Germans for their use of gas, they were quick to adopt it as a weapon. By the time of the battles of 1918, the clumsy wind-borne clouds of chlorine had been replaced by shells dispersing mustard gas, a blistering agent, and gas masks had become relatively sophisticated. It is even possible to argue that gas, which tended to disable and inconvenience rather than kill, was a more humane weapon than high explosive. Seventy years after the war's end, there were still old men suffering from the effects of mustard gas – but they were alive. At Ypres in April 1915, the secret of this new weapon – one of the greatest strategic surprises of the war – was thrown away on a strictly limited offensive, when, if used imaginatively, it could have unlocked the deadlocked front. Instead, the German gains were paltry – a flattening out of the Ypres salient, and 58,000 British casualties (the Germans suffered 47,000). OHL's handling of Second Ypres constituted a colossal strategic error.

May Offensives of 1915

The German line in Artois included a salient, three miles deep. Here, the Germans had anchored their line on Vimy Ridge, an impressive physical feature which rises 400 feet above the Plain of Douai. It was the unenviable task of General Pétain's French XXXIII Corps to attempt to capture the Ridge. With the Central Powers embroiled in Poland, it was hoped that a blow struck in the West would catch the Germans off balance; at the very least it would take pressure off the Russian army. Joffre's plan was to attack on a narrow front with D'Urbal's Tenth Army of nine divisions; Pétain's corps of three divisions was to attack in the center; three more divisions were to attack to the north, and three to the south. Nine more divisions, and three cavalry divisions were to form the reserve. The assault began on 9 May 1915.

At the outset, the attack was successful. The German garrison on the Ridge was weak, in contrast to the physical strength of the feature. The 5th Bavarian Reserve Division collapsed under the weight of a five-day bombardment from 1200 guns (including 293 heavy guns). The French XXXIII Corps surged forward almost to the crest of the Ridge, having covered 2½ miles. Like the British at Neuve Chapelle, the assaulting battalions had trained intensively, and all ranks were thoroughly conversant with their role in the attack. Ninety minutes after the battle had begun, the 77th and Moroccan Divisions were able to look out onto the industrial plain below them, and back toward their own lines to watch for the reserves.

No reserves arrived. The tragic pattern of Neuve Chapelle was repeated. D'Urbal's reserves were eight miles away. It took hours for the news of the break in to filter back first to Corps and then to Army and even longer for the reserves to be activated and to pick their way through No Man's Land and up to the crest of the ridge. The 18th Division arrived at 1830 hours; by then Kronprinz Rupprecht, the commander of German Sixth Army, was able to throw in local counterattacks and stabilize the line. The moment for a breakthrough had passed, and the struggle degenerated into the usual battle of attrition, using up the lives of 100,000 Frenchmen and 60,000 Germans. The French had gained a strong foothold on Vimy Ridge, but that was a poor substitute for a decisive breakthrough.

Haig's British First Army also attacked on 9 May, at Aubers Ridge on a nine-mile frontage. This was a complete failure, costing 11,000 casualties for no gains of any significance. Aubers Ridge was a disaster in more than one sense, for the hurricane bombardment became discredited as a result of the failure of the assault. Drawing what appeared to be the obvious conclusions from Aubers Ridge, the BEF's next battle – at Festubert on 15 May – was preceded by a four-day bombardment. The BEF had only limited objectives, of fighting an attritional battle, to 'wear out the enemy' and pin down reserves that could otherwise oppose the French, and in this French and Haig were reasonably successful. As a result of Festubert, they deduced that greater weight of bombardment was the key to successful offensives. This line of thinking – which appeared to be fully supported by recent military lessons – led inexorably to the tragedy of the Somme.

The second battle of Artois failed to effect a breakthrough on the Western Front, and failed even to draw off German troops from the Eastern Front; in fact, two divisions (103rd and 8th Bavarian Reserve) were sent from the West to the East during the course of the battle. Separately, both the French and British General Staffs were groping toward the same conclusions, that it might be necessary to fight a deliberate battle of attrition to destroy the enemy's reserves before a genuine breakthrough could be achieved. The problems of devising efficient tactics were temporarily ignored; instead the maxim that 'artillery conquers, infantry occupies' became an article of faith among British generals. The BEF was to pay a heavy price for this under-standable, but misguided, interpretation of the 'lesson' of May 1915.

RIGHT: *The prizes of war: French prisoners are paraded down the Boulevard de la Liberté in Lille, Belgium, 1915. Note the fixed bayonets of the guards. The crowd looks on with indifference.*

RIGHT: *German cavalry near Arras, 1915. The Germans took a calculated risk in making their main effort in the East in 1915, but were able to hold on in the West even with weakened forces.*
BELOW RIGHT: *A German machine-gun team. The weapon is the MG08, a version of the Maxim. Note the gunners' assortment of weapons, waterbottles and other equipment.*
BELOW: *A French* poilu *with an improvised aerial torpedo. The French were quick to develop trench-warfare weapons, but many were unsuccessful.*

ABOVE: *German propaganda picture of British troops surrendering. They are festooned with unlikely looking bandoliers.*

LEFT: *German dressing station, 1915. Casualties went through a series of medical posts before reaching a major hospital. Germany, along with Britain, was well-organized in providing medical facilities.*

RIGHT: *In the Trenches, by Frank Dobson. Note the corrugated iron roof to the dugout and the improvised brazier.*

Third Artois, Second Champagne and Loos

Between the close of the Artois campaign in June and the opening of the September offensive, there were no major actions on the Western Front. These months were, however, far from peaceful. Trench warfare continued with varying degrees of intensity; and in Alsace, the Argonne and Flanders bitter local operations were fought, all taking their toll of lives. At Hooge in July, for example, the Germans first used flame-throwers, or 'liquid fire' as it was known. During this period, the BEF continued to grow in size as Territorial and the first Kitchener units arrived in France, allowing the formation of a Third Army, under Monro, which in July relieved the French on the Somme.

Joffre's strategy for the September campaign was a more ambitious version of that of May. The Noyon Salient was to be attacked by 35 divisions in Champagne, while a simultaneous thrust was to be launched by 18 French and 12 British divisions in Artois. Joffre was confident of success: the German line was weakly held; only six divisions were available in Artois, 17 in Champagne, and a further six divisions were held in reserve, spread thinly along the Front. GQG's optimism filtered down to the *poilus*. There was a widespread feeling that the coming battle would end the war: Joffre proclaimed to his army that, *'Votre élan sera irrésistible'* – and he was believed. French troops attacked on 25 September with drums beating and colors flying: a gesture which now seems as poignant as it seems archaic. The men of the BEF shared this confidence – some Territorials of 47th (London) Division were even seen dribbling a football towards the enemy – but both French and Haig were pessimistic. They would have preferred to attack further north, or even delay until 1916, but Joffre insisted on the BEF fighting at the side of the French. In order to preserve inter-Allied harmony, and to relieve the pressure on the Russians and Italians, Sir John French reluctantly agreed to adopt this approach. As a result, Haig's First Army was committed to an attack across the difficult terrain of the Loos/Lens area – a landscape which was scarred by slagheaps and dotted with mining villages.

RIGHT: *German 7.7cm field gun at maximum recoil, Champagne. It could fire a 15-pound shell 9200 yards.*
ABOVE RIGHT: *Men of B company, 1st Scots Guards, in Big Willie Trench, October 1915. The Guards Division was formed in 1915 and played a prominent role at the Battle of Loos.*

ABOVE: *Field Marshal Earl Kitchener of Khartoum visiting France, during the shell crisis, 1915. Kitchener began his career as an officer in the Royal Engineers and succeeded Lord Roberts in command in South Africa during the Boer War. In August 1914 he happened to be on leave in England and was made Secretary of State for War, but despite being a national hero, his appointment was not a success. He was killed in 1916 while on a visit to Russia; his ship was sunk in the North Sea.*

The main French blow fell in Champagne. After exhaustive preparations, including a three-day-long bombardment, the Second Army (now commanded by Pétain) attacked at 0915 hours on 25 September. The French advance was aided by the use of poison gas, and the first wave of attackers penetrated as far as 3000 yards into the German defenses. When they came up against the second German line, which was being held as their main position, the attack foundered. The French continued to try to break through these strongpoints until 28 September, when Joffre suspended operations. A further series of attacks on 6 October were also unsuccessful. The Second Army had taken 25,000 prisoners, but nowhere had the fighting risen above the level of trench fighting.

The attack in Artois was equally disappointing. The town of Souchez, at the northern end of Vimy Ridge, was taken by the Tenth Army, along with a sliver of land on the Ridge itself; but, generally, the German garrison of two divisions tenaciously clung to the crest. The French attempted to learn from their experience of May by holding their reserves in readiness close to the front. Consequently, they took heavy casualties from artillery fire. The problem seemed insoluble.

Although the British were still suffering from a shortage of artillery ammunition (heavy guns were able to fire only 96 rounds in 24 hours), Haig hoped that the use of gas would prove an effective substitute for a heavy bombardment. Five thousand cylinders had been installed in the front line, and at 0500 hours on 25 September Haig had to decide whether or not to release the gas. The strength and direction of the wind was all important, for, if released when the wind was unfavorable, the gas could prove to be as much of a hazard to the British as to the Germans. After some hesitation, Haig ordered the gas to be released. This was one of the most controversial incidents in his career.

At 0630 hours six divisions attacked in line. On the extreme left, where the wind was negligible, the gas blew back onto the 2nd Division, whose attack failed completely. A brigade of 1st Division was similarly held up by the British gas. In other places, the gas did drift over the German lines, but the dramatic impact that Haig hoped for did not materialize. Nevertheless, the British were making steady progress everywhere except on the front of 2nd Division. The 15th Division, one of two Scottish New Army formations in the First Army, broke through the second, and final German line. Now was the time for the reserves to come forward and exploit the opening; the Germans fully expected to be defeated, and were preparing to retreat.

The British reserves for the battle had originally been under the control of French at GHQ. Haig protested, but it was not until 1320 hours that they were released to the First Army commander. The reserves, two raw New Army divisions, the 21st and 24th, had already endured three successive marches by night, and reached the front line too late to attack on that day. On the following day, they advanced at 1100 hours and were repulsed. The newly formed Guards Division had to be thrown in to hold the British line as the 21st and 24th fell back in confusion. French's judgment was at fault not only in holding the reserves 16 miles behind the battle front, but also in choosing two untried formations for the battle, when there were plenty of experienced Regular and Territorial divisions, including the 46th (North Midland) and 51st (Highland) Divisions, holding quiet sectors of the line. His insistence on prolonging the battle until 4 November compounded these errors. Haig, who enjoyed good relations with the King, intrigued to have French replaced. As senior Army commander, he stepped into French's shoes – an act for which French never forgave him. The Chief of the General Staff, General Sir William Robertson, who was to become the first 'Other Rank' to rise to Field Marshal, was appointed as Chief of the Imperial General Staff (CIGS). The year 1915, which had begun with the 'Easterners' in the ascendant, ended with the British army in the grip of 'Westerners.'

ABOVE: *A column of French prisoners is marched away past a cemetery.*
RIGHT: *A German Red Cross poster. The caption reads, 'Friend or foe, we help.' The German medic is carrying a Scottish soldier, visual evidence of the truth of the caption.*
ABOVE LEFT: *General Sir William Robertson, drawn by Francis Dodd in 1918. He was appointed Chief of the Imperial General Staff in 1915.*
LEFT: *German heavy artillery in action at Reims, 1915. The lack of similar guns greatly handicapped the British in the early part of the war.*

The Air War on the Western Front, 1914-16

In 1914 the military aircraft was in its infancy. It was not expected to fight; it was seen as a kind of 'flying cavalry,' scouting ahead of the ground forces. The airplane had impressed several influential observers at prewar exercises, notably General Grierson, commander designate of the British II Corps, but few foresaw any other role than reconnaissance. Aircraft very quickly proved its value in this role when Allied airmen were able to detect von Kluck's critical wheel before Paris, which exposed his flank to an Allied counterthrust. The sheer effectiveness of the airplane as an aerial scout inevitably led to a struggle for 'mastery of the air,' to prevent the enemy from carrying out reconnaissance while protecting friendly aircraft. This battle was waged between the pilots of the belligerents, and also between the scientists of both sides, who strove to build increasingly sophisticated aircraft. The 'technological pendulum' swung to and fro between the Allies and the Germans until the Armistice.

The earliest attempts at aerial combat took the form of observers firing at each other with pistols or carbines, or by pilots staging threatening mock attacks to force an opponent down. The next step was to fit machine guns to airplanes, although it was only possible to mount a forward-firing machine gun in 'pusher' aircraft, where the propeller was situated at the rear. The first significant advance toward creating a true 'fighter' aircraft was made by a Frenchman, Raymond Saulnier, who fitted 'deflector plates' to the blades of a propeller. This allowed a machine gun to fire through the propeller arc, the plates deflecting stray bullets. The French capitalized on this by forming *Escadrilles de Chasse*, or hunting squadrons, dedicated to fighter duties. On 1 April 1915 a Morane-Saulnier Type L monoplane piloted by Roland Garros shot down a German two-seater using the new device. It was the first of five victories in 18 days. The advantage that this gave the Allies was not allowed to go unchallenged for long. By July, a revolutionary new aircraft had begun to appear over the battlefield – the German Fokker E1 (Eindecker, or monoplane). It was equipped with an interrupter gear, a device which prevented a forward machine gun from firing when the propeller blade was directly opposite the gun muzzle. The Fokkers were to dominate the skies over France in the remaining months of 1915.

ABOVE: *'The Eagle of Lille,' Oberleutnant Max Immelmann, winner of the Iron Cross First and Second Class and the Pour le Merité, or 'Blue Max.' He was a pioneer of aerial tactics and was killed in June 1916 while flying a Fokker EIII.*
LEFT: *The instrument of the 'Fokker Scourge' of 1915: the Fokker EIII monoplane. It had a 100 hp Oberusel rotary engine and was an improved version of the original EI Eindecker.*

ABOVE: *Georges Guynemer, the French ace who flew with the famous 'Cigogne' unit. He claimed a total of 89 kills, 54 of which were confirmed.*
ABOVE LEFT: *Captain Albert Ball VC, DSO, MC, pictured early in his flying career, as a Second Lieutenant in 1915.*
LEFT: *One of the earliest aircraft designed to destroy other aircraft, the Morane-Saulnier Type N 'Bullet,' fitted with deflector plates on the propeller.*

KNIGHTS OF THE AIR

LOOK HINDENBURG! MY GERMAN HEROES!

ABOVE: *A German 'Knight of the Air' over the Western Front. First used only for reconnaissance, aircraft were soon developed for the fighter and bomber roles.*
LEFT: *A bitterly sarcastic comment on the German policy of strategic bombing. In fact, the British were to follow the German lead eagerly.*
RIGHT: *A De Havilland 'pusher' biplane of the type used successfully against the Fokker biplane early in 1916. Note the pennant on the strut of the aircraft; this indicates a flight commander's machine.*

Although in comparison to aerial combat between individual 'aces' reconnaissance was a distinctly unglamorous task, it nevertheless remained the principal role of the aircraft – indeed, the *raison d'être* of the struggle for command of the air. Both sides produced improved aerial cameras, signal devices and wireless sets; as early as March 1915 the BEF had obtained the important asset of an accurate map of the enemy trenches opposite their sector, compiled by photoreconnaissance. Another invaluable form of aerial reconnaissance was 'artillery co-operation,' spotting targets and observing the fall of shot for the gunners. Later came co-operation with the infantry in the form of 'contact patrols,' in which aircraft would attempt to report on the whereabouts of ground forces during an offensive. It was, however, the exploits of the fighter pilots, romantically envisaged as modern 'Knights of the Air' by the popular press, that caught the public imagination during the war.

The year 1915 saw the beginnings of the evolution of fighter tactics, particularly by the German pilot Hauptmann Oswald Boelcke, who pioneered the technique of hunting in pairs, and attacking the 'blind spot' on the tail of an enemy aircraft by diving out of the sun. 'Beware of the Hun in the Sun' became the watchword of the Royal Flying Corps (RFC). Another German, Oberleutnant Max Immelmann, developed what became known as the 'Immelmann Turn,' a surprise tactic which allowed an airplane to maintain height while in the process of a turn. German superiority was such that, despite an overcautious approach by High Command to the use of the E1, by late 1915 RFC pilots bitterly called themselves 'Fokker Fodder.'

81

LEFT: *A German observer in a 'sausage' balloon. Note the camera. Unlike most pilots, balloon observers were equipped with parachutes, but observation was still a hazardous task.*
BELOW: *A Caquot kite balloon being hauled down by a motor-winch. Note the horse-lines in the background. This is an RFC balloon section near Fricourt, on the Somme, 1916.*

The war in the air over Verdun in 1916 witnessed the next major shift in the aerial balance of power. The French massed their fighter aircraft into large units and began to pursue an aggressive policy that gradually pinned the Eindeckers back behind their own lines, allowing French reconnaissance planes to operate over the battlefield. It was over Verdun that the Nieuport scout, flown by men such as Guynemer, first showed its potential. The RFC, by now led by Major General Trenchard, also adopted an essentially offensive policy. Their faithful BE2cs were supplemented and replaced with superior aircraft; the Nieuport, Sopwith 1½ Strutter, and, in August 1916, the French Spad VII. Captain Albert Ball VC, DSO, MC, perhaps the greatest British ace of the war, achieved his finest victories while flying a Nieuport. At the time of his death in May 1917, he had amassed 44 'kills.'

A task that was particularly unpopular with most fighter pilots was 'balloon busting,' or shooting down the fat, sausage-shaped observation balloons that were situated just behind the front lines. They were invariably heavily defended by anti-aircraft fire ('Archie' to the RFC pilot) and were thus difficult targets to attack, despite their ungainly appearance. However, some pilots specialized in attacking them, men such as Gontermann, a German who in a seven-month spell in 1917 destroyed 18, in addition to 21 planes; the American, Frank Luke, and the Belgian ace, Willy Coppens, who accounted for 28 balloons and nine aircraft.

The Allied command of the air began to be seriously challenged in the autumn of 1916, when new German models began to reach the front. Faced by Albatros DIIs and DIIIs organized into elite fighter units called *Jagdstaffeln*, Allied losses began to mount up. Among the pilots of *Jagdstaffel (Jasta) II* was a young officer who was to become the highest scoring ace of the war with 80 victories. His name was Manfred Freiherr von Richthofen.

TOP: *Bristol Scouts of the Royal Naval Air Service on a French airfield, 1914. The RNAS had a fine record of service and served on the Western Front as well as in direct support of the Royal Navy. It was amalgamated in 1918 with the RFC to form the Royal Air Force. The Royal Navy later re-created its own air service, the Fleet Air Arm.*

ABOVE: *A gun mounting developed by Lieutenant Strange to enable the pilot of a BE2 to fire a machine gun. It was mounted at an angle to clear the airscrew, but was not a great success. The pilot had to fly 'crabwise' to aim and fire.*

RIGHT: *An illustration of an early, primitive method of bombing.*

The Eastern Front in 1915

At the beginning of 1915, Austria-Hungary's strategic position appeared to be parlous. Russian troops were in position on the crest of the Carpathian Mountains, poised to sweep down onto the Hungarian plain, and deliver a blow which might well force the Hapsburg Empire to sue for peace or even break up altogether. An Austrian offensive in January achieved little, and the fall of Przemysl on 22 March released three Russian corps for offensive operations. The 'Westerner' Falkenhayn was thus forced to mount a major offensive to rescue his ally by forcing the Russians off the Carpathians.

The Russians, too, were beset by problems. Their army was suffering from a chronic shortage of weapons and munitions; it required 250 million shells every month, but only 550 million were being produced annually. Much effort was spent in rectifying the situation – by September 1916 Russia was producing three-and-a-half times as many shells as Austria, which was also suffering from a munitions crisis – but the immediate prospects for the army in the spring of 1915 were bleak. Even rifles were in short supply – as a result of the losses of 1914, perhaps as many as one-third of the infantry of some divisions did not possess this basic side arm. Yet a Russian victory against Austria-Hungary remained a real possibility, particularly in view of the impending declaration of war on the Hapsburg Empire by Italy (which occurred on 23 May).

ABOVE: *Czar Nicholas II (next to car, on foot) and his uncle, Grand Duke Nicholas, the Russian commander in chief (in car, on the right). Despite the success of Lemberg, the loss of Poland in 1915 seriously undermined the Czar's confidence in his uncle.*

BELOW: *Hindenburg, the 'Wooden Titan,' being acclaimed by German troops during the Winter Campaign in Masuria. Hindenburg proved the perfect foil for his younger colleague Ludendorff and, like Kitchener in Britain, became a national hero.*

Two plans were considered by the Germans. Hindenburg proposed an offensive southeast from East Prussia into Poland (the Russian Tenth Army had been expelled from East Prussia in the Masurian Winter Campaign, in January-March 1915). Conrad argued for a blow to be launched against the Third Army in Galicia, to be launched on a 30-mile front between Gorlice and Tarnow. The Kaiser chose Conrad's scheme, without being aware of its provenance, and the offensive was planned to begin in May. The Austrian Fourth Army and the German Eleventh Army, which had been recently formed from a nucleus of eight divisions withdrawn from the Western Front, were to make the attack. The Eleventh Army's commander was von Mackensen. His principal staff officer was Hans von Seeckt, who was to be the architect of Germany's postwar army. The Eleventh Army was to advance, after a four-hour bombardment, with the right wing of the Austrian Fourth Army, while the remainder and the Austrian Third Army covered their flanks. A diversionary attack was made, far to the north, when a small German force advanced 75 miles into Lithuania. On 2 May 1915, 700 guns opened fire on the positions of the Russian Third Army.

Along the front as a whole, the Russians had a numerical superiority of the order of 35 percent. In the Gorlice-Tarnow sector, however, the Central Powers attacked with 22 divisions against 14 Russian divisions. The feeble Russian artillery was suppressed by the Austro-German barrage, and at 1000 hours assault troops, having crossed 3000 yards of No Man's Land under the cover of the bombardment, stormed the Russian trenches and without difficulty broke into the front line. Large numbers of Russians surrendered and others were routed. Complete surprise had been achieved, and, by sending in the reserves close on the heels of the first wave, they were able to maintain the momentum of the attack. The defenders, unlike the German defenders on the Western Front, were able to put up only a weak resistance; worse, the Russian reserves were placed too far back to be able to stem the advance of the Austro-German forces. On 3 May the second line was taken, and the Germans had broken through into open country. The defeated Third Army reeled back toward Przemysl, as did its neighbor, Brusilov's Eighth Army. Russian reinforcements, arriving piecemeal, were caught up in the general retreat. In the course of the next two weeks Mackensen advanced 95 miles; in the month of May, the Russian Southwest Front lost 412,000 men, a third from the Third Army. The Russians only escaped envelopment by a precipitate retreat. It was the most dramatic breakthrough of the war. By 15 May Mackensen had reached the River San.

The Germans had not expected success on this scale, and a heated debate arose between Conrad, OHL and the Hindenburg/Ludendorff team about the strategic aims of the offensive. Falkenhayn, who had to keep one eye firmly on developments on the Western Front, wanted to bring the offensive to a halt east of Lemberg. Hindenburg wanted to advance in the north, into Russia proper, enveloping the retreating Russians. Conrad argued for the continuation of Mackensen's offensive. Eventually, a modified version of Conrad's plan was adopted, with the armies of the Central Powers advancing along the entire front; about 1⅓ million Austrians and Germans faced 1½ million Russians. Poland was abandoned by the Russians. Warsaw fell on 6 August, and the important railway junction of Brest-Litovsk on 26 August, severing Russia's lateral communications with her northern armies. The Russian armies had been tested almost to destruction, but remained intact. At the beginning of September Falkenhayn decided to break off the offensive.

RIGHT: *German artillerymen in the Baltic area. Note the 24.5cm minenwerfer (trench mortar), range finder and field telephone.*
BELOW: *German transport crossing the River Vistula, Poland, 1915. The spectacular success of the Central Powers' 1915 campaign led Falkenhayn to discount the possibility of a Russian offensive in 1916. In the event, the Russians achieved a major strategic surprise.*

Falkenhayn's decision has been criticized, and yet appears to have been correct. His armies were at the end of a long logistic chain and the Franco-British offensives in Artois, Champagne and Loos were about to begin. Hindenburg's northern offensive and an Austrian attack in the south had not brought a decisive victory, but the Central Powers' achievements were far from negligible. Two million Russians had been killed, wounded, or taken prisoner; Russian morale had taken a fearful battering; Hungary had been freed from the threat of invasion; and German troops were dug in on Russian soil. In desperation, the Czar dismissed his uncle, Grand Duke Nicholas, as commander of his armies and took on that role himself. This was a mistake. In future, every defeat suffered by the Russian armies reflected badly on the Czar himself. Previously, he had been virtually immune from criticism; in many ways, by denting the mystique of the Russian Royal Family, the Revolution was brought a step closer.

Austria, too, had suffered immense casualties – in the unsuccessful September offensive alone, 230,000 – and the failure to break Russia in 1915 brought about the necessity for another campaign in 1916, while the Western Allies grew stronger and prepared for their own 'war winning' offensive. Austria-Hungary had been saved – for the moment – but the struggle on the Eastern Front was far from over.

One of the Allies had been knocked out of the war: Serbia. Her strategic importance had grown with the entry of the Ottoman Empire into the war, for Serbia blocked the land route by which supplies could reach the Turks from Germany. Having remained unmolested for most of 1915, by October the Serbs faced invasion by Austrian,

LEFT: *Russian casualties after the Battle of the Masurian Lakes. The outlook for the survivors was bleak: Russian medical services were at best rudimentary.*
BELOW LEFT: *The realities of war: a dead Austrian soldier.*
BELOW: *Serbian artillery in action on the plain of Kosovo, 1915. Although poorly equipped, the Serbs put up a heroic fight against the invading armies.*

German and Bulgarian forces. 'Foxy' Ferdinand, the King of Bulgaria, had adhered to the Central Powers on 6 September 1915, having decided that Germany's bribes of Serbian territory were more attractive than the Franco-British inducements to remain neutral. This decision effectively sealed Serbia's fate. The Austrian Third Army (which included three German divisions) and the German Eleventh Army (von Gallwitz) lay to the north, and the Bulgarians to the east.

The Serbian forces fought bravely, but they were faced by the formidable Mackensen, a rather better commander than the feeble Potiorek who had led the Austrian forces in 1914. In contrast to the earlier invasion, the German staffwork, which was mainly undertaken by Colonel Hentsch (of Marne fame) was excellent, and the Central Powers soon crushed the five weak Serbian armies of General Putnik.

On 7 October, the Austro-Germans crossed the barriers of the River Save and Danube. Belgrade was taken two days later, and Putnik began to retreat. The *coup de grâce* was delivered by the movement of the Bulgarian First Army across the border, which acted as the eastern jaw of a vice (Mackensen's forces acting as the western jaw). The Bulgarian Second Army deployed to prevent any reinforcements arriving from Greece (where two Allied divisions had landed at Salonika on 5 October). Putnik's broken armies fled southwest into the mountains of Albania and Montenegro, where the terrain was as inhospitable as the inhabitants. The vestiges of the Serbian army struggled to the Adriatic coast, where they recuperated at Corfu before joining the Allies at Salonika. Some 100,000 Serbs had died; 160,000 were captured. Serbia had been eliminated.

Gallipoli: the Naval Overture

By early 1915, it was clear that the deadlock in the West was not going to be easily broken, and two schools of thought emerged among the British leadership. The Westerners, who included French, Haig, and Robertson (who was to be appointed CIGS, Chief of the Imperial General Staff, in November 1915) held that the German army had to be defeated for the war to be won; and since the German army was to be found on the Western Front, operations elsewhere were a dangerous dissipation of resources. The Easterners, led by Churchill (and later in the war by Lloyd George), were heirs to a more traditional strategy based on a limited military commitment to the Continent and the use of sea power to exert British influence. They were convinced that there was a way round the deadlock in France, through the Mediterranean. After the Russians appealed to the British on 2 January 1915 to make a naval demonstration against the Turks, the eyes of the Easterners began to be drawn to the point where Europe meets Asia.

An operation against the Straits had many attractions. The Turkish capital, Constantinople, and Turkey's two main munitions plants were situated there; thus a successful attack might have forced the Ottoman Empire out of the war. Most tantalizing of all, a new supply route to Russia would have been opened up. The huge stocks of Russian wheat could have reached the West, and Western supplies could have been sent to the beleaguered Russians, reinvigorating her war effort. It is even possible that the 1917 revolutions could have been averted. The strategic concept of the Dardanelles expedition was sound, but its planning and operational handling were not. When the idea was first mooted, Kitchener insisted that no troops could be spared for the enterprise. The original plan thus was a compromise; the Dardanelles would be forced, but by the Navy alone. This was the first of many missed opportunities, for the Gallipoli peninsula was defended by only one division in early 1915. Between 27 February and 3 March parties of British Marines, landed from the Fleet, were able to roam almost at will over the peninsula. The Turkish Staff History candidly admitted that, up to about 25 February, the capture of the Straits by a small land force would have been a relatively easy undertaking. By 4 March, reinforcements were reaching Gallipoli and the opportunity vanished.

ABOVE: *Allied transports, the Dardanelles expedition at Lemnos, April 1915. Only a power with control of the sea could have mounted such a logistical effort.*
LEFT: *The old battleship HMS* Canopus *steams into harbor off the island of Mudros. Obsolete warships such as the* Canopus *were incapable of operating effectively in the North Sea 'battleground' but it was hoped that they would prove useful in subduing Turkish shore batteries along the Dardanelles.*

RIGHT: *Vice-Admiral Sir John de Robeck, KCB. Sir William Birdwood, commander of the ANZACs, said he was 'worth a dozen of Carden,' de Robeck's predecessor as* *the Allied naval commander. The failure of the attack of 18 March was clear evidence that the mine and the torpedo had brought the era of undisputed battleship supremacy to an end.*

LEFT: *The crew of HMS* Grampus *cheer the submarine* E.11 *as she leaves the Dardanelles Straits after sinking the Turkish battleship* Babarousse Hairedine. E.11 *was commanded by Lieutenant Commander Nasmith, whose exploits included bombarding a railway with a 12-pounder gun, and landing an officer, Lieutenant D'Oyly-Hughes, to complete the demolition with explosive obtained by dismantling a torpedo.*

LEFT: *French cartoon showing the Turkish Sultan cringing with his harem when the guns of the Allied fleet were heard in Constantinople. The Sultan was little more than a cipher, with the 'Young Turks' ruling the moribund Ottoman Empire.*
BELOW: *The Allied fleet bombard the Dardanelles. For the naval assault on 18 March Admiral de Robeck had a powerful force of 18 British and French battleships – an impressive sight as this painting indicates.*

LEFT: *The effect of the Allied bombardment on the Turkish shore defenses. Three French staff officers pose beside Turkish guns in the old fort at Sedd-el-Bahr after the cessation of hostilities.*
RIGHT: *The naval assault of 18 March 1915. The failure of the surface fleet contrasts strongly with the success of the operations of the Allied submarines, and indeed those of the German U-Boats in the area.*

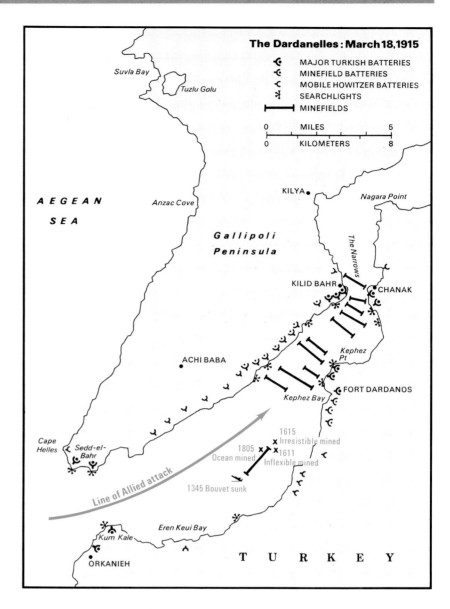

The Dardanelles: March 18, 1915

⚓ MAJOR TURKISH BATTERIES
⚓ MINEFIELD BATTERIES
⚓ MOBILE HOWITZER BATTERIES
⚓ SEARCHLIGHTS
▬ MINEFIELDS

MILES 0 — 5
KILOMETERS 0 — 8

Suvla Bay
Tuzlu Golu
KILYA •
Nagara Point
A E G E A N
S E A
Anzac Cove
G a l l i p o l i
P e n i n s u l a
The Narrows
KILID BAHR
CHANAK
• ACHI BABA
Kephez Pt
FORT DARDANOS
Kephez Bay
Cape Helles
Sedd-el-Bahr
1615 ✕ Irresistible mined
1805 ✕ ✕ 1611
Ocean mined Inflexible mined
1345 Bouvet sunk
Line of Allied attack
Eren Keui Bay
Kum Kale
ORKANIEH •
T U R K E Y

Even without military support, naval power alone could have knocked Turkey out of the war. In early 1915, civilian morale in Constantinople was extremely low. The authorities feared that the arrival of the Allied Fleet would spark off a revolution, and opened secret negotiations with the British. A successful attack would almost certainly have led to Turkey's withdrawal from the war. However, it was not to be. Preliminary bombardments of the Outer Forts began on 19 February, but inaccurate gunnery and bad weather prevented completion of this task for three weeks. Then the job of clearing the channel of mines began. However, only slow progress was made because the shelling by Turkish mobile howitzers caused serious morale problems among the minesweepers' civilian crews. Nonetheless, the British commander, Admiral Carden, decided to move to the third stage of the operation with the minesweeping unfinished.

On 18 March, de Robeck (Carden's deputy, Carden having fallen sick) sent 18 battleships in to reduce the Inner Defenses. At first, they made good progress. At 1100 hours the four leading ships began to bombard the shore installations from a range of 14,000 yards. By 1400 hours many of the forts were severely damaged, and with the rupturing of communications, Turkish fire began to slacken. Then disaster struck: a French battleship, *Bouvet*, exploded. Two hours later the British battle cruisers *Inflexible* and *Irresistible* were holed by mines, and at 1805 hours the battleship HMS *Ocean* was sunk. In all, the Allied Fleet lost six capital ships that day: three were sunk, and three were disabled. De Robeck was badly shaken by this loss of a third of his fleet and refused to renew the attack without military support. Had he possessed the same ruthless attitude toward his ships that Haig, for instance, was to show toward his men's lives, that attack would probably have succeeded. A German general in Constantinople at the time considered that the Allies could have broken through for the sacrifice of 10 ships. Only the Super-Dreadnought *Queen Elizabeth* and the battle cruiser *Inflexible* were modern ships. The rest were obsolete and should have been regarded as expendable. This was contrary to every instinct of the early twentieth-century officer of the Royal Navy.

Gallipoli: the Allies Invade

On 25 April 1915 Allied troops began landing on the Gallipoli peninsula at dawn. Even before de Robeck's failure to force the Straits with the Fleet, it had become clear that land forces would have to be committed to the area. The Westerners objected that these would be sent at the expense of the BEF; this obstacle could have been overcome, had not the Russians vetoed the offer of three Greek divisions, on the grounds that they feared the Greeks had designs on Constantinople (which had been promised to the Russians themselves). By 10 March Kitchener had finally been persuaded to release troops for service in the east, and Sir Ian Hamilton was appointed as commander of the Mediterranean Expeditionary Force (MEF) of 75,000 men.

This commitment of troops to the Dardanelles can be seen as an example of 'too little, too late.' Hamilton's force consisted of two divisions of the Australian and New Zealand Army Corps (ANZACs), and the hastily raised Royal Naval Division (RND). Both formations were totally inexperienced and only half trained, although the ANZACs were to gain a formidable reputation during the course of the campaign. The French also contributed a division, and the MEF's order of battle was completed by 29th Division. This was composed of Regular battalions who had been on colonial garrison duty at the outbreak of war, and was in effect the last of the old prewar army. Although individually each battalion was of excellent quality they had never served together as a formation. Apart from these drawbacks, the MEF was short of artillery and Hamilton had had only 40 days in which to create a staff from scratch. Above all, Hamilton was being asked to carry out one of the most difficult of maneuvers – an opposed amphibious landing – with these mainly inexperienced troops.

During World War II, such landings had the benefit of amphibious vehicles and tanks, radio and specially designed landing craft. The MEF had no such equipment. It had also forfeited the element of surprise. Turkish morale had been boosted by the Turks 'victory' over the Allied Fleet; even before the arrival of Liman von Sanders, the German general appointed to command the forces on the peninsula, work had begun on coastal defenses. Von Sanders' intention was to hold the beaches with light forces, and to concentrate the bulk of his troops inland. Of his six divisions (about 62,000 effectives), he deployed two on the Asiatic shore, one at the tip of the peninsula, one at Gaba Tepe, and the remaining two divisions, as a reserve, in the north near Bulair.

The attack of 25 April was a disaster, although this was not the fault of Hamilton's original plan, which was reasonably sound. The ANZACs were ordered to land about a mile north of Gaba Tepe and strike inland, capture the surrounding heights, and then make for the town of Maidos, thus sealing off the southern part of the peninsula. Unfortunately, 1st Australian Division, leading the assault, was deposited about two miles north of the intended point – whether through human error or a strong north-flowing current, it is uncertain – resulting in a confusing mixture of units on a strange beach surrounded by almost sheer cliffs. Unperturbed by this inauspicious beginning, parties of Australians pushed inland and reached the commanding height of Chunuk Bair; a resounding victory against the few Turks in the area seemed within their grasp. Only the prompt reaction of the future President of postwar Turkey, Mustapha Kemal, then a lieutenant colonel commanding 19th Division, halted the Australian advance. He organized a series of makeshift counterattacks which pushed the ANZACs back and bought time for the Turkish reserves to arrive. By nightfall, the ANZACs were fighting to simply retain their toehold on the beach. Their line, although battered, held, and 'ANZAC Cove' was to witness some of the most bitter fighting in the entire campaign in the months to come.

Two feint attacks worked well. The RND's demonstration at Bulair succeeded in tying down the Turkish reserves situated there, and the

RIGHT: *Lieutenant General Prezhevalsky, commander of the Turkestan Army Corps during the capture of Erzurum in 1916. It is often assumed in the West that the Dardanelles was the major Turkish theater of operations. In reality, the Turkish battles against the Russians were on a far larger scale.*

ABOVE: *Liman von Sanders, the German commander of the Turkish forces.*
TOP: *The landing at Anzac Beach, 25 April 1915. In 1915, amphibious operations were crude, improvised affairs with much left to chance.*
LEFT: *Lord Kitchener at Anzac Beach, 13 November 1915. Behind him is Birdwood. Note the informal attitude of the Anzac soldiers on the right.*

French diversionary landing at Kum Kale deflected the attention of the enemy artillery from the landing at S beach, just across the sea at Cape Helles. Likewise, troops landing at three of the five beaches – lettered S, X, and Y – at Cape Helles encountered only minimal opposition. At V and W beaches, scene of the main landings, it was a very different story. On the former, an old collier, the SS *River Clyde*, was to be run aground and the attacking troops were to jump out of the pre-prepared 'sally ports,' having been protected from enemy gunfire right up to the beach. That was the theory. In practice, the men of 2nd Hampshires and 1st Royal Munster Fusiliers found the water too deep to wade ashore, and many drowned or were hit by the heavy fire that the Turkish defenders – a mere three platoons of the 3rd Battalion of the 26th Regiment – were able to bring to bear on the assaulting troops. The 1 Royal Dublin Fusiliers, landing from small boats, fared no better. The corpses were heaped up at the water's edge.

At W beach a similar tragedy was being enacted: there the 1st Lancashire Fusiliers won 'six VCs before breakfast.' The Turkish defenders, displaying considerable courage and fire discipline, withheld their fire until the armada of small boats was only 100 yards away. Then they unleashed a devastating series of volleys into the ranks of the attacking Fusiliers. As they struggled to create a gap in the wire laid in the shallow water, the British were simply cut down. Amazingly, a small party did reach the beach, which they attempted to clear at the point of the bayonet. However, it was the landing of a company further up the shore, on the initiative of Brigadier-General Hare, that forced the Turks to retire, fearing that they were about to be outflanked. As the defenders skillfully withdrew, they left 533 casualties of the Lancashire Fusiliers behind them. British reinforcements landing on W beach had to wade through sea that was literally crimson with blood.

In spite of the disasters on two of the Cape Helles beaches, victory still could have been obtained by reinforcing the successful landings at the other three. However, Hunter-Weston, the commander of 29th Division, had tactical control of the available reserves, and his attention was focused almost exclusively on the grim struggle for W and V beaches. Thus he insisted on reinforcing the failures there, rather than the successes elsewhere. Hamilton, at sea in HMS *Queen Elizabeth*, saw 'Hunter-Bunter's' error, and offered the latter some trawlers to transport reserves to Y beach instead of their intended destinations. Hunter-Weston declined this offer, and he also ignored a later suggestion of Hamilton's that two French brigades should be sent to Y beach. Hamilton's Staff College training had taught him that a commander in chief should not overrule the judgment of the 'man on the spot,' and as a result of his self-restraint, Hamilton exerted little or no influence on the course of the battle.

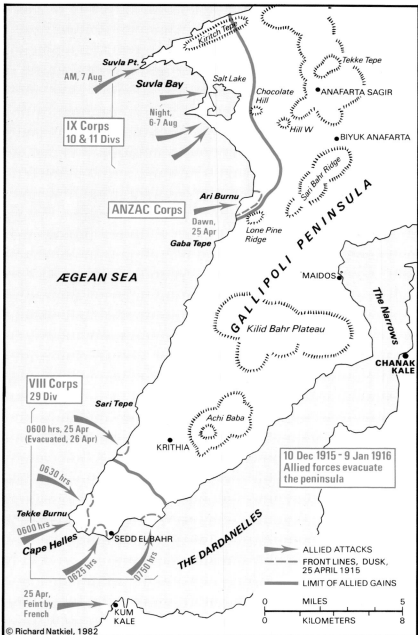

A similarly dismal standard of leadership was displayed on Y beach. There, there was confusion as to which of two battalion commanders was really in command of the landing, and Hunter-Weston's orders left little scope for individual initiative. Even after taking these factors into account, it must be said that remarkably little urgency was shown in attempting to link up with X beach, or even in digging in. At the time of the landing, the Turkish defenders in the area were weak and scattered. By the evening, the Turks had surrounded Y beach, and were throwing in increasingly threatening counterattacks. On the following day, Y beach was evacuated.

Thus the attempt to pull off a *coup de main* failed. Instead, the conditions of the Western Front were repeated, with the additional complications created by the narrowness of the Allied bridgehead and the extremes of climate, which caused sickness and disease on a vast scale. A savage series of battles began, between enemies whose trenches were sometimes as little as 30 yards apart. By the end of May, British casualties alone exceeded 38,000. In July, Hamilton finally received reinforcements, and another attempt was made to break the deadlock.

On 6 August 11th Division, a raw New Army formation, landed at Suvla Bay, three miles to the north of Anzac Cove. Simultaneously, Birdwood's ANZACs attempted to break out of their bridgehead. The Suvla force achieved complete surprise, but was commanded by a general who was supine even by Gallipoli standards. Although opposed by minimal Turkish forces, Lieutenant General Stopford's corps made virtually no attempt to take any aggressive actions. Once again, Hamilton was content to offer advice and suggestions to his subordinate, and would not give Stopford, who had never commanded troops in battle before, a direct order. By 8 August Stopford had still not moved. By that date, the Turks were in the Suvla Bay area in some force. Yet another clear opportunity for a breakthrough had been allowed to develop into a stalemate through the incompetence of the British military leadership. The heroic efforts of the ANZACs, who won 15 VCs in the fighting for the Lone Pine position, were wasted. The failure at Suvla sounded the death knell for both the Gallipoli expedition and the military career of Sir Ian Hamilton. He was recalled on 16 October and his replacement, Sir Charles Monro, recommended that the peninsula should be evacuated – an eminently sensible

ABOVE LEFT: *Part of the Allied armada off the Dardanelles. Allied ships provided fire support for the troops on shore.*
LEFT: *The campaign on the Gallipoli peninsula. Although Turkey was a second-class military power, its army proved a formidable opponent for the armies of the French and British Empires.*

ABOVE: *Australian troops practice bomb throwing. Grenades or 'bombs' were manufactured on the beaches from old cans. Note the varied campaign dress of the men.*
TOP: *The aftermath of the Allied landing: a lighter packed with dead and wounded, off Sedd-el-Bahr, April 1915.*

decision. For once, this operation was a complete, and almost bloodless, success. The final stage, the evacuation of Cape Helles, was accomplished on the night of 8 January 1916. The Dardanelles adventure was over. In retrospect, it seems clear that even had the operation succeeded, it would not have proved the 'key' that would have unlocked the Western Front; the hope of a resurgent 'Russian Steamroller' was a mere chimera. As it was, the failure of the Dardanelles campaign discredited the Easterners among the British generals. For the rest of the war, the Westerners were definitely in control; and their eyes were firmly fixed on the area where they faced their main enemy: the Western Front.

Turkish armies stood on the defensive at Gallipoli, but in the Caucasus they carried the fight to the enemy, prompting the Russian appeal to the Allies in January 1915. Enver Pasha, the Minister of War, believed that a successful invasion would cause a general uprising among the Czar's Islamic subjects, and on 21 December 1914 he led the Third Army across the Russian frontiers. The expedition was a disaster. The Caucasian Mountains were inhospitable in the extreme, and easily defended by the Russians. The rudimentary Turkish logistics severely depleted the Third Army's numbers even before the fighting began, and when the Russians counterattacked, at Sarikamish in January 1915, the Turks were badly beaten; one entire corps surrendered, and two others were forced back. By the time Enver fled back to the safety of Constantinople in mid-January, the Third Army could muster between 12,000 and 18,000 bayonets. It had commenced the campaign with 66,000 effectives.

Apart from some see-saw fighting around Malazgirt in July, the Caucasus remained generally quiet in 1915. On 17 January 1916, however, the Russian commander, General Yudenich, launched a surprise attack which punched a deep hole in the Turkish defenses. Advancing steadily forward, Yudenich won a series of battles, culminating in the victory at Erzincan (captured on 25 July) which crippled the Third Army. The Second Army, which had been hastily dispatched from the coast of Asia Minor, launched a counteroffensive which was fended off by Yudenich. He was unable to repeat his victories in 1917; although the army of the Caucasus remained loyal to the Czar during the turmoil of that year, it was starved of supplies, and, by the time of the Bolshevik putsch of November, was beginning to crumble away.

1916

The Year of Attrition

Chronology 1916

January 7	Evacuation of Gallipoli completed
February 21	First German attack on Verdun
March 18	Russian Offensive around Lake Narotch
April 29	Townshend capitulates at Kut
May 14	Austrian Trentino Offensive begins
May 31	Jutland
June 4	Brusilov Offensive begins on Eastern Front
June 5	Kitchener drowned
July 1	Battle of the Somme begins
July 23	Pozières falls to Australians
August 8	Fall of Gorizia to Italians
August 27	Rumania enters wars
August 27	Falkenhayn replaced by Hindenburg and Ludendorff
September 15	Flers-Courcelette: tanks used for the first time
September 24	Fort Douaumont recaptured by French at Verdun
November 16	Battle of Somme closed down
December 6	Bucharest falls; most of Rumania occupied by Central Powers
December 6	Lloyd George becomes British Prime Minister
December 12	German Peace note
December 18	US Peace note
December 20	Battle of Verdun closed down

LEFT: *A British 12-inch gun blasts away at German positions from its railway mounting at Meulte during the Battle of the Somme, August 1916. Guns of this caliber were essential for the destruction of a well-fortified trench redoubts which formed the keystones of the German defensive system.*

Ireland: the Easter Uprising

The outbreak of war in August 1914 brought Ireland back from the brink of civil war. Asquith's Liberal government had attempted to grant a measure of Home Rule to Ireland, which infuriated the mainly Protestant province of Ulster. The Ulster Unionists feared that any transfer of power to the Catholic south of the country would bring about 'Rome Rule' by the hated Roman Catholic Church; and, perhaps most importantly, they feared that any loosening of the economic tie with Britain would ruin Ulster's booming industries. The Ulster Unionists, egged on by the Conservative opposition, raised their own private army to resist Home Rule by force of arms and the Nationalists raised their own force in response. Even the British Army's attitude was uncertain, as the so-called Curragh Mutiny of March 1914 revealed. However, the coming of war in Europe rallied all of Ireland behind the British government. The Ulster Volunteers became a part of the British Army as the 36th (Ulster) Division. The German invasion of Catholic Belgium outraged Nationalist opinion to such an extent that an entire division, the 17th (Irish), was raised from the South. When Private Michael O'Leary of the Irish Guards won the VC in 1915, he became a national hero in Ireland. The prospect of an independent Irish state looked remote.

On Easter Monday 24 April 1916 a group of 40 men seized the Central Post Office in Dublin and proclaimed the Irish Republic, taking prisoner a surprised British officer who had been sending a telegram to his wife. The rebels then occupied some other key buildings and sat back to await the reaction of the Irish people and the British Army. The former responded disappointingly. The general reaction of Dubliners to the coup was amazement, and even annoyance at the disruption of daily life. The latter reacted slowly at first, but soon began to exceed expectations. One of the insurgent leaders, James Connolly of the socialist Irish Citizen Army, had declared that the British would never use artillery against the rebels out of respect for private property in the center of Dublin; but British guns soon began to pound the rebel positions. The ultimate result was never in doubt. By Sunday, 30

April, the last of the insurgents had surrendered to the British forces. One hundred British soldiers and 450 Irish rebels and civilians had been killed.

At first, the uprising appeared to have failed completely. Militarily, the insurgents had been crushed; more importantly, they had failed to rally popular opinion behind them – the Dublin crowd had even shouted abuse as they were led away as prisoners. All this changed as the British executed 14 of the rebel leaders, including Connolly and Patrick Pearce of the Irish Volunteers. Sir Roger Casement, a former British colonial official who had been negotiating with the Germans for aid for the insurgents, was also hanged. A wave of revulsion swept the country and the 'Easter rebels' became popular heroes. From that point on, the Union between Great Britain and Ireland was dead. Five years later, the Irish Free State came into being after a bitter Anglo-Irish war, with Ulster remaining as a persistently troubled part of the United Kingdom.

ABOVE: *A panoramic view of Sackville Street and Quayside, Dublin. This area was heavily shelled by a British gunboat from the River Liffey. Britain, committed to total war in Europe, felt compelled to crush this challenge to its authority with the upmost speed and severity.*
LEFT: *Ulster extremists protest against Home Rule, Portadown, September 1912.*
RIGHT: *The illusion of victory: British soldiers march a Sinn Fein prisoner to Dublin Castle, the symbol of British rule in Ireland.*

Verdun: Phase I

The last month of 1915 was spent in planning for the coming year's campaigns. At Chantilly on 6 December the Allies agreed to launch offensives roughly simultaneously on the Western, Italian and Eastern fronts. Falkenhayn was not, of course, privy to these counsels, but it took little imagination to guess the general thrust of the *Entente*'s strategy for 1916. He decided to pre-empt them by striking first. On Christmas Eve he presented a memorandum to the Kaiser, setting out his ideas. He rejected an Austrian scheme to knock Italy out of the war, and similarly dismissed the idea of an attack on Russia which he (wrongly) believed was incapable of taking offensive action in 1916. Germany's main enemy, he argued, was Britain, and the way to defeat her was to 'knock her best sword . . . out of her hand,' that is, to cripple the French Army.

Falkenhayn intended to achieve this by striking at the fortress of Verdun, which, in the eyes of the public, was the lynchpin of France's defenses. Traditionally, historians have accepted his claim – made in his postwar memoirs – that all along he intended to bleed the French Army to death by forcing them to fight for a national symbol, thus achieving his aim even if Verdun did not fall. Recently, some historians have challenged this view. Falkenhayn could not hope to 'win' a prolonged war of attrition, simply because the Germans had fewer human resources than did the *Entente*, and the German army was likely to suffer heavily in the process of bleeding France white. It is possible that Falkenhayn originally intended to promote a French collapse by seizing Verdun. The government would have been unlikely to survive this blow to its prestige, and a compromise peace might have resulted. In that case, a limited period of attrition against an enemy already weakened by the campaigns of 1915 might hasten the process. Alternatively, it has been suggested that Falkenhayn hoped to draw French reserves to Verdun and then attack in Champagne, or even to force the British to launch their 'big push' prematurely in Artois, which could then be followed by a counteroffensive. The taciturn German Chief of Staff gave few hints as to his true intentions but it is most likely that he intended the battle of Verdun to remain limited.

ABOVE RIGHT: *The death of a French soldier at Verdun; a dramatic 'action' photograph.*
RIGHT: *Erich von Falkenhayn, Chief of the General Staff and de facto German commander in chief in the West. He ordered the commencement of the attack at Verdun but was replaced as the German casualties began to mount.*
FAR RIGHT: *A German 25cm* minenwerfer, *one of the thousands of artillery pieces that battered the French positions around Verdun.*

LEFT: *French* poilus *cower as a shell explodes. Men could be killed in many ways by shellfire. Some were literally blown to pieces; others were outwardly unmarked, killed by concussion.*
BELOW: *A German flame-thrower attack on the Western Front. Although a terrifying weapon, flamethrowers were clumsy to carry and easy targets for snipers. They had some success on 21 February 1916, the first day of the struggle for Verdun.*

The strength of Verdun was illusory. Most of the forts had been stripped of their heavy artillery, which had been sent to the field armies. The public was unaware of this. To them, Verdun remained the unassailable fortress of prewar propaganda. In reality the trench systems were far from satisfactory and, in February 1914, only 270 guns and four divisions of XXX Corps, which included aged Territorials, defended the sector. Against them, the Germans deployed Kronprinz Wilhelm's Fifth Army, backed up by 1400 guns. Falkenhayn planned a limited attack on the eastern bank of the Meuse (which ran through Verdun itself), to be launched firstly by parties of assault troops, some armed with flame-throwers, who would infiltrate the French front line. Only if these probing parties found the defenses thoroughly destroyed would the main attack go in, thus minimizing casualties. The attack was planned for 12 February 1916, but had to be delayed because of bad weather. Had the Germans attacked on that day, they would have had a five-to-one advantage in infantry. The weather on that occasion was most certainly an ally of the French infantry.

At 0715 hours on 21 February the German bombardment began. For nine hours the defenders cowered under the heaviest barrage the world had ever witnessed. At 1700 hours the infantry attack began. To reach the city of Verdun, the Germans had to break through two lines of forts. The results of the first day showed just how difficult it was going to be to reach that target. The French, stunned from the barrage, were given enough time to recover before the main attack reached them. Ironically, this was one occasion on which a shoulder-

LEFT: *The German bombardment of Fort Douaumont, 1916. The Germans had pounded the fort with huge 42cm shells twelve months before the attack of February 1916 and had drawn the erroneous conclusion that it had been heavily damaged.*
BELOW LEFT: *A German infantryman shelters beside a dead Frenchman at Verdun.*
BELOW: *A German 15cm howitzer (known to the British as a 5.9-inch gun) in the Vosges. At the end of the first four months of the battle, 24 million shells had been fired at Verdun.*

to-shoulder advance might have broken through. By the end of the day, the Germans had taken only part of the French front line, but their resistance cost the defenders dearly: Colonel Driant's two battalions of Chasseurs, for instance, suffered 1800 casualties out of 2000 effectives in the first days of the fighting. On 22 February and subsequent days, the Germans made some progress. The entire front line fell, and sections of the second line were captured. Moreover, French morale was causing some alarm in GQG. On 23 February, colonial troops of 37th African Division had been routed, and the spirits of the white soldiers were little higher. General Langle de Cary, the Commander of Central Army Group, decided to cut his losses and abandon the right bank of the Meuse to the Germans. De Castelnau – Joffre's second in command – immediately went to Verdun where, on 25 February, he took the fateful decision to defend the right bank. Herr, the old and dispirited local commander was removed, and his Army Group Commander followed him in April. Langle de Cary's decision, in purely strategic terms, had been the correct one. It was, however, politically impossible for Verdun to be abandoned; it would have been a devastating blow to the self-esteem of the French nation and army. Indeed, as Alistair Horne has suggested, it was uncertain whether the French army was capable of carrying out an orderly withdrawal. So de Castelnau picked up the gauntlet Falkenhayn had hurled – and thus condemned the French army to a slow death. General Philippe Pétain was appointed to command at Verdun. He was promptly faced by a disaster: on 25 February the central bastion of the defenses of Verdun, Fort Douaumont, had been captured by the enemy.

Verdun: Phase II

The fall of Fort Douaumont was the result of a catastrophic French mistake. The fort had been scarcely damaged by the German siege artillery; yet it was captured by a party of nine pioneers from 24th Brandenburg Regiment, led by Sergeant Kunze – who obtained access by forming a human pyramid to reach an embrasure. Douaumont contained a mere 57 Territorial gunners; an administrative error had left it virtually undefended. The news provoked a further crisis of morale in the French army, and ecstatic celebrations in Germany. Victory appeared to be at hand.

Pétain took command at midnight on 25 February and at once set about transforming the situation. He raised morale by declaring *'Ils ne passeront pas'* (They shall not pass), and, more practically, threw in what Falkenhayn described as 'violent – one might say desperate' counterattacks, which reduced the German advance to a crawl. The French reinforcements which reached Verdun were sustained by supplies brought along specially constructed light railways and along the *Voie Sacrée* (Sacred Way), a single road along which, although under shellfire, 35,000 lorries carried 4,000 tons of supplies and up to 20,000 men every day. The French line held.

Falkenhayn was faced with a choice: either to admit defeat or to extend the still-limited battle. He chose the second option. The first attack west of the Meuse began on 6 March. This initiated a new phase of the battle, a struggle for possession of the *Mort Homme* (Dead Man), and Hill 304. French and German battalions continued to be sucked inexorably into the 'mincing machine' of Verdun. Falkenhayn tried to break off the battle on 30 March; Kronprinz Wilhelm insisted on continuing. With all restraints cast to the wind, amid the shattered

trenches and shellholes, ceaselessly pounded by artillery, two mighty nations were locked in a struggle to the death. It raged until December. Fort Vaux fell on 7 June; by employing lethal phosgene gas the Germans came close to capturing Fort Souville 13 days later. This was the highwater mark of the German effort at Verdun. On 11 July they attacked for the last time, and failed to break through. With the Germans now having to fight another battle, on the Somme, Falkenhayn ordered the army onto the defensive. Pétain was given the opportunity to make good his boast of *'On les aura'* ('We'll get 'em'). At the end of March he had been promoted to command the Central Army Group and a new name began to appear on French lips – General Robert Nivelle, who took command of the Second Army at Verdun.

The German defenders in the second half of 1916 were not of the same caliber as the men of February. Heavy casualties at Verdun and on the Somme had sapped their morale, and caused the loss of many of the most experienced men. On 24 October General Charles Mangin, a Colonial soldier and a close associate of Nivelle, recaptured Fort Douaumont, and took 6700 prisoners. The enormous weight of the bombardment played a large part in this success. With their airmen tightening their control over the skies, the French were now pushing the Germans back. Fort de Vaux was abandoned in November, and on 15 December Nivelle launched eight divisions against the German positions. Nine thousand prisoners were taken, and by the conclusion of the battle the German front line had been pushed back three miles.

Verdun gained the reputation as being the worst battle of the War, a battle of attrition *par excellence*. Approximately 362,000 Frenchmen and 340,000 Germans became casualties. There were other casual-

LEFT: *Anglo-French unity in the third year of the war: from left to right, Joffre, President Poincaré, King George V, Foch and Haig. This photograph was taken at Château Val Vion, Beauquesne, 12 August 1916. The opening of the mainly British offensive on the Somme in July forced the Germans onto the defense and allowed the French to launch offensive operations at Verdun.*

RIGHT: La voie sacrée *(the sacred way). Troops rest while in the background an endless stream of lorries carries supplies to the front at Verdun. Vehicles which broke down were simply tipped off the road.*

BELOW: *Some of the many French prisoners taken at Verdun. In the later stages of the battle equally large numbers of Germans were captured. The Germans tended to keep units in the line until exhausted, while their enemies practiced a system of rotating* *troops in and out of the battle. While this may have had some short-term advantages, it also ensured that large sections of the French army underwent the morale-sapping ordeal of fighting at Verdun. The mutinies of 1917 were a consequence.*

ties, too. Joffre and Falkenhayn were replaced by Nivelle (on 27 December) and the Hindenburg-Ludendorff team (on 29 August) respectively. The morale of the French army had suffered, but the extent of the wounds did not become clear until the following spring. The German army, too, was not the force it had been before Verdun and the Somme.

Many years later, in 1984, Verdun, the setting for the most bitter Franco-German struggle in history, witnessed a symbolic act of reconciliation. Hand in hand, the President of France and the Chancellor of the Federal Republic of Germany stood in silence on the battlefield where 700,000 of their countrymen had become casualties.

The Clash of the Dreadnoughts, 1915-16

The German strategy of attempting to isolate and destroy British squadrons was continued into 1915. On 24 January, Rear Admiral Hipper led 1st Scouting Force out to attack the Dogger Bank Patrol. Forewarned by Room 40, Beatty's battlecruisers lay in wait for Hipper. The German force consisted of the battlecruisers *Seydlitz, Moltke* and *Derfflinger*, and the old cruiser *Blücher*. As it steamed forward, Beatty attempted to interpose his ships between Hipper and his base. The Germans turned for home, with the British pursuing them. At 0900 hours, at a range of 20,000 yards, Beatty opened fire. Twenty minutes later, *Seydlitz* had been severely damaged and *Blücher* crippled. A confused series of signals from Beatty led to four of the five battlecruisers (*Tiger, New Zealand, Princess Royal* and *Indomitable*) concentrating their fire against the doomed *Blücher*, which allowed the German battlecruisers to escape. Nevertheless, the British trumpeted the Battle of the Dogger Bank as a convincing victory. The Germans also had some reason for private, if not public, satisfaction. They had badly damaged *Lion*, Beatty's flagship, and in general, their gunnery had proved superior to that of the Royal Navy – the German battlecruisers had scored 2.1 percent of hits per shells fired, as against the British score of 0.5 percent. Perhaps most importantly of all, valuable lessons were learned from the near-disaster on *Seydlitz*, when a flash fire had come close to igniting the ship's magazines. Immediate precautions were taken, which were to be of enormous benefit at Jutland, 16 months later.

For the remainder of 1915, the naval fleets avoided each other. The Kriegsmarine concentrated on its U-Boat campaign, while the Grand Fleet continued to launch endless 'sweeps' of the North Sea from its bases at Rosyth and Scapa. The appointment of the aggressive Vice-Admiral Scheer to command the High Seas Fleet in January 1916 marked an end to this period of inactivity. On 31 May, the two fleets clashed off Jutland, in the only large-scale battle in history fought between two forces of Dreadnoughts and battlecruisers, without the intervention of aircraft.

The rival commanders possessed fundamentally different ideas about how a major fleet action should be fought. Jellicoe was convinced that the battle would be won by superior gunnery, and was to maneuver so as to allow the heavy guns of the Grand Fleet to bear on Scheer's vessels. Conversely, Scheer had no intention of engaging in a gunnery duel with Jellicoe. If outnumbered, the High Seas Fleet would disengage, using torpedo boats to cover the withdrawal; for Scheer, the torpedo, not the gun, was the decisive weapon. As the intentions of the two commanders were diametrically opposed, it is not surprising, in retrospect, that the battle of 31 May 1916 was inconclusive.

Hipper's battlecruisers were the bait to be used to trap an unwary British force. They were to cruise off Norway, with Scheer's battleships following 50 miles astern, ready to close in. The Grand Fleet actually set sail before Scheer – having been given advance warning once again by Room 40. Beatty was dispatched to reconnoiter the Jutland area, with two squadrons of battlecruisers and one of fast battleships, and at 1428 hours made contact with Hipper's escorting destroyers. Hipper swung southeast, back toward Scheer's main force, with Beatty following. The first salvos were exchanged at 1548 hours. By 1626 hours Beatty was facing disaster. Of the ships under his command *Lion* had been hit and *Indefatigable* and *Queen Mary* had blown up and sunk, causing the deaths of over 2000 British sailors and prompting Beatty to comment, 'there's something wrong with our bloody ships today.' The German battlecruisers had also sustained heavy damage, but they were all still afloat.

At 1640 hours Beatty sighted Scheer's battleships and turned to the northwest to avoid the trap. The High Seas Fleet pursued him. After Beatty turned to shield the Grand Fleet from Scheer's gaze at 1726 hours, Jellicoe gave his battleships the order to form a line of battle.

LEFT: *Vice-Admiral Reinhard Scheer, commander of the German High Seas Fleet at Jutland. One of the most able German sailors, he was respected and feared by his British counterparts.*

RIGHT: *The German cruiser* Blücher, *photographed in 1910. To send such a slow ship to sea in the company of fast, modern battlecruisers was to prove an error. In many ways, the Germans were fortunate to escape so lightly from the Dogger Bank action.*

BELOW RIGHT: *The German battlecruiser* Moltke, *one of Admiral Hipper's fleet at Dogger Bank.*

BOTTOM: *The British battleship HMS* Agincourt *saw action at Jutland. She had seven 12-inch gun turrets – the largest number of turrets of any Dreadnought.*

ABOVE: *The stern and bow of HMS* Invincible; *she was torn in two when she blew up. The destroyer HMS* Badger *can be seen searching for survivors. Battlecruisers were built for speed and were thus relatively thinly armored.*

ABOVE LEFT: *HMS* Invincible *explodes at Jutland. She sank with the loss of 1026 men.*

LEFT: *The German battlecruiser* Seydlitz *in port at Wilhelmshaven after the Battle of Jutland. Seydlitz was severely damaged at Jutland, being hit by 21 heavy shells.*

RIGHT: *Rear Admiral Goodenough (right), commander of the First Light Cruiser Squadron at Jutland, with Admiral de Robeck. Goodenough was one of the most capable British naval commanders of the war and his conduct at Jutland was exemplary, providing his superior, Admiral Jellicoe, with much-needed information and support.*

Scheer seemed to be about to place his neck in a noose; Jellicoe would be able to endanger Scheer's line of retreat and 'cross his T,' that is, allow his battleships to fire broadside at the advancing German columns. Scheer awoke to the danger and ordered a 'battle turnaway' – through 180 degrees – and attempted to escape. In the process, another British battlecruiser, *Invincible*, was sunk, going down with Rear Admiral Hood on board.

As daylight faded, Scheer headed for home. He was not yet clear of danger; at 1915 hours he once again came up against the center of the British line after a maneuver went badly awry. To cover his precipitate withdrawal, a salvo of 32 torpedoes was fired at the British battleships, prompting the most controversial order of the day: Jellicoe ordered the line to turn away from the torpedoes, thus sacrificing the chance of inflicting a decisive defeat on Scheer. The High Seas Fleet, after further alarms, escaped into the darkness and the ships reached the safety of their bases.

In purely numerical terms, the Germans were able to claim a victory, for they sank three British battlecruisers and lost only one of their own, *Lützow*, and a pre-dreadnought, *Pommern*. The British ships had revealed grave deficiencies, and, as Beatty pithily remarked 'There is something wrong with our system' – a remark that pinpointed the Grand Fleet's poor staff work and overcentralization of command. And yet in strategic terms Jutland was a British triumph, albeit of a negative kind; the Grand Fleet was substantially intact, and the Royal Navy retained its command of the seas; the blockade of Germany had not been broken. Despite the disappointment of the British public that Jutland had not been another Trafalgar, the battle was a decisive victory, the German fleet never ventured out again on a large scale. In the words of an American newspaper, 'The German Fleet has assaulted its jailor; but it is still in jail.'

The Opposing Armies on the Somme, 1916

The French army had borne the brunt of the Allied offensives in 1914-15; from 1916 onward, the British army began to take over this role. The BEF of 1916 was a very different organization from the four-division-strong force of August 1914. It had grown to 58 divisions, organized into 18 corps and four armies. Supporting arms had also undergone massive expansion; the number of heavy artillery batteries, for instance, had increased from 36 in January 1915 to 191 in July 1916 (and 12 months later there were to be 400 batteries). In addition to the regular units, which as a result of the battles of 1914-15 consisted largely of wartime volunteers stiffened by the few remaining 'old sweats,' there were two other types of infantry units: Territorial Force and New Army (or 'Kitchener') battalions. The original Territorials had been part-time soldiers, intended for Home Defense. They had been rushed out in 1914 to reinforce the BEF, and their ranks had also been heavily diluted by wartime recruits. A number of fresh Territorial units were raised, drawing on the same pool of recruits as Kitchener's Army.

On 7 August 1914, the newly appointed secretary of State for War, Lord Kitchener, issued an appeal for volunteers for the army. The resulting flood of recruits overwhelmed the authorities, and as an emergency measure private individuals, organizations and especially municipal bodies began to raise battalions which were later taken over by the War Office. One of the most remarkable armies in history came into being, providing the BEF with such unlikely units as the 23rd Royal Fusiliers (1st Sportsmen), 11th East Lancs (Accrington Pals) – raised by the Mayor of that town – and 16th Highland Light Infantry (Glasgow Boys' Brigade). This unique army of 'Pals' was destroyed on the Somme; and the BEF was never the same again.

RIGHT: *Men of the Sheffield City Battalion (12th Yorks and Lancaster Regiment) in training in 1914. This battalion suffered heavy losses on the first day on the Somme. One party simply vanished: their remains were found in a German trench five months later. The losses of 1 July 1916 are by far the highest that the British army has ever sustained in a single day. The French and Germans had been suffering immense casualties since 1914 but never quite on this scale.*

RIGHT: *German troops snatch some rest in a trench. They are wearing the 'coalscuttle' pattern of steel helmet introduced in early 1916 and the wartime issue M.1915 tunic.*
BELOW LEFT: *Men of 10th East Yorks (Hull Commercials), 31st Division moving up to the trenches, 28 June 1916. This division attacked at Serre, north of Beaumont Hamel on 1 July, and found the enemy barbed wire uncut in many places. The division was composed of 'Pals' battalions from the north of England, including the Sheffield City Battalion.*
BELOW: *A German sentry of 127th Regiment, armed with the famous potato-masher hand grenade and looking through a trench periscope in the Ypres area, 1916.*

The BEF of 1916 was an amateur army; enthusiastic, but poorly trained and inexperienced. Few of the generals had had the opportunity to command anything larger than a brigade in the small prewar army, and battalion and company commanders were frequently 'dugouts,' or retired officers with little knowledge of modern warfare. Most junior officers held a temporary wartime commission and were as ignorant of the realities of war as the men they commanded, although an increasing number of experienced 'Other Ranks' were receiving commissions. Many of the temporary officers of the New Armies were mature men, who had perhaps 10 years experience in civilian professions, but the popular image of the subaltern of 1916 remains that of the ex-public schoolboy, in his late teens or early twenties, who saw the war in terms of duty, patriotism, and adventure. Such an officer was Lieutenant W N Hodgson of the 9th Devons, who concluded a poem written on the eve of battle with the words: 'Help me to die, O Lord.' He was killed on the next day, 1 July 1916.

In sharp contrast, the German army of 1916 still retained many of its prewar officers and NCOs. This gave it a depth of experience that was to prove invaluable in the fighting on the Somme. Unlike the British, the Germans often left units holding the same sector of the line for months on end. Thus units on quiet sectors could avoid the gradual attrition of experienced men that occurred when battalions were rotated through active sectors. In addition, the Germans treated their officers as precious assets, allocating many of the duties performed in a British battalion by an officer to a senior NCO; in an attempt to avoid giving commissions to socially inferior men, promising soldiers were instead promoted to *Offizier Stellvertreter* (literally, 'substitute officer'). The organization of the infantry battalion had changed relatively little since 1914, but sweeping changes were to occur in late 1916 and in the following year, as the lessons of Verdun and the Somme were assimilated and acted upon.

The Somme – 1 July 1916

At the Chantilly Conference in December 1915, Joffre proposed that the Anglo-French armies should attack together on the Somme front in the following summer. The French wanted this to be preceded by a series of battles to 'wear down' the enemy. Haig rejected this idea, but agreed to an offensive on the Somme, although he would have preferred to attack in Flanders, for the Somme offered no major strategic goals; its main virtue was that it would allow the Allies to attack side by side. Initially, it was to be a predominantly French affair, but the maelstrom of Verdun drew increasing numbers of French divisions south to reinforce the weak line, and the British took the leading role in a major offensive for the first time.

Two men dominated the first stage of the Battle of the Somme: Sir Douglas Haig, the Commander in Chief, and Sir Henry Rawlinson, commander of the Fourth Army. The former laid down general objectives for the Fourth Army, and left 'Rawly' to do the detailed planning. Haig's plan was for an advance parallel to the straight road that ran southwest to northeast, from Albert, behind the British lines, to German-held Bapaume. The German positions on Pozières Ridge would be captured, and then a force of cavalry and infantry (the Reserve Army, under Sir Hubert Gough) would exploit the gap and swing to the north. Accompanied by the victorious infantry, the entire German position would then be rolled up.

ABOVE: *Men of 1st Lancashire Fusiliers are addressed by Major General de Lisle, commander of 29th Division, on the day before the battle. This Regular division was the only one to serve at Gallipoli and to attack on the opening day of the Somme offensive.*
RIGHT: *The British bombard German trenches before the Battle of the Somme.*

RIGHT: *Lieutenant General Sir Henry Rawlinson, the commander of the Fourth Army. Although his handling of the first day of the Somme battle has been heavily criticized, his successful campaigns in 1918 have gone some way to restoring his reputation.*

FAR RIGHT: *A British newspaper reports the opening of the Battle of the Somme. Strict censorship kept the British public in ignorance of the true state of affairs at the front.*

BELOW: *The entrance to a deep German dugout captured in Bernafay Wood, 3 July 1916. Dugouts like this one enabled sufficient defenders to survive the shelling and blunt the British attack.*

Rawlinson did not share Haig's optimism about the possibility of a breakthrough. He planned that the heaviest artillery bombardment the British had ever been able to mount would pulverize the German positions, which would then be occupied by the infantry. The artillery would then switch to the next line – and so on, until the British reached open country. Thus the British plan for 1 July suffered from a fundamental difference in opinion as to its purpose. Haig saw it as an attempt to break through; in Rawlinson's view, it was to be a battle of attrition, à la Joffre. Haig's Staff College training had taught him not to interfere with the 'man on the spot,' who was, in any case, an infantryman, while Haig was a cavalryman. Like Hamilton at Gallipoli, he did not feel able to impose his ideas on his subordinate.

This dissension among the generals did not filter down to the British troops on the Somme. This was their first battle and their morale was excellent. The sick list of 1/16th Londons (Queen's Westminster Rifles), who had never seen action before, was one of the smallest of the war, with every man eager to fight. The men were told that the shelling would destroy all the enemy positions, and the battle would be a walkover. The evidence of their own eyes appeared to show that this was true. Some 455 heavy guns were massed on the 18-mile front, a concentration of one gun every 57 yards, although the French had one to every 20 yards. For seven days the British gunners pounded the enemy positions, but of the impressive number of 1,700,000 shells fired, about a million were shrapnel shells fired by the field guns, useless for destroying trenches, and not very effective at cutting barbed wire. An alarming number were 'duds.' The bombardment failed to destroy the German trenches. Military historian John Keegan has calculated that each 10 square yards received only one pound of high explosive. Although the bombardment was terrifyingly noisy and, to the observer, apparently effective, thousands of the defenders survived in their deep dugouts, which the Germans had constructed over the course of the previous two years.

Rawlinson had ordered his infantry to attack in line; as early as the Battle of Loos, 'Fire and Movement' tactics had been abandoned in favor of a close-formed linear advance because it was thought that the amateur soldiers of Kitchener's Army could not cope with more sophisticated tactics. So, at 0730 hours on 1 July, waves of close-formed troops from 14 divisions began to advance slowly, heavily

117

laden, across No Man's Land. The German machine guns which had survived the bombardment then opened up. It was a massacre. The 16th Highland Light Infantry (Glasgow Boys' Brigade), attacking opposite Thiepval with 32nd Division, lost half of its strength in the first 10 minutes; 1st Newfoundland Regiment later lost 684 men. That day, the British suffered losses of 57,470 – about a third of which were killed. Courageously, the devastated units re-formed and tried to reach their objectives. Almost everywhere, the Germans had the advantage of higher ground. At La Boiselle, on the Bapaume road, 34th Division had to advance into 'Sausage Valley'; the Germans were able to pour fire into the assaulting battalions of the 103rd (Tyneside Irish) Brigade before they reached the British front line; although reduced to only 50 men, they still attempted to reach their final objective, Contalmaison. All four battalion commanders became casualties; the 1st and 4th Tyneside Irish alone lost 1159 men.

Some units had initially done well. In the north, 56th (London) Division had taken their objectives in a diversionary attack at Gommecourt, and in the center, 36th (Ulster) Division had penetrated almost to the second line, but both were forced to withdraw, partly because of the failure of adjacent formations to make any headway. A common, disheartening sight was of the British barrage racing ahead of the beleaguered infantry, as the gunners stuck to their rigid time-tables; there was no way of recalling it.

Only in the south was there success. There, a 'creeping' barrage was used (see below), and the 18th (Eastern) Division, commanded by Maxse, had sent their men out into No Man's Land before the barrage lifted. Thus the 18th Division were able to win the race to the parapet which those of their comrades who started in their trenches lost. One battalion of the 18th, the 8th East Surreys, attacked kicking footballs to divert the minds of their men from the terrors ahead. The 18th and the neighboring 30th took all their objectives, including Montauban, as did the French attacking to the south. Controversially, Rawlinson passed over the opportunity to attempt to exploit this success, which could have changed 1 July from a catastrophe into a victory. Thus the total achievement of that day was the destruction of many fine battalions, and the bringing of sorrow to thousands of homes, humble and grand, across the British Isles. The enthusiasm and patriotism of so many of the volunteers of 1914 led them to their deaths on a hot July day in eastern France.

ABOVE: *British infantry pick their way through their own barbed wire at the beginning of the Somme offensive. This is a still from the official film of the battle.*
LEFT: *A British 15-inch howitzer. Note the winch for the shell. The British had all too few of these weapons in 1916.*
RIGHT: *The 18th Indian Lancers on the march. Indian cavalry joined the attack on High Wood.*

The Somme: Phase II

After the failure of 1 July, Haig still hoped for a breakthrough on the Somme but effectively the battle became one of attrition. Like Falkenhayn, Haig was later at pains to convince posterity that he had intended to fight a *battaile d'usure* all along. In his Final Dispatch he presented his – unquestionably brilliant – campaigns of 1918 as being the culmination of the attritional battles of 1916-17, a line that has been since followed by Haig's apologists. While there is some truth in that assertion, Haig had undoubtedly planned for a decisive breakthrough on 1 July and as late as 15 September was still trying to achieve one. Yet in his dispatch of 23 December 1916, no mention appears of his original concept of a breakthrough. Haig referred to the campaign as 'the opening of the wearing-out battle,' a phrase that graphically captures the essence of the fighting on the Somme in the second half of 1916.

On 14 July, Rawlinson overcame Haig's objections and launched a bold stroke by attacking Trônes Wood with four divisions at night, after a bombardment of only five minutes' duration. The Germans were taken by surprise, and the attacking infantry overran their front line before they could react.

Although a breakthrough did not materialize, the new British tactics worked brilliantly, particularly the 'creeping barrage,' which had been used by Maxse's 18th (Eastern) Division on 1 July. This was a 'curtain' of shells, usually shrapnel, which moved slowly 100 yards in advance of the assaulting infantry. It was far more effective than the rigid 'lifts' that had raced ahead of the infantry on 1 July.

The battle continued, with the British attempting to claw their way onto Pozières Ridge. The devastated town of Pozières fell on 23 July to the Australians, who rapidly established a reputation equal to the Canadians for gallantry and efficiency. The flavor of much of the fighting of July and August can be gauged from an examination of one episode, the capture of Delville Wood. It had been captured by the South African Brigade of 9th (Scottish) Division, but mostly it was lost on 18 July. The casualties of the period can be judged from the fact that one battalion, 4th Royal Fusiliers, lost 352 men in 13 days clinging to a toehold at the southern end of 'Devil's Wood,' without participating in an attack. At 0710 hours on 27 July Brigadier General R O Kellett's 99th Brigade of 2nd Division attacked the German positions, with 23 Royal Fusiliers (1st Sportsmen) and 1st King's Royal Rifle Corps in the lead, and 1st Royal Berks in support. By 0940 hours their final objectives had been taken. Then the real trouble for 99th Brigade began. The Germans threw in counterattack after counterattack, which came perilously close to succeeding. Parties of the fourth battalion in the brigade, 22nd Royal Fusiliers (Kensington) came up to reinforce the battleline. Originally they had been used as carrying parties, bringing supplies to the front, but now they were organized into a fighting unit. The reinforced British beat off a strong German attack at 1500 hours; in this the Brigade Machine Gun Company, commanded by an officer of the 22nd, Captain Grant, played a prominent role. At the end of the day casualties in the company were so heavy that it was commanded by a lance corporal. Losses in the infantry had also been fearful; 194 in the 22nd, 289 in the 23rd. Many had been caused by shellfire. An officer of the 23rd described the effect of the bombardment: 'Trees were torn up by the dozen, and fell blazing. By the end of the day there was nothing but shattered stumps.' The wood was held; it never again left British hands.

Similar scenes were enacted at dozens of other unhealthy spots on the Somme in the summer of 1916: Leuze (Lousy) Wood, High Wood, and Guillemont to name a few. Everywhere, the general pattern was the same: heavy shelling, German counterattacks and the steady, remorseless but deadly slow advance of the British. By the end of July, the Germans had lost 160,000 men, and they were forced to go onto the defensive at Verdun. That, if nothing else, was a solid achievement for the British on the Somme.

ABOVE: *British machine gunners, wearing gas helmets, aim a Vickers Mark 1 at Ovilliers, July 1916.*
ABOVE RIGHT: *A column of French infantry. The French, in contrast to the British, were reasonably successful on 1 July.*
LEFT: *A French machine gunner armed with a Cauchat light machine gun in the Somme area, August 1916.*
RIGHT: *British and German wounded near Bernafay Wood, July 1916.*

The Somme: Phase III

On 29 August 1916, Falkenhayn was replaced by Hindenburg, with Ludendorff as his deputy, as First Quartermaster General. Too many casualties, and too few tangible gains, had fatally undermined Falkenhayn's position. His fall had two important consequences. The military command of the Central Powers was unified under Hindenburg, despite Conrad's opposition. Secondly, the Germans began to develop a form of flexible defense and to erect a massive, fortified position in the rear (see below). In the meantime, the British began another 'push' on the Somme: the Battle of Flers-Courcelette. This marked the introduction of a major new weapon – the tank. The Mark I tanks available in September 1916 were slow, ungainly armored boxes, armed with two 6-pounder guns in the 'male' version or four machine guns in the 'female.' They were designed to traverse No Man's Land, crash through barbed wire and straddle trenches. Only 49 were available to Haig on the eve of Flers-Courcelette, and he decided to commit them to battle in 'penny packets' to support the infantry. Haig's detractors – including Churchill, who had a large hand in their development while at the Admiralty – have compared this decision with the German misuse of gas in April 1915, arguing that there were too few tanks to be decisive, and by revealing the secret he squandered the opportunity to achieve one of the greatest surprises of the war. In fairness to Haig, while it would have been preferable to use them en masse, there were too few to have done so, and it is far from certain that the weapon could have remained secret until large numbers arrived in France in mid-1917. Also, *pace* his Final Dispatch, Haig believed that a breakthrough was possible and the Somme might have been the last opportunity to use the tank.

On 15 September, 12 divisions, including Canadians and New Zealanders, attacked on a 10-mile frontage, utilizing a creeping barrage. Results were far more impressive than on 1 July; the appearance of the tanks produced a satisfying degree of terror in some German units, but on the whole the six-and-a-half defending divisions fought as stubbornly as ever. The British line advanced 2500 yards but the prospect of open warfare was as far away as ever. All hope of a breakthrough had vanished. The battle settled down into a form of attrition. Unlike Joffre's strategy in 1915, attrition was not primarily seen by Haig as the means to a limited territorial end. Haig's design was grander, he wanted to 'wear out' the German army by inflicting as many losses as possible.

The Somme was a predominantly British affair, but the French contribution should not be ignored. In the first weeks of September, the French Tenth Army joined their comrades of the Sixth in the battle. A further Franco-British effort began on 25 September. Thiepval, which had been a British objective on 1 July, fell to British II Corps and the Canadians. Perhaps in acknowledgment of the intensity of the fighting, which was bitter even by the standards of that terrible summer, an enormous and ugly memorial to the missing of the Somme was inaugurated by the then Prince of Wales (later King Edward VIII) in 1932. By early October, a new enemy had appeared on the battlefield: mud. Torrential rain turned the ground to a glutinous swamp. An artillery officer remembered seeing one of his drivers return from a trip to collect rations. Only the man's face was visible, 'the rest was mud – fresh, moist mud on mud that was lighter in color, and dry.' His horse had to be hauled out of a sump by a chain attached to a truck.

ABOVE: *A British 6-inch howitzer in a sea of mud epitomizes the later stages of the fighting on the Somme.*
LEFT: *Gordon Highlanders putting on rubber thigh-boots at Bazentin-le-Petit, November 1916. Some veterans of the Somme thought that the mud in Picardy was worse than in the Flanders campaign of twelve months later.*
FAR LEFT: *A clogged road near Fricourt. Note staff-cars, mule-limbers, lorries, an ambulance, marching infantry, and pioneers widening the road.*

ABOVE: *The British secret weapon: a Mark 1 tank, in Chimpanzee Valley, 15 September 1916. The wire-mesh protective screen for the crew was not popular and was soon removed.*

The final push came on the River Ancre, after a further month of attritional fighting. The bad weather caused the attack to be delayed day after day, which placed an enormous strain on the nerves of the troops waiting to begin the assault. J F C Fuller gave evidence to the postwar Committee of Enquiry into Shellshock that the conditions on the Ancre drove substantial numbers of British soldiers to desert to the enemy, the only time in the war that this occurred. German morale was also noticeably poor. Eventually, Gough's Fifth Army (formerly called the Reserve Army) attacked Beaumont Hamel on 13 November – another objective of the Fourth Army on 1 July. This time, the British had one gun every 35 yards. The final lunge of the BEF on the Somme brought success; 63rd (Royal Naval) Division took Beaucourt and 51st (Highland) Division entered the ruins of Beaumont Hamel itself. Haig pronounced himself satisfied and on 19 November the battle of the Somme was closed down. It had lasted for two-and-a-half months. One-and-a-quarter million men had become casualties.

What had the battle achieved? Verdun had been relieved, but in terms of ground gained there were few tangible results. One can walk in a day from Albert to the furthest point reached by the British in 1916, a distance of only seven miles. The Germans were voluntarily to retire more than double that distance when they withdrew to the Hindenburg line in early 1917. Judged by Haig's criterion of 1 July, the battle had been a failure for no breakthrough had been achieved. By his later standards, the campaign was a limited success. The Germans (although it is difficult to arrive at precise figures) lost about 650,000 men; the Allies, 614,105, and of those 419,654 were British. In an attritional sense, this was a victory, for the Allies, with the longer 'purse' of men, could afford to accept equal casualties, in the knowledge that German manpower would become exhausted first. Moreover, German morale was suffering: 'Life here is absolutely ghastly,' wrote an officer in August, 'six weeks ago Martinpuich was . . . inhabited and secure. Now it is a region of horror and despair.' He went on to recount how his men had to be driven into the attack at gunpoint. He was killed in October. The Somme was, in the words of one German staff officer the 'muddy grave' of the old German army. Most of the prewar NCOs and privates were killed or wounded, reducing the army to the status of a 'militia,' similar to the BEF of 1916. One historian has calculated that the Germans made 330 counterattacks; as a result, the life blood of the German army seeped into the ground. As for the morale of the BEF, the enthusiasm of July had gone, but in its place was a dogged determination to 'stick it,' which, combined with the experience gained, was to see it through another gruelling attritional battle in 1917. The Somme was a 'victory,' but how many more 'victories' could the British army survive?

LEFT: *British and German wounded withdraw from the front line during the Battle of the Somme.*
RIGHT: *British gunners watch wounded prisoners being marched to the rear after the capture of Guillemont by 16th (Irish) Division, September 1916. The Easter Uprising had little effect on Irish troops serving with the British army in France. As well as the Irish regiments in British service, there were large numbers of Irishmen serving in nominally English regiments.*

The Eastern Front in 1916

The overall direction of the Russian war effort in 1916 nominally rested with the Czar. In reality, most decisions were taken by Alexeiev, the Chief of Staff, who had some reason to feel cautiously optimistic at the turn of the year. The Russian army had survived the 1915 campaign more or less intact, and the worst shortages of arms and ammunition were beginning to be mastered. New conscripts were filling the gaps in the ranks, and the army was shortly to prove that Falkenhayn's assessment in his Christmas Eve Memorandum that Russia was incapable of taking the offensive was wishful thinking. Much was to change before the year was out.

Russia prepared to fulfill her part in the Chantilly agreement, with three army groups (or fronts). She responded sympathetically to France's anguished cries for relief when the Germans attacked at Verdun by starting an offensive on either side of Lake Narotch, 80 miles northwest of Minsk. The two northern fronts (Kuropatkin and Evert), attacked on 18 March 1916 at odds of five to one. For the first time, the Russians had rough parity with the Germans in artillery. Although each gun could fire 100 rounds a day, the Russians achieved little at the expense of 110,000 casualties. This compares with a total of 20,000 Germans lost.

Stavka was undeterred. One front had not yet seen action in 1916; this was Brusilov's Southwest Front. Although he had originally been allotted a secondary role in the next offensive, planned for May, Brusilov obtained permission to plan a campaign of his own. The resulting battle became known simply as 'The Brusilov Offensive.' It was to be the greatest Russian victory of the war.

Brusilov's plan was simple, but effective. He attempted to mislead the enemy as to where the blow was to fall by ordering each of his four army commanders each to begin preparations for an attack. Intensive reconnaissance was carried out, ammunition dumps were established, and reserves moved up behind the lines in over 26 active sectors. The Central Powers were unable to concentrate their reserves to counter the coming offensive. They had no doubt an offensive was about to be launched, the question was – where?

ABOVE: *General Brusilov, the most able commander in the Russian army. Unlike many high-ranking Czarist officers, he remained in Russia after the Revolution, and in fact before the 'October' Revolution he declined an offer to become Dictator of Russia.*
LEFT: *Sunlight streams through the window of a church in Russian Poland, commandeered by the Germans as a temporary billet.*
RIGHT: *The telephone communications section of the Austrian General Staff. As the war went on, Austria became increasingly subservient to her German partner.*

On 5 June, Brusilov revealed his hand. Evert had postponed his offensive, so Southwest Front attacked alone. The night before the preliminary bombardment began, Alexeiev lost his nerve and demanded that Brusilov attack at one point, instead of on a broad front. Brusilov held his ground, and the Chief of Staff finally capitulated, saying, 'God be with you. Have it your own way.' Hours later, the Russian guns erupted in a violent 'hurricane' bombardment that destroyed the Austrian trenches and tore gaps in their wire. At dawn on 5 June, Kaledin's Eighth Army attacked at Luck; the opposing Austrian Fourth Army promptly collapsed.

The Central Powers had 37 divisions, mostly Austrian, on this front; Brusilov had one more. Had there been more German divisions present, Brusilov's campaign may have succeeded, but probably not in such a spectacular fashion. Archduke Josef Ferdinand's Austrian Fourth Army bore the weight of Kaledin's attack. One corps gave way almost immediately, and the Russians advanced into the gap. The Austrian front crumbled. By 6 June 44,000 prisoners had been taken and the Fourth Army was retreating to the River Styr in disarray. In the south, Shcherbachev's Seventh Army broke through Pflanzer-Baltin's Austrian Seventh and chased it across the River Strypa.

Where were the reserves that could have converted the Austrian retreat into a disaster? They were assembled in Evert's sector, away to the north, and few reached Brusilov while the Austrians were in rout; Alexeiev, as well as the Austrians, was the victim of strategic surprise. Evert could have capitalized on the situation by striking in the north, but wasted the opportunity by attacking only half-heartedly on 2 July. The Germans were given time to reinforce the area, where, on 16 June, six German and three Austrian divisions counterattacked Brusilov's northernmost thrust and slowed his advance. Once again, the Carpathian Mountains proved to be the furthest point reached by the Russian armies in the south. Brusilov attacked again in July, and the campaign dragged on into September, but by this time the momentum had been lost.

The Brusilov Offensive could be called 'The Battle that destroyed two Empires.' Austria-Hungary, having lost 450,000 prisoners, had been dealt a blow from which it never recovered. The Russians, too, had suffered stupendous losses: 1 million casualties, and, even more ominously, the same number of troops had simply deserted and returned home. The morale of the Czarist army was shattered for ever: revolution was but a step away.

Just when the campaign was winding down, Rumania had declared for the Allies, bribed by the promise of Austrian territory in Transylvania. The timing of Rumania's entry into the war is one of the great 'might-have-beens' of the conflict. In the summer of 1916, the Central Powers were under enormous strain, fighting at Verdun, on the Somme, in Italy and in Galicia. Had Rumania joined the Allies at the beginning of July, rather than the end of August, it is conceivable that the balance would have tipped decisively in favor of the *Entente*. Instead, Rumania paid a harsh penalty.

LEFT: *Von Mackensen, the German commander of the southern force that crushed Rumania.*
BELOW LEFT: *A Russian heavy howitzer in position near Przemysl. By 1916 Russian gunners were at last receiving sufficient quantities of ammunition: nearly 3 million rounds were manufactured in September alone.*
RIGHT: *An Austrian crew sighting a 30.5cm mortar at Simemakowce.*
BELOW: *Ferdinand of Bulgaria. Having assisted in the overthrow of one neighbor, Serbia, in 1915, Bulgarian forces invaded another neighbor, Rumania, one year later.*

The Russians advised the Rumanians (who, like Italy, had been in 1914 a nominal ally of Austria but had chosen to stay neutral) to remain on the defensive. Instead, they invaded Transylvania, in the fond hope that the Allied force at Salonika would neutralize hostile Bulgarian forces to the south. The Salonika force was quite unable to influence the course of the Rumanian campaign. Instead, the Central Powers delivered a devastating riposte.

This campaign was one of the most efficiently planned, orchestrated and executed operations of the war. The key figure was none other than Falkenhayn, the deposed German Chief of Staff. He launched a brilliant campaign which involved German, Turkish, Austrian and Bulgarian troops, invading Rumania from three directions. The Bulgarian Third Army drove into the Rumanian coastal province of Dobruja; while Falkenhayn's Ninth and the Austrian Fourth Armies counterattacked in Transylvania. The Rumanians were defeated at Hermannstadt and Kronstadt on 30 September and 8 October, but evaded Falkenhayn's attempted envelopment and fell back through the passes of the Transylvanian Alps. Falkenhayn had bludgeoned his way through the Vulkan Pass by 26 November and set out for the Rumanian capital, Bucharest. He entered it on 5 December, just ahead of Mackensen, who had invaded from the south, over the River Danube. The Rumanians retreated to their Moldavian province, the only strip of territory which remained to them. They had suffered 310,000 casualties.

The campaign was a virtuoso performance, not least because it provided a model example of how to conduct coalition warfare. For the second time, the *Entente* had to stand by and watch a small Balkan ally trodden underfoot. At the end of 1916, the French and British were slowly coming to realize that the war in the East had been lost.

Italy 1915-16

Italy's decision to remain neutral on the outbreak of war did not come as a surprise to her erstwhile allies Germany and Austria. Even before 1914, Conrad, the Austrian Chief of Staff, is reputed to have referred to the Triple Alliance as a 'pointless farce.' Popular sympathy in Italy lay with the *Entente*. Anti-Austrian feeling was rife, thanks to irredentist claims on Trieste and in the Trentino. In the secret Treaty of London in April 1915, Italy agreed to enter the war in return for receiving these territories in the postwar settlement. She declared war on Austria-Hungary on 23 May 1915, although the Italians delayed beginning hostilities with Germany until August 1916.

Armchair strategists were enthusiastic about the addition of 36 divisions to the *Entente*'s order of battle, and the apparent opportunity to strike at the weaker of the Central Powers from Italian soil. This was a chimera. Italy lacked the raw materials to undertake a sustained war without assistance from the Allies, and the frontier with Austria was a mountainous area which favored the defender rather than the attacker. There were only two areas even remotely suitable for an offensive: the Trentino in the north of the country, and across the River Isonzo in the northeast.

The Italian Chief of Staff and *de facto* Commander in Chief was General Luigi Cadorna. He planned to cross the Isonzo and capture the town of Gorizia and the barren region of the Carzo. Trieste, and eventually the Danubian plain, were Cadorna's ultimate objectives in the Isonzo campaigns. Even to take Gorizia proved to be beyond the Italians in 1915; yet Cadorna fought 11 times on the Isonzo, which must earn him a place alongside Haig and Falkenhayn as one of the arch-attritionists of the war.

LEFT: *General Luigi Cadorna, Italian Chief of Staff and effective Commander in Chief.*
BELOW LEFT: *A symbolic Bersaglieri rifleman and his slavering Roman hound (note collar) manhandle a scraggy Imperial eagle. The Austrian resistance to the numerous Italian offensives was rather more stubborn than this Allied propaganda would suggest.*
RIGHT: *The influence of Leete's 'Kitchener' poster of 1914 can be seen in this Italian example. The caption reads 'Do your whole duty.'*
BELOW RIGHT: *The formidable terrain of the Italian theater is well illustrated by this photograph of a gun position in the mountains.*
BELOW: *War in the mountains: an Austrian patrol passes through a snow-bound forest.*

The first two battles of the Isonzo (which were really only phases of one protracted campaign, separated by a pause) ran from 23 June to 4 August 1915, when a shortage of shells forced Cadorna to prorogue the campaign. When the Third and Fourth Battles (18 October to 2 December) were halted, small gains had been made, but at the cost of 177,000 Italian and 117,000 Austrian casualties. The Austrians had been forced to divert 12 divisions from the Eastern Front, but this brought scant relief to Italy's hard-pressed Russian ally. The year 1916 began with both Cadorna and Conrad (who nursed a particular hatred for the Italians) planning to take the offensive. The Sixth Battle of the Isonzo (1 March 1915) was begun to fulfill Italy's undertakings at the Chantilly Conference, but was as unsuccessful as its predecessors. One month later, the Austrians attacked in the Trentino.

Conrad failed to persuade the Germans to co-operate in this campaign for Falkenhayn remained profoundly skeptical about the strategic value of an offensive in Italy, even if it succeeded. However, two Austrian armies – the Eleventh and Third – were assembled, partly by denuding Boroevic's Fifth Army on the Isonzo. It was impossible to conceal the arrival of 14 divisions and 1000 guns from the Italians. Nevertheless, the attack on 15 May was successful. The Austrians advanced five miles in as many days, reaching a line between the towns of Arsiego and Asiago; but then the familiar pattern reasserted itself. Cadorna used his interior lines of communication to rush reinforcements to the Trentino Front, and the Austrians were stopped short of their objective, the North Italian plain. Archduke Eugen, the Army Group Commander, wisely retired to lessen the impact of the inevitable counterblow. The Austrians had taken 45,000 prisoners, but they had not broken the stalemate.

The Asiago campaign had an immediate repercussion on other fronts; on 4 June the Brusilov Offensive was begun by the Russians as a response to Italian pleas for help. On the Isonzo, too, Cadorna was able to take advantage of the depletion of Boroevic's force by switching troops back from the Trentino and capturing Gorizia and a bridgehead over the river (6-17 August). The Seventh, Eighth and Ninth Battles of the Isonzo (14 September-4 November) attempted to broaden this bridgehead, but with little success. The 'Butcher's Bill' this time was 75,000 Italians and 63,000 Austrians, evidence that refuted Conrad's belief that a decisive victory could be gained more easily in Italy than in the West. Curiously, Lloyd George, who became the British Prime Minister in December 1916, was about to fall into the same trap.

LEFT: *Campaigning in the Alps posed a different set of logistic problems to those familiar from the Western Front. Here, an elite Italian Alpini soldier slides down a mountainside. He is armed with a 6.5mm Mannlicher-Carcano rifle.*
RIGHT: *An Italian Alpini detachment armed with machine guns poses for the camera. The Italian army had fought against Turkey over Libya in 1912 but the experience of this war was of limited use for the European conflict.*
BELOW RIGHT: *Artillery positioned on a mountain peak with a connecting trench dug into the snow.*

Mesopotamia 1914-16

The British campaign in Mesopotamia (modern-day Iraq) had its genesis in the modest and sensible aim of securing the Royal Navy's supplies of oil. In November 1914, the Indian 6th (Poona) Division landed to safeguard the refinery on Abadan Island in the Shatt-al-Arab. A Turkish counterattack was brushed aside, and by 9 December, Basra, 20 miles away, and Qurnah, at the confluence of the Rivers Tigris and Euphrates, had been captured. Thus the approaches to the Persian Gulf were firmly in British hands. There the campaign should have been halted. Instead, in the vague hope of encouraging the local Arabs to revolt against their Turkish overlords, a further advance was authorized; the strategic towns of Amarah (on the Tigris) and Nasiriyah (on the Euphrates) were to be taken.

The strategic rationale behind this campaign is difficult to fathom. Mesopotamia was too remote for it to constitute a direct threat to Turkey, or even to draw off many reserves. The logistical problems of an advance inland were formidable, with all supplies having to travel by water in the absence of roads. To the difficulties of the terrain were added an unhealthy climate and, above all, the Indian government (which was administering the campaign) was ill-equipped to sustain an expeditionary force overseas. Nevertheless, an army corps under Sir J E Nixon was assembled, and prepared to advance. Nixon first heavily defeated the Turks at Shaiba (11-13 April 1915).

The 6th Indian Division and a cavalry brigade moved up the Tigris on a flotilla of small boats (nicknamed Townshend's Regatta, after the commander of the division) and captured Amarah on 3 June. Nasiriyah fell to Gorringe's 12th Indian Division on 25 July. The weakness of the Turkish opposition bred overconfidence. Nixon asked for, and received, permission for Townshend to advance a further 40 miles up the Tigris to Kut al Amara, which fell on 28 September, after Townshend had efficiently defeated a Turkish force. Baghdad, with all its romantic connotations of the Arabian Nights, was only 40 miles away, and the Indian authorities saw the capture of the city as a wonderful 'Christmas present' to offer the British people, who had been starved of good news throughout 1915. Nixon ordered an advance in the full knowledge that he would take the blame if the venture ended in failure.

Before Baghdad lay the ancient town of Ctesiphon. There a Turkish force, under Nur-ud-Din, was entrenched, and Townshend's column was too weak to dislodge it. Townshend was forced to retreat to Kut. Nur-ud-Din followed him cautiously. On 7 December 1915 the Siege of Kut began. It was to last for five terrible months. Even before Ctesiphon, sickness was rife in the Anglo-Indian force; in temperatures of 120°F, the troops suffered from dysentery, malaria and even cholera. Logistic problems were such that barely 75 percent of the supplies the Mesopotamian force needed were ever received. It is clear that Townshend had been hopelessly overambitious in marching on Baghdad, and his men suffered for his incompetence.

Having Townshend cornered in Kut, the local commander – von der Goltz, an aged German – first assaulted the town and then sat back to starve the British out. By the end of the siege, 3000 cases of disease had been reported among the garrison. The rations had been progressively reduced; the Indian soldiers, in particular, became extremely emaciated, being unwilling to eat the horsemeat which became a staple of their diet. Townshend had taken a ridiculously pessimistic view of the food supplies, claiming that the garrison could last out for only two months. This forced the relief column – 3rd (Meerut) and 7th (Lahore) Divisions, newly arrived from France – into attacking in January, before preparations were complete. The attempt to relieve Kut failed, as did other attempts made in March and April. On 29 April 1916, Townshend surrendered, and passed into comfortable captivity. Twelve thousand others were not so lucky; nearly three-quarters of the British, and probably more of the Indians, died in, or on the way to, Turkish prison camps.

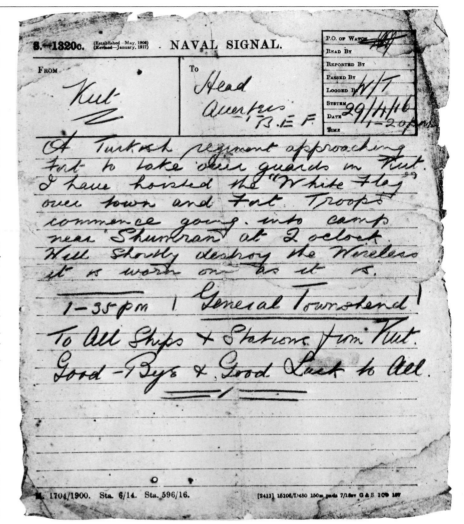

ABOVE: *British cavalry pass the Roman arch at Ctesiphon, which marked the high water mark of Townshend's advance.*
RIGHT: *An artillery battery with a mixture of Turkish and German personnel in Mesopotamia.*
ABOVE LEFT: *A signal from Townshend announcing the capitulation of the Kut garrison, dated 29 April 1916.*
LEFT: *Major General Townshend, who was responsible for the most humiliating British defeat of World War I. In October 1918 he was sent by the Turks to ask the British for armistice talks.*

1917

The World in Conflict

Chronology 1917

February 1	Germans recommence unrestricted submarine warfare
February 1	Washington severs diplomatic relations with Berlin
March 11	Fall of Baghdad
March 18	Beginning of 'February Revolution' in Russia
March 26	First battle of Gaza
April 6	USA enters war
April 9	Arras Offensive begins: Vimy Ridge stormed
April 16	Nivelle Offensive begins
June 7	Messines
July 1	Kerensky Offensive begins
July 31	Third Ypres begins
August 17	Eleventh and last battle of Isonzo
September 3	Riga captured by Germans
October 24	Caporetto
November 7	'October' or Bolshevik Revolution in Russia
November 9	Clemenceau becomes French Prime Minister
November 20	British armored attack at Cambrai
November 20	German counterattack at Cambrai
November 29	Lord Lansdowne's Peace Letter
December 16	Allenby enters Jerusalem
December 16	Armistice between Bolsheviks and Central Powers

OPPOSITE: *Women engaged in the assembly of airplane wings in a British aircraft factory. Britain was quick to utilize its female workforce in war industries; for the first time women were engaged in work that had traditionally been the exclusive preserve of men.*

The War at Sea: Beneath the Waves, 1914-18

Unlike the struggle between mass armies on land, the war at sea was fought by small elite groups, in ships and in submarines. The latter proved a highly cost-effective weapon, being small and cheap to produce, yet capable of sinking a large, expensive battleship. It could be used to project naval power into an 'enemy lake' (an area where the surface vessels of a belligerent could not penetrate), such as the Baltic Sea, where British submarines caused disruption out of all proportion to the small number involved. Similarly, Royal Navy submarines caused havoc in the otherwise inaccessible Sea of Marmara during the Dardanelles campaign: the *E-11* under Martin Nasmith VC even torpedoed a Turkish transport in Constantinople harbor. By the new year of 1916, over 200 Turkish vessels had been accounted for, including two battleships and 16 transports, and sea traffic in the Sea of Marmara was effectively paralyzed.

In the same way, German U-Boats were able to operate in areas where the High Seas Fleet could not reach, such as the Mediterranean and the Atlantic. U-Boats achieved a number of victories against enemy warships – for instance, *U-21* sank the pre-Dreadnoughts *Majestic* and *Triumph* off the Gallipoli peninsula. However, it was after the Germans declared the waters around the British Isles a War Zone in February 1915 that the U-Boat began to demonstrate its potential. Germany hoped to break the strategic deadlock by striking at the merchant shipping that kept open Britain's trans-Atlantic lifeline, and thus starve Britain into submission – which was a mirror image of Britain's naval strategy. Despite the partial success of this policy, in September 1915 the U-Boats were switched to 'legitimate' targets for fear of provoking the United States into the war.

ABOVE: *A German U-Boat supply ship with torpedo craft and submarines, c 1917. The U-Boat crews enjoyed extremely high morale and were less affected by revolutionary sentiments in 1918 than sailors of the surface fleet, despite the fact that one in three of all submarine personnel were killed or wounded.*

ABOVE LEFT: *Lieutenant Commander Arnaud de la Perière and crew members man the conning tower of* U-35, *the most successful U-boat in the history of submarine warfare. Altogether this submarine sank 224 Allied vessels during World War I.*

LEFT: *A U-Boat attacks an Allied merchantman. Unarmed merchant ships were sunk by surfaced U-Boats, to save torpedoes to attack armed ships. Sometimes the crew of the victim would be warned and allowed to take to the lifeboats.*

RIGHT: *The entrance to the Bruges Canal at Zeebrugge after the British raid, showing the sunken* Thetis, Intrepid *and* Iphigenia. *These obsolete vessels successfully sank themselves in the entrance to the canal, but U-Boats were able to slip past at high tide.*

TOP: *An Allied convoy, with two destroyers in the foreground. The First Sea Lord, Jellicoe, opposed convoys because of the difficulties involved in organizing them, and argued that they would simply provide larger targets for the U-Boats. Had his views prevailed, it is quite possible that Britain could have been forced out of the war in 1917.*

ABOVE: *The torpedo room of a German submarine. Germany had shown little interest in the submarine before 1914, being more concerned with building a surface fleet to challenge the Royal Navy. During the war its potential was realized, as it was a potent weapon able to threaten Britain's mercantile lifeline.*

RIGHT: *A small German submarine of the UB type comes alongside U-35 in the Mediterranean. The figure on the right in British military uniform is Captain Wilson, a King's Messenger, who had been taken prisoner by the U-Boat. German submarines operated in the Mediterranean from the Adriatic port of Cattaro.*

As the stalemate in the West dragged on into 1917, the German government, now dominated by Ludendorff, announced the reintroduction of unrestricted submarine warfare from 1 February. They had few illusions as to the likely reaction of the United States; they gambled that the U-Boats would knock Britain out of the war before the American war machine could make its presence felt in Europe. The gamble almost succeeded. By April 1917 British losses were running at nearly 90,000 tons of shipping a month (January's figure had been 110,000 tons) and she was down to only 6 weeks reserve stock of food. The Royal Navy could suggest no adequate countermeasures. Depth charges had been developed, as had the hydrophone, an acoustic listening device. The Royal Navy even deployed Q-ships, apparently innocuous merchantmen with concealed armament – these enjoyed some success at sinking surfaced U-Boats. However, in the end, it was the reintroduction of the convoy system, at Lloyd George's insistence but in the teeth of the Admiralty's opposition, that finally mastered the U-Boat menace.

By sailing merchant ships in convoy, the British were able to give them adequate protection with the limited number of destroyers available, although the US Navy played an increasingly important role as the war neared its end. In the period September to December 1917, less than 1000 tons of British shipping was lost; the first Battle of the Atlantic had been won.

There was a dramatic coda to this campaign: the attempt to deny the inland port of Bruges to the U-Boats. On 23 April 1918, St George's Day, Rear Admiral Sir Roger Keyes led a naval force in an attack on Zeebrugge. He succeeded in the difficult task of sinking three blockships in the canal that led to Bruges, but within three weeks the canal was again being used by U-Boats. Although a military failure, the raid was a psychological victory; in Churchill's words, 'the finest feat of arms in the Great War' raised Allied morale at a critical stage of the German spring offensive. By mid-1918, with the U-Boat threat contained, and the British blockade of Germany biting hard, the scene was set for the final, tragic act of the war at sea.

Total War: the Home Fronts 1914-18

The nations of Europe went to war in 1914 expecting that it would be over by Christmas. Instead, it dragged on for four years, and the trends noticeable in some previous wars – particularly the Napoleonic and American Civil Wars – were brought to a logical climax. All the resources – economic, technological, human – of modern industrial states were eventually directed to one end: the achievement of political aims by military means. 'Total War' thus became a reality, with enormous consequences for the political, social and economic structures of the states involved.

The outbreak of war in 1914 was greeted with an outburst of popular enthusiasm which served to unite, if only superficially, the unequal and divided societies of Europe. In France, the *Union Sacrée* was set up; a patriotic coalition composed of activists of every political hue from extreme left to extreme right. Germany had its *Burgfrieden* (Fortress Truce), which temporarily halted industrial unrest, and even in Russia, the militancy of the work force subsided. In Britain, where a general strike was threatened for the autumn of 1914, the Labour Party and labor movement threw its weight behind the war effort, although some of its leaders, including Ramsey MacDonald, opposed the war and went into temporary political exile. The great hope of socialists such as Karl Liebknecht in Germany and Keir Hardie in Britain, that an international syndicalist strike would bring the preparations for war grinding to a halt, was itself sabotaged by the workers of Europe, who proved to have a stronger loyalty to their nations than to international proletarian solidarity.

Few people had expected the war to be anything but short in August 1914. One who thought otherwise was Field Marshal Kitchener, who became British Secretary of State for War and set about raising a mass volunteer army, announcing that the war would last for three years. He benefitted from this universal belief that the war would be short. Asquith's Liberal government gave him almost unlimited control of Britain's war effort, on the assumption that affairs would swiftly return to normality. This usurpation of civilian political power was a widespread phenomenon. Joffre assumed virtually dictatorial powers in the 'Zone of the Armies' in eastern France, largely untrammelled by civilian ministers. His additional ascendency in national affairs was

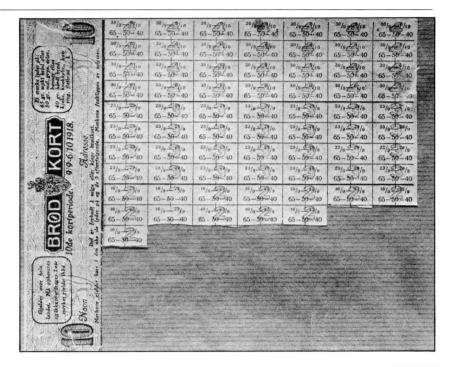

Eat Less Bread

—— ▪ ——

Waste None

ABOVE: *A British poster from 1917. In Britain the better-off classes were worst affected by food shortages; for the poor, a monotonous diet was scarcely a novelty. Some middle-class recruits to the army were shocked to meet other, unhealthy, working-class recruits, the victims of industrial capitalism.*
TOP: *A German bread ration card. Staple foodstuffs were rationed from 1915 onward. By the end of the war food supplies in Germany were very short as a result of the Allied blockade.*
LEFT: *Patriotic Germans subscribe to the war-loan at the Savings Bank of Charlottenburg, 1915.*

RIGHT: *An idealized image of German womanhood, supporting the soldier fighting for the Kaiser and the Fatherland. In fact, the Germans were slow to mobilize women in the war effort.*
BELOW: *Americans too were encouraged to invest in war loans.*

THEY KEPT THE SEA LANES OPEN

INVEST IN THE VICTORY LIBERTY LOAN

aided by the flight of the government to Bordeaux in September 1914. It did not return until the following December. This casual consent to military domination of the executive was at least partially the product of a general acceptance of the truth of a misleading interpretation of Clausewitz. 'War is the continuation of state policy by other means' was believed to mean that, in time of war, military needs must take precedence over civilian. In the militaristic empires of the east, this only confirmed and accelerated the general political and social trends.

In France and Britain, the civilians attempted to claw back their lost political power. In 1916, the French Chamber of Deputies reasserted its position as the elected representative of the nation, managing to gain the right to visit the army at the front. Briand, the Prime Minister, manipulated the crisis brought about by Verdun to topple the autocratic Joffre by elevating him to a Marshal of France and replacing him as *de facto* Commander in Chief with Nivelle. Briand's successor, Ribot, in turn sacked Nivelle after his promises of a breakthrough proved to be illusory. Kitchener, too, rapidly outlived the initial enthusiasm for his appointment among politicians, although he never lost the adulation of the British army and public. Kitchener was by nature an autocrat, and his secretive habits and abrasive manner alienated many of his civilian colleagues, including Lloyd George. His powers were gradually whittled away during 1915, culminating in the appointment of General Sir William Robertson as CIGS, with greatly increased powers. This transference of power from one soldier to another created as many problems as it raised. Although Kitchener conveniently drowned in June 1916 on his way to Russia, when Lloyd George became Prime Minister in December 1916, he promptly came into conflict with Robertson and Haig over their Western policy of attrition. Robertson was finally removed in February 1918 (Lloyd George claimed, unconvincingly, that 'Wully' was contemplating a military dictatorship) and replaced by Sir Henry Wilson. Lloyd George never dared to attempt to remove Haig himself: he was reliant on Unionist (Tory) support to maintain himself as Prime Minister. The Liberal Party having split, Haig enjoyed the support of the Tories.

In the Central Powers, the military increased its grip on the government. Before the war, the Reichstag had had an important influence on German policy: it could refuse to vote credits. Its power diminished during the years 1914-16. The 'All Highest,' the Kaiser, remained in theory an autocrat but in practice became little more than a cipher as, what has been described as the 'silent dictatorship' of

Ludendorff and Hindenburg, took over not only OHL, but also effectively the direction of the war effort at home. This represented a defeat for the German moderates. The decision to reopen unrestricted submarine warfare in February 1917 was taken against the wishes of the civilian Chancellor, Bethmann-Hollweg, who resigned in July 1917 and was replaced by the pliable Dr Georg Michaelis.

The Hindenburg-Ludendorff partnership did much to fulfill the trend toward total war in Germany. Centralized direction of the economy was undertaken in Germany from the very beginning of the war, largely because of the foresight of German industrialists (notably Walther Rathenau of AEG). The Germans had naively expected to be able to import vital foodstuffs and raw materials through the Netherlands, which had thus been deleted from the original Schlieffen Plan. When the Allied naval blockade began to take effect, Germany had reason to be grateful to Rathenau. In August 1914 the Ministry of War set up an infrastructure for co-ordination and planning of the German economy; trade, the search for synthetic materials, allocation and distribution of resources were all included. Food was also controlled, although less successfully, with the rationing of staple foods being introduced during 1915. 'War Socialism,' as it was called, was greatly extended by the Hindenburg-Ludendorff dictatorship. A 'Patriotic

LEFT: *A team of dogs pulls a harrow at a farm near Reninghelst, April 1916. In the last two years of the war, the German successes in Russia brought fresh supplies of wheat from the newly captured agricultural lands in the Ukraine but in insufficient quantities to prevent widespread hunger in Germany during the last winter of the war.*

BELOW: *A carefully posed German photograph of an all-too-familiar event on the home front of every belligerent: a wife receives notification of her husband's death in action. The picture on the wall is of the Kaiser, Hindenburg and Ludendorff.*

ABOVE: *Walther Rathenau, who helped to organize the German economy.*

LEFT: *In order to save space on shipping, Britons were encouraged to grow their own food. Pictured here is an allotment in Dulwich, a suburb of London.*

ABOVE LEFT: *A dead horse is being cut up on the street for food. The original caption reads 'Hungerwinter 1917/18 in Deutschland.' By this date the Allied naval blockade was causing great suffering in Germany. Germany was forced to use animal fodder to feed her population. As a result, dairy products became scarce, and swedes and turnips became the German staple diet at a time when industrial workers were in greater need of a healthy diet than ever before.*

Auxiliary Service Law,' promulgated at the end of 1916, introduced industrial conscription. All males between 17 and 60 years were pressed into service. Ironically this law – introduced in order to fulfill the 'Hindenburg Program' of munitions production – led to the German state taking the Trades Unions into junior partnership, the better to control the workers. As a corollary, the unions were able to obtain social and political reforms that would be difficult to reverse after war. As John Gooch has pointed out, the German authorities were forced to make short-term concessions on these matters, against all their political instincts, in order to win the war; defeat would almost certainly bring about revolution. Tirpitz expressed this paradox succinctly: 'Victory or defeat, we shall get democracy.' The question was, how violent would be the transition?

RIGHT: Woolwich Arsenal, 1918 by Sir George Clausen. The initial rush to enlist in Britain denuded the factories of many skilled men needed for war work, and some were transferred out of the army back to their old jobs. Many women left domestic service and entered the factories, for work in munitions, although unpleasant and sometimes dangerous, was much better paid than work as a domestic servant.

LEFT: A poster inviting citizens of Frankfurt to show the gratitude of the Kaiser and people to the army and navy at Christmas by making a donation to a fund-raising drive. There was an enormous gulf between the men who had served at the front and those who remained at home, who found it impossible to grasp the reality of trench warfare.

RIGHT: The howitzer shop in the Coventry Ordnance Works. The British labor movement made significant advances during the war as the government and industrialists sought to make allies of the people who actually produced war materiel. Industrial relations had been particularly bad in the last years before 1914.

LEFT: *A woman bus conductor (or 'clippie') in London during the Great War. The prewar Suffragettes had failed to win the vote for women in Britain by protest but the women's contribution to the war effort helped them gain political rights after the war.*

ABOVE: *Spy mania gripped America in 1917, as it had the other combatant nations in 1914. Here German suspects are rounded up in New York in 1917.*

RIGHT: *A British engineering worker, 1917. In 1914 only 212,000 women were involved in such work; by 1918 there were nearly one million. Many women, especially those who had taken the place of skilled men, lost their jobs in 1919, but there was still an increase of about 250,000 women in permanent employment over the total of 1914.*

This intelligent centralized direction of the economy was not adopted in Austria-Hungary. There, an internecine trade war developed between the two halves of the Dual Monarchy, which led to the industrial cities of Austria being denied Magyar wheat, leading to paralyzation of the war effort. In Italy, a serious effort to achieve a war economy was not made until after the Battle of Caporetto, and Orlando's ministry came to power. The strains of the war on the fabric of Italian society destroyed democracy, which was in 1922 replaced by Mussolini's authoritarian Fascist regime.

Britain's drift to a war economy also began slowly, the popular slogan being 'Business As Usual,' but by 1917 it too was adapting to the demands of total war. Much of the credit for the British transformation is due to David Lloyd George, the Chancellor of the Exchequer in 1914, who became Minister of Munitions in June 1916. He persuaded the Trades Unions to accept the dilution of skilled labor by unskilled men, and even women, and thus increased shell production dramatically. When he became Prime Minister, he presided over a small War Cabinet of five members, including a Labour Party representative (first Arthur Henderson, later George Barnes). The impact of the German U-Boat campaign in 1917 brought Britain even closer to total war, as food shortages brought in their wake stringent rationing. Georges Clemenceau, nicknamed 'The Tiger,' became French Prime Minister in November 1917, and had a similar galvanizing effect across the Channel. The French had also been initially slow to organize for war. Provisions for industrial conscription were made as early as July 1915, but not rigorously enforced until 1917. Joffre, in spite of his commanding position, did not have the vision of a Ludendorff.

For the ordinary citizen of the belligerent powers, perhaps the greatest impact of total war was the erasure of the dividing line between 'combatant' and 'non-combatant.' His very diet was a legitimate target of the enemy; by 1918, the shortage of food in Germany

was severe. Ersatz (substitute) coffee, made from acorns, and numerous other ingenious replacements were introduced; the winter of 1916-17 was remembered as the Turnip Winter. It has been suggested that one of the causes of the breakdown in German army morale in 1918 was capturing plentiful supplies of British food, after having been told that the British were starving. Morale at home collapsed shortly afterward. A wave of strikes and other symptoms of popular unrest had swept the country as early as January. France and Britain also experienced disturbances. Some 9344 men had gone on strike in France in 1915; 293,810 in 1917. Civilians were also thrust, literally, into the firing line; the destruction of enemy morale by bombing became a legitimate military aim. The freedom of citizens to change their job, to buy luxuries or oppose the war was affected by laws such as DORA (the British Defence of the Realm Act), centralized direction of the economy or public pressure. Pacifists had a hard time, as did enemy aliens; an unhealthy element of racism was injected into the war, with the Germans being called 'Huns' by the British and *les Boches* (rascals) by the French. A German composed a 'Hymn of Hate' which included the lyric, 'Hate by water and hate by land/ . . . We have but one foe alone, England.' Shops with foreign-sounding names were sacked in London's East End. By far and away the worst racial atrocity of the war was committed far from the Western Front: more than 1½ million Armenians perished as the result of a Turkish policy of genocide. Yet paradoxically it is possible to argue that the people of Britain, at least, did well out of the war: social and political changes brought the working classes a general level of prosperity higher than at any time previously, and the ground was laid for major initiatives in housing and health. If Wilhelmine Germany had survived the war, there too, the social structure would have been markedly different from 1914. As it was, Germany was transformed into a liberal Republic, and 'Prussianism' appeared to have been destroyed.

The Nivelle Offensive and the French Mutinies

The military plans of the *Entente* for 1917 originally contained little of novelty. Joffre proposed that the Somme offensive should be reactivated, as soon as possible, although on a somewhat wider front; and his view prevailed. It was also agreed, at Chantilly on 16 November 1916, to launch offensives on all the Allied fronts, including the 'side shows.' Later in 1917, Haig's brainchild of an offensive in Flanders would at last become reality.

The 'kicking upstairs' of Joffre – he was elevated to a Marshal of France and replaced by Nivelle – caused these plans to be drastically modified. The Somme offensive was abandoned – probably wisely, as the actions of the British Fifth Army in the Ancre valley in early 1917 highlighted the problems of campaigning in severe winter weather. Instead, Nivelle wanted to make the major effort on the Aisne, with the British making a preliminary push to the north around Arras, to attract the enemy reserves. Nivelle came as a breath of fresh air to the politicians, who were used to dealing with the taciturn and stolid Haig and Joffre. Nivelle was eloquent, even garrulous. He charmed even Lloyd George, who, at the Rome conference in January, had advocated that the major effort of 1917 should be made in Italy. Nivelle spoke perfect English – he had a British mother – and for a short time, Lloyd George, a dedicated Easterner, became an enthusiastic supporter of the French Commander in Chief. He even attempted, by devious means, to permanently subordinate Haig to Nivelle at the Calais Conference of 26 February 1917, which had been called ostensibly to discuss transport. As a compromise, Haig was to act under Nivelle's orders for the duration of the offensive. This episode poisoned civil-military relations in Britain for the rest of the war.

Nivelle's popularity with the politicians was a result of his bold declaration that he had discovered a 'secret' which would unlock the Western Front. He proposed to return to the offensive *à l'outrance*. A violent, surprise bombardment would disrupt and disorientate the enemy, who would then face a headlong frontal infantry assault, protected by a creeping barrage. The line would be pierced, and rapid exploitation would reopen mobile warfare. Nivelle's success at Verdun lent plausibility to this plan, but his army commanders, Micheler, Pétain and d'Esperey had grave reservations, which were deepened when on 14 March the Germans began to withdraw to the *Siegfriedstellung*, which the British called the 'Hindenburg Line.' This was a strongly fortified position 15 to 25 miles in the rear of the German lines, which had begun construction in the autumn of 1916. The withdrawal shortened the German line by 26 miles, and allowed 10 divisions to be withdrawn from trench-holding duties. The abandoned territory was devastated; buildings were ruined, trees cut down, and booby traps plentifully scattered around the resulting waste. At first, the Allies believed that the retreat signified the collapse of German morale; they were to be strongly disabused of this notion.

Nivelle had planned for the BEF and Northern Army Group to attack the sides of the German salient, which no longer existed. Nevertheless, the BEF's attack went ahead. Nivelle made no major changes to his plan, despite the forfeiture of strategic surprise. His inability to keep quiet forewarned the Germans. By April, they had massively reinforced the sector to be attacked, from 18 divisions in January to 42. Ten days before the battle began the complete order of battle of the French Fifth Army was captured. Incredibly, even then Nivelle chose not to change his plans.

The British diversion at Arras began on 9 April 1917; the main French attack on the 16th. The French infantry was supremely confident, as it had been before the autumn offensive of 1915. In all 46 divisions attacked, supported by 3810 guns. The assault troops came up against the new German defenses, which absorbed the French blows. The Germans then counterattacked. The Chemin des Dames Ridge proved as unassailable as it had in October 1914. Although

ABOVE: *General Robert Nivelle, French Commander in Chief in 1917. Nivelle was an artilleryman by background and believed that the secret of victory lay in combining a scientific artillery barrage with a surprise infantry attack. He promised to win the war and succeeded in convincing the* poilus *that they were on the point of victory. His Napoleonic eve-of-battle message to them was: 'The hour has come! Confidence! Courage! Vive la France!' Nivelle's plan broke down within hours of the opening of the battle when the attackers became bogged down in the German front line. Instead of bringing victory, Nivelle brought the army to the edge of disintegration.*

BELOW: *French deserters, 1917. The French succeeded in concealing the extent of the mutinies from their British allies and their German enemies. It has been suggested that the Germans could have won a great victory if they had attacked in the spring of 1917, but it seems that most of the mutineers were prepared to defend their trenches if attacked. A few extremists tried to convert the mutiny into a revolutionary movement, but they were not typical.*

ABOVE: *The Kaiser decorating German guardsmen after the Allied spring offensives of 1917.*
ABOVE RIGHT: *Marshal Pétain being decorated by George V, July 1917. In World War II Pétain led the collaborationist Vichy government. This overshadowed his success in nursing the French army back to health in the aftermath of the 1917 mutinies – an outstanding achievement.*

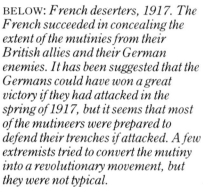

Mangin's Sixth and Mazel's Fifth Armies took over 10,000 prisoners, no decisive breach was made in the German position. An attack using tanks was a disappointing failure; they proved to be as unreliable as the British model, and suffered heavily from the German guns. Nivelle had previously promised to break off the offensive within 48 hours if the French did not succeed in reaching open country. Instead, he continued the battle, launching the Fourth Army forward in Champagne on 20 April. This force bit deeply into the German line, but could not pierce the enemy positions. Nivelle, in desperation, threw the Tenth Army, which had been the formation held in the rear to exploit the breakthrough intended for 16 April, into a series of headlong assaults on the Aisne on 25 April. These attacks, like the others, could break into, but not out of, the enemy defenses. Nivelle's 'secret' had proved to be worthless on the battlefield. He was *limogé* or sacked. Pétain took his place.

Judged by the standards of the Western Front, Nivelle's campaign on the Aisne had been a limited success. Some 29,000 prisoners had been taken, and a salient four miles deep on a 16-mile front had been created. A total of 187,000 Frenchmen and 163,000 Germans had been lost. Nivelle had promised much more than this. He had promised a decisive victory, and he paid the price for his vainglorious boasting. So did France. Disillusioned, and sickened by the casualties, large sections of the French Army mutinied.

The first case seems to have been on 17 April; isolated cases were still occurring in January 1918. Professor Pedroncini, a French historian, has concluded that the worst period was in June 1917. In all, there were 250 cases of 'collective indiscipline,' affecting 68 divisions. But 44 were unaffected; a total of perhaps 35,000 men, or one mutineer for every 100 soldiers. Even in the most mutinous divisions, actual mutineers were in a minority. At the time, there was much talk of pacifist/defeatist agitators stirring up discontent among the ranks. While this played a part, it seems that general war-weariness and disillusion were the major factor in the mutinies. Indeed, the very term 'mutiny' is misleading; in most cases, the disturbances took on the character of a 'strike,' with men being willing to hold trenches but not to take part in any futile offensives. The Russian Brigades in France proved to be an exception – but they were affected by the tumultuous events in Russia herself.

Fortunately for the Allies, the Germans did not find out about the mutinies until the worst of them were over. Pétain rectified many of the grievances – ensuring regular leave for the *poilus*, for example. Only 55 mutineers were executed, out of 23,385 men found guilty of various crimes. Pétain attempted to heal, rather than punish, the army. One thing was clear: with the French incapable of undertaking a major offensive in 1917, the main Allied effort on the Western Front would have to be made by the BEF.

Arras and the Storming of Vimy Ridge

'The news is excellent and as we marched forward today, we saw all manner of troops going in the same direction, including a division of cavalry . . . it's extraordinary how good news bucks up the men . . .' So wrote a British officer on 10 April 1917. The 'good news' he referred to was the beginning of the Battle of Arras. On the previous day, the bastion of Vimy Ridge had been stormed and captured by the Canadian Corps. At last it appeared that the British army had the enemy on the run.

Arras was intended as a diversion to aid Nivelle's main thrust on the Aisne. Horne's First Army was to take Vimy Ridge and thus safeguard the flank of Allenby's Third Army, which was to pierce the Hindenburg Line. Allenby's objective was strongly fortified, consisting not only of the new style 'zonal' defense, but also of the old German trenches. Gough's Fifth Army was available to attack further to the south if the initial assaults achieved their objectives.

The attack on Vimy Ridge was entrusted to the Canadian Corps, which was commanded by Lieutenant General Sir Julian Byng, a British cavalryman. Like other white Dominion troops, the Canadians combined a disregard for the niceties of King's Regulations with a fine record as fighting troops. The 'colonials' were the finest soldiers in the BEF, tending to display a higher level of individual initiative than the average British Tommy, which was perhaps a reflection of the open nature of Australasian and Canadian society. They would need all their martial skills to capture Vimy Ridge, which was reputed to be impregnable. The Germans had three main defensive lines, linked to a labyrinthine system of deep dugouts by tunnels. The Ridge was in fact honeycombed by underground passages. Beneath the earth, tunnellers of all nations along the whole front waged a private, subterranean war, seeking to construct mines to destroy the positions above. Countermining and even hand-to-hand combat beneath the earth were part of the hazards faced by these brave men. For the operation against Vimy Ridge, effective use was made of tunnels to move troops up to their start-lines unmolested by artillery. In well-lit and properly ventilated underground chambers, reserves could be sheltered close to the front line, ready to exploit any penetration of the enemy positions.

In many ways, Arras was an old-fashioned battle. Haig insisted that the German positions were 'softened up' by a five-day pounding by 2879 guns, with one heavy piece every 21 yards, despite Allenby's request for a short bombardment. The 40 available tanks were again distributed piecemeal to the attacking forces. Nevertheless, the opening day of the battle was a major success. Attacking north of the River Scarpe, XVII Corps advanced 3½ miles into the German positions, establishing themselves on the third line; 9th (Scottish) Division and 4th Division had made the furthest single advance achieved in one day since trench warfare began in the West. Along the entire front of the Third Army, a minimum of 2000 yards was taken, and in some places three times as much territory was gained. The Canadians captured Vimy Ridge although hampered by snow, and earned four VCs in the process. Allenby was convinced that the Third Army was now 'pursuing a beaten enemy,' and the cavalry was brought up for the chase, but the battle, frustratingly, became stalemated.

BELOW LEFT: *A naval gun fires from behind the Canadian lines on Vimy Ridge, May 1917. Much of the heavy artillery supporting the Canadian assault was provided by the British: the XIII, XVIII, XXVII, XLIV, LXX and LXXVI Heavy Artillery Groups were present, in addition to the 1st and 2nd Canadian Groups. This huge concentration of firepower was a significant factor in the Canadian victory.*

RIGHT: *Some of the many German soldiers captured by British Empire troops in 1917. These are the staff of a battalion, including the commander and adjutant. Note the guard visible in the background. He is wearing a small box respirator which also contained his gas mask.*

BELOW: *Canadian 29th Infantry Battalion advances toward its objective during the Battle of Vimy Ridge.*

Uncharacteristically, the German defenders (Falkenhausen's Sixth Army) had made some important errors in their dispositions. The principle of 'elastic defense' does not seem to have been fully understood. The front posts were too strongly held, while the reserves assigned to the counterattack role were positioned too far back. The British and Canadians, advancing deep into the German positions, were held up by the uncut wire of the rear defenses – which had been built beyond the range of the British 18 pounders – and were then faced by the German reserves belatedly arriving on the battlefield.

The remaining days of the battle were disappointing for the British. An imaginative joint infantry/tank assault by the Fifth Army at Bullecourt on 12 April broke into the Hindenburg Line, but a brigade of 4th Australian Division suffered heavily from counterattacks. An attempt to feed cavalry through a gap created south of the Scarpe at Monchyle-Preux, captured on 11 April, was a bloody failure. Haig continued to fight until 17 May. The last phase, the Battle of Bullcourt, was described by the British Official Historian as 'pure attrition.' However,

it served its purpose of preventing German reserves from being sent south to oppose Nivelle. Arras cost the British about 150,000 men; the Germans over 100,000. A total of 20,000 German prisoners were taken as well as the strategic prize of Vimy Ridge, which was to prove invaluable in the 1918 campaigns. The British and Canadians had performed brilliantly in the initial, 'set piece' phase, although when faced with the unforeseen problems of a semi-fluid battle, the BEF's skill was found wanting. But it is certainly true that the BEF of April 1917 had a much higher level of tactical ability than the BEF of April 1916. The Canadians, in particular, had reason to be proud of their achievements; Vimy Ridge became the symbol of their efforts in 1914-18. After the war, 250 acres of land on Vimy Ridge were given by the people of France to the people of Canada. On it stands an enormous and beautiful Memorial. It is sometimes said that Canada's nationhood was consecrated in blood on the battlefields of the Western Front. If so, it paid a high price: the names of 66,000 dead are inscribed on the twin pylons of the Vimy Memorial.

Messines and Third Ypres – Phase 1

ABOVE: *Wounded German prisoners taken by the French. Note the German medical orderly. Although non-combatant, medical personnel were frequently called upon to undertake dangerous tasks. One of the very few soldiers to win a Bar to a Victoria Cross was a British Medical Officer.*
LEFT: *Oppy Wood, 1917, by Paul Nash. Canadian and British troops attacked this wood at the end of the Arras campaign. A British staff officer described it as 'almost impregnable' and one British unit, the 22nd Royal Fusiliers, suffered 75 percent casualties in a single attack on the position.*

Sir Douglas Haig, who became a Field Marshal in December 1916, had been in favor of an offensive in Flanders since 1915. The genuine strategic objectives that had been absent on the Somme could be found in Flanders. If Passchendaele Ridge could be taken, the pressure on the Ypres Salient would be greatly eased. A breakout from Ypres along the coast would outflank the entire German line, and by 1917 it was believed that it would have a decisive effect on the war at sea. Jellicoe, the First Sea Lord, believed (erroneously) that the capture of the ports of Ostend and Zeebrugge was essential, if the Royal Navy was not to lose the Battle of the Atlantic and, with it, the war. Finally, Haig firmly believed that the German army had been seriously weakened by the campaigns of 1916. One more major push might cause it to collapse. After the spring battles of 1917, it was clear that the BEF would have to undertake the Flanders campaign with only the minimum of assistance from the French, even though the full extent of the French army's problems was concealed from the British. Haig was confident that the offensive could be launched by the British alone, and indeed was essential to keep the enemy off the French's backs, but the War Cabinet only reluctantly gave its assent. The dramatic triumph of Messines Ridge seemed to show that Haig's confidence in the BEF was well founded.

The capture of Messines Ridge was an essential precondition to the storming of the main German positions. General Sir Herbert Plumer's Second Army undertook the planning and execution of the operation. 'Daddy' Plumer formed a perfect partnership with his Chief of Staff (and future biographer), Sir Charles Harington. Plumer had the reputation as a humane man, who was sparing of his men's lives, in spite of his command of the notoriously dangerous Ypres Salient. The Battle of Messines was a typically methodical operation. For over a year, a series of tunnels had been bored under the ridge, and packed with ½ million pounds of high explosive. On 7 June 1917, at 0310 hours, 19 mines were blown. The crest of the ridge was literally wrenched off. Simultaneously, an intense bombardment straddled the German positions, and nine divisions assaulted the ridge. The operation was a complete success, marred only by the crowding of the ridge which caused some unnecessary casualties on subsequent days. This was hardly new; it was a species of siege war that would have earned the approval of Vauban, the great seventeenth-century siegemaster.

LEFT: *The battle of the mud: an Australian mule team stuck in the morass, Flanders, October 1917. A bullet in the head was often the fate of animals stranded in the mud. Mules were the only animals – apart from humans – capable of standing the strain of shelling.*

RIGHT: *The shattered remains of Ooattaverne Wood, showing trenches taken by the British during the capture of Messines Ridge in June 1917.*

Haig then proceeded to make the first of his many errors in this campaign: he took the responsibility for the main attack from the Second Army and gave it to Gough's Fifth Army. Gough, a young, thrusting cavalryman, was unfamiliar with the terrain of the salient and adopted a plan almost diametrically opposed to Plumer's. Plumer's scheme was designed to seize the low ridges around Ypres in a series of limited attacks covered by the artillery. Gough instead gave units objectives as much as 6000 yards away, seeking to achieve the breakthrough that he had been denied in July 1916. Gough's change of plan and the delays caused by the arrival of a small French force (Anthoine's First Army), sent by Pétain as part of his policy of restoring French confidence by fighting small-scale actions, caused a delay of seven weeks between the end of Messines and the opening of the offensive on 31 July. This time was not wasted by the Germans. Ypres was reinforced and the defenses, based on a series of ferro-concrete 'pill boxes,' were improved.

The first phase of the Third Battle of Ypres was preceded by an aerial offensive, in which the British gained control of the air; the RFC played a significant, if rarely mentioned, role in the campaign. At 0350 on 31 July 1917, nine divisions went 'over the top.' At first they made some headway: Gough's left-hand corps and the French advanced nearly two miles and took most of Pilckem Ridge. But in the center, German counterattacks forced the British back to only 500 yards from their start line. The use of tanks was not a success. Out of 19 of II Corps' tanks that reached the battlefield 17 were knocked out, and the muddy, lunar landscape was hard going. Gough had been hopelessly optimistic in his objectives, but compared with 1 July 1916, progress had been reasonable, and casualties were lighter: 17,000 instead of 57,000. And 7500 prisoners and 67 guns had been taken. The situation would have been hopeful except for one factor: in late afternoon, the heavens opened and it began to rain.

Rain in late summer in Belgium was hardly a novelty. Haig had been warned by the meteorologists that he could expect a maximum of three weeks of good weather, and the Tank Corps HQ had provided GHQ with daily reports of the sodden state of the ground, until ordered to stop. Even before the rains began, the intensive bombardment which began on 18 July – by 1400 guns, including one heavy gun every 23 yards – had cratered the ground, destroying the drainage system and filling the shell holes with water, which naturally enough, lies close to the surface in the Low Countries. Haig had been warned of this consequence, but he chose to ignore it, believing a heavy bombardment was essential to success. The heavy rain of early August turned the 'wet Flanders plain' into a quagmire. On 2 August the campaign was suspended, to await dry weather.

ABOVE: *An Australian mortar team in a flooded trench. The mortar provided the infantry with close-range fire support. However, service in a trench mortar battery could be dangerous – in the British army they were known as 'Suicide Clubs' and mortarmen were unpopular with line infantrymen because they drew fire onto their positions. Prior to the arrival of mortars a variety of improvised weapons capable of lobbing grenades and bombs across No Man's Land were invented, including giant catapults that drew their inspiration from medieval siege warfare.*

RIGHT: *Australian troops of Plumer's Second Army study a large contour map of Messines Ridge before the battle. Note the mixture of slouch hats and steel helmets. Australian and New Zealand troops took a leading role in the Battle of Messines Ridge. In all, the Germans suffered 17,500 casualties and had 7500 men taken prisoner, while Allied losses amounted to 17,000 men. Careful preparation before the attack was a special feature of Second Army operations.*

Third Ypres – Phase II: Passchendaele

The Canadian Corps won a brilliant victory at Lens in mid-August, capturing Hill 70 and engaging five German divisions that could otherwise have been sent to Flanders. At Verdun Pétain launched another 'healing attack,' which took 10,000 prisoners. Up at Ypres there was little to cheer about. The second phase of the offensive, the Battle of Langemarck (16-18 August) achieved little. Haig then gave Plumer responsibility for the main attack. The Second Army began to plan a painstaking campaign. It would edge forward by fighting strictly limited actions, under a massive umbrella of shells. Infantry objectives would be set at only 1500 yards or so, each advance taking place behind a creeping barrage. The middle phase was the most successful of the campaign.

The battle came very close to being permanently halted: Haig had to fight hard against those in the War Cabinet who were horrified by the casualty rate. Once it recommenced, with the Battle of Menin Road Ridge (20-25 September) Plumer's tactics were justified. The British moved steadily forward, gained their objective, and then waited for the guns to move up and pummel the next objective. 'Elastic defense,' to the consternation of OHL, was not working. They began to reinforce the front line, where the extra men simply made additional targets for

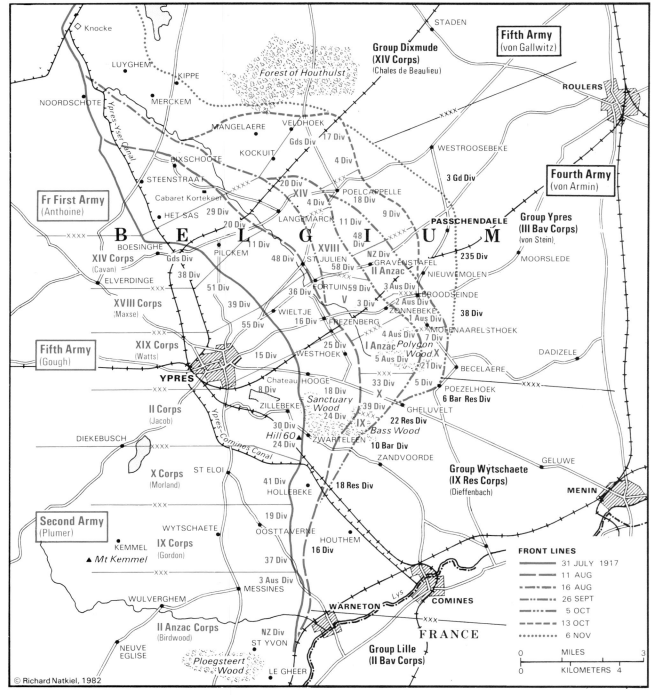

ABOVE: *Commander of the British Second Army, General Sir Herbert Plumer decorates women ambulance drivers for bravery under fire. Plumer was generally considered to be the ablest army commander of the Western Front, highly regarded for his meticulous attention to detail.*
LEFT: *The British advance during the Third Battle of Ypres failed to live up to its planners' expectations; the offensive ground to a halt near the village of Passchendaele: the place which gave the battle its popular name.*

LEFT: *Canadian machine gunners hold an improvised front line on Passchendaele Ridge, the furthest point of the Allied advance in November 1917. Repeated artillery bombardments turned the battlefield into a sea of mud, giving Third Ypres its particularly grim character.*
BELOW LEFT: *A British soldier passes the iron framework of a German pillbox at Waterloo Farm, Broodseinde.*
BELOW: *German troops endure a British bombardment in the comparative safety of a dug-out. Fully armed, they are ready to rush back to the front line once the artillery barrage ceases.*

the British guns. Menin Road Ridge was followed by Polygon Wood (26 September) and Broodseinde (4 October). All were tactical triumphs in which the ANZACs, among other formations, distinguished themselves. However, the original strategic rationale for the campaign, the clearance of the Flanders coast, was forgotten. Now Haig was content to secure an advantageous line for the winter – and, of course, to subject the German army to attrition. By the Battle of Broodseinde, the first 'Black Day' of the German army, it seemed that Haig was about to break the enemy's morale. The British Official Historian went as far as to claim that the Germans were 'beaten,' and that Rupprecht, the German commander, was preparing to retreat. At the very least, it is clear that the Germans were dreading a renewal of the battle.

Then the weather intervened. Broodseinde was fought in the rain, but 'rain' is not an adequate word to describe the deluge that began on 12 October. The ground once more liquified. Both army commanders wanted to halt the campaign, but Haig elected to fight on. This decision

was perhaps the most damning of Haig's misjudgments. He was condemning men to fight in a morass. 'Up to the present I have seen only one aspect of this part of France – Mud,' wrote a British officer in November. He went on to compare it to 'a stretch of grey water.' Private George Brame of 2/5 East Lancs (66 Division) was wounded at Poelcappelle and fell into a shell hole 'full of mud, slime and barbed wire.' He was gradually sucked into the mud and would have drowned had he not been rescued. Many others were not so lucky. The last three battles of 'Third Ypres' – Poelcappelle, (9 October) First and Second Passchendaele, (12 October and 26 October-10 November) – have indelibly stamped their mark on the Anglo-American folk memory of World War I. The name Passchendaele has become synonymous with the whole campaign, and similarly the entire battle is remembered as a mudbath. It was the Canadians who had the empty honor of capturing the rubble of Passchendaele itself on 6 November. Four days later, most of Passchendaele Ridge had been captured and the battle came to an end.

ABOVE: The Menin Road by Paul Nash. Later to become an official war artist, Paul Nash had been commissioned into the Hampshire Rifles in 1916 and in February 1917 was posted to the Ypres Salient. There he made numerous sketches of life in the Salient which formed the basis of the series of oil paintings that made his reputation.

TOP: Brother of Paul, John Nash's Over The Top depicts an actual event, the attack by the 1st Artists' Rifles at Welsh Ridge, Marcoing on 30 December 1917. An officer in B Company, Nash commanded a bomber section which took part in the attack. The raid was a disaster, however, with 68 of the 80 men involved either killed or wounded.

ABOVE: The Ypres Salient at Night by Paul Nash. The painting depicts a burst of starshell over No Man's Land, a regular occurrence during nocturnal operations on the Western Front. He was injured in May 1917 and fortunately missed his regiment's attack on Hill 60, during which most of the officers became casualties.

Was the battle worth the sacrifice? Undoubtedly, the convalescent French army had bought time in which to recover, but the five-mile extension of the Ypres Salient made, if anything, the defense of the area more difficult. Casualties were probably equally shared between the Allies and the Germans – approximately 250,000 apiece. The morale of both armies undoubtedly suffered; the British army forfeited its 'spirit of optimism,' according to Philip Gibbs, the War Correspondent, although vastly exaggerated claims have been made about the mutiny at Etaples base camp in the autumn of 1917. A major casualty of the Third Ypres was the reputation of Sir Douglas Haig.

Much of the postwar assault on his reputation by people such as Liddell Hart, Lloyd George and Churchill was based on his handling of this battle. It was alleged that Haig so terrified his staff that they fed him only information that he wanted to hear, and he ignored any uncomfortable fact that did not fit in with his opinion. In the 1960s, Haig's reputation was ably refurbished by John Terraine; but in the 1980s, scholars are once again returning to an essentially damning view of Haig's generalship. Tens of thousands of members of the Second and Fifth Armies were unable to contribute to the postwar debate on the handling of Third Ypres. They were the dead.

The Russian Revolution 1917-18

All sections of Russian society were exhausted and war-weary by the end of 1916. The huge casualties suffered in the campaigns since 1914, culminating in the Brusilov Offensive, had left the army demoralized. The peasantry, burdened by heavy taxation and scared by inflation, began to keep their produce to themselves, thus creating a food shortage in the cities which only added to the problems of the urban proletariat, already suffering from the traumas of rapid industrialization. The middle class and intellectuals were deeply disillusioned with the government's conduct of the war, and, indeed, with the entire Czarist system of government. The Duma (parliament) was toothless, and, until his murder in December 1916, the monk Rasputin exercised his baleful influence over the Czar and Czarina. That a mystic charlatan could have such influence epitomized the inability of czarism to cope with a modern industrialized society and a total war. In 1914, the strains on Russian society, some of which dated back to the reforms of Alexander II in the 1860s, had temporarily been submerged beneath a tidal wave of patriotism. On 8 March 1917, they resurfaced with a vengeance, and the February Revolution, so called because the Russian Calendar was 11 days behind the Western one, broke out.

The Revolution began with a series of violent strikes in Petrograd (which had been known by its German name, St Petersburg, until 1914). A revolution in 1905 had foundered largely because of the loyalty of the troops to the government. This time, Imperial Guards-

ABOVE: *Alexander Kerensky, charismatic leader of the new Provisional Government which replaced the autocracy of Czar Nicholas in March 1917. Kerensky advocated the continuation of the war and this decision alone ensured the early demise of his government in November 1917.*

LEFT: *Bolshevik troops stand on a street corner reading propaganda leaflets in October, shortly before the Bolshevik Revolution overthrew the Provisional Government.*

LEFT: *Once in power the Bolsheviks sued for peace and negotiations with the Germans were instigated in the old Polish town of Brest-Litovsk. This photograph shows the Russian delegation; they were eventually forced to accept humiliating terms at the hands of the German victors.*
BELOW: *A Russian officer speaks to his men at a front-line position in March 1917. By this time the war-weary soldiers of the Imperial Army had reached breaking point and mass desertions were becoming commonplace. In Lenin's famous phrase: 'They voted with their feet.'*

men fraternized on the streets with the rioters. The fall of the monarchy could not be long delayed. On 12 March a 'Soviet' (revolutionary council of workers, soldiers and Duma members) met in Petrograd and set up a Provisional Government. Three days later, Nicholas abdicated, and the Romanov dynasty was effectively at an end.

The leader of the new, liberal Provisional Government was Prince Lvov, but the dominant personality was Alexander Kerensky, the Minister of War, who was determined that the war against Germany should go on. The February Revolution was therefore enthusiastically received in Britain and France, where it was believed that the war in the East would now be more efficiently prosecuted. With the United States on the brink of war, it was possible to talk of a war 'to make the world safe for Democracy,' now that the *Entente* was free of an embarrassingly autocratic ally. The Germans initially hoped that the Provisional Government might be willing to negotiate peace, although they hedged their bets by allowing a dedicated revolutionary to return to Russia from exile in Switzerland. A sealed train containing Vladimir Ilyich Ulyanov crossed Germany into Russia; under the pseudonym of Lenin, this man was to play a central role in subsequent events.

Kerensky ordered a fresh offensive for 1 July 1917. If the Germans had attacked during the turmoil of the spring, it is possible that they could have achieved a resounding success. Instead, the new Russian offensive – masterminded by Brusilov, the new Commander in Chief – began reasonably well. Thirty-one divisions attacked on a 40-mile front at Brody and made little headway, but a second attack in the Carpathians begun on 7 July by Kornilov's Eighth Army thrust back the Austrian Third Army. This success was not exploited. Each unit had established Soviets, who rapidly usurped the authority of the officer. As early as May, Brusilov recalled, 'the troops . . . began to definitely disobey orders, and no steps could be taken to stop them. Even the Commissars they themselves appointed were only given a hearing when they were in agreement with the men . . .' Units simply refused to advance. Not surprisingly, the German counteroffensive which began on 19 July, under the effective command of Hoffmann, pushed the Russians back to beyond their starting line. Similarly, an attack in the south by the Fourth Army and the Rumanians on 22 July was driven back and the front stabilized. Kerensky, by now head of the Provisional Government, replaced Brusilov with Kornilov, but the decline of the Russian Army was too far advanced to be checked merely by reshuffling the personnel at the top.

LEFT: *As an orator, Lenin had few equals and his skills of public persuasion were an important factor in the success of the Bolsheviks in 1917. This example of Soviet Realism bears out Lenin's abilities in this field. A remarkable leader by any standards, Lenin's rise to power was helped by the indecision of his opponents.*

ABOVE: *Led by a sailor waving the red flag, Bolsheviks storm the Winter Palace, 7 November 1917. Masterminded by Trotsky, the Bolshevik coup was an almost immediate success, Kerensky's government having been discredited in the eyes of the masses.*
LEFT: *A Soviet painting of the storming of the Winter Palace. In fact, the Bolshevik assault was a virtually bloodless affair.*

The blow which toppled Kerensky was delivered by von Hutier's German Eighth Army at Riga, on the Baltic. Colonel Bruchmüller organized a devastatingly effective five-hour bombardment, without previously registering his guns, and on 1 September Hutier pushed forward and took the city and 9000 prisoners. The Russians offered little resistance. The repercussions were dramatic. Petrograd itself appeared to be under threat; Finland, an Imperial province just across the Gulf of Bothnia, had been occupied by the Germans since April. Kornilov attempted to launch a *putsch*, which failed; but the threat of a military dictatorship and fear of a German attack gathered support for Lenin's Bolshevik party, which had been growing in strength since March. Trotsky, Lenin's right-hand man, planned a *putsch* for 7 November (25 October, old style, hence the October Revolution).

The Bolsheviks were successful. Kerensky was forced to flee, and in 8 November 1917 Lenin became the leader of the world's first government of Workers and Peasants. The October Revolution was perhaps the most important event of the twentieth century, but for the moment it will suffice to note its impact on the war. Trotsky, Commissar for Foreign Affairs, began to negotiate with the Central Powers at Brest-Litovsk. The Germans held out for punitive terms; autonomy for Poland, the Baltic provinces, the Ukraine and Finland, which would naturally fall into the German sphere of influence, thus realizing the prewar dreams of the pan-German annexationists. Trotsky refused to

agree, and on 10 February 1918 announced a unilateral compromise, by refusing to continue to negotiate, but also refraining from participation in the war. The German response was simple. They abrogated the armistice (which had began on 2 December 1917) on 18 February and advanced deep into Russia. Moreover, the previous day the Central Powers had signed a separate peace with the former Imperial province of the Ukraine by which Ukrainian wheat supplies would be sent to Germany and Austria-Hungary rather than to the Bolsheviks. Trotsky's bluff had been called. On 3 March 1918, the Bolsheviks signed the treaty; for the Russians, World War I was over. This did not bring immediate peace to the war-weary Russian people; the Russian Civil War, which was to claim millions more lives, was about to begin.

The Western Allies angrily denounced the Bolsheviks as collaborators and traitors to the Russian people. In truth, Lenin and Trotsky spoke for virtually all the common people in desiring peace. In retrospect, the Provisional Government might have survived had it immediately sought peace in March 1917. Instead, it continued the war, and thus signed its own death warrant. Even in its death-throes, pre-Bolshevik Russia served its allies well. On the Eastern Front in 1917, 99 divisions, which were badly needed by the Germans in Flanders, were tied down. The reward for Russia's unselfish loyalty was a casualty list of over 9 million men, and an army of occupation sitting on Russian soil, 600 miles east of the 1914 frontier.

The Awakening Giant: The USA 1914-17

The United States remained neutral on the outbreak of war in 1914, neutral, but not 'Isolationist.' Long before its entry into the war in April 1917, the United States had begun to play an increasingly important role as a world power. Since the end of the nineteenth century, the United States had begun to acquire colonies and military bases (such as the Philippines, Cuba and Hawaii), and to intervene in the affairs of other states. In 1916, for example, a punitive expedition was sent into Mexico, and from 1912 to 1932 Nicaragua was virtually under American control. Germany, as an economic rival, had been identified as a serious military threat as early as the mid-1890s, and military and naval plans for a war were prepared and constantly updated. The United States had no part in the July crisis of 1914, but immediately afterward began to play a vital role in the Allied war effort.

President Woodrow Wilson had no wish to go to war on behalf of Franco-British Imperialism. He was a genuine idealist who feared that the New World would become corrupted by the Old if the United States became embroiled in what he saw as a squalid European civil war. Wilson was also a shrewd politician, and 1916 was an election year. Pro-Isolationists, and anti-British voters, such as German- and Irish-Americans, supported Wilson as the 'peace' candidate who was re-elected largely thanks to the slogan 'He Kept Us Out of War.' The slogan would have been more accurate had it said, 'He Kept Us Out of the Fighting' for the United States had, by 1916, become essential to the war effort of the *Entente*. Americans were broadly sympathetic to the Allied cause (with obvious exceptions). This was largely due to the boost given to the American economy by Allied orders for war materiel. Trade with Germany had dwindled away to almost nothing as a result of the British blockade, but trade with the *Entente* boomed,

and American prosperity depended on Franco-British orders. The American economy benefited from the war in another way. Both Germany and the United States had overtaken Britain as industrial powers before 1914, but the United States used the war years to draw decisively ahead of both her rivals. Of prewar Latin American imports 31 percent had been British, 22 percent German and only 15 percent American: by 1929, the respective figures were 22 percent, 16 percent, and 38 percent. From 1914, the United States was fighting an economic war with Britain, and winning it.

The route that led the United States to war was marked with the wrecks of victims of Germany's submarine campaign against British commerce. Inevitably, American ships were lost and American lives were taken. The torpedoing of the British trans-Atlantic liner *Lusitania* in May 1915 was merely the most notorious example; 1195 lives were lost, including those of numerous Americans. The first unrestricted U-Boat campaign was suspended by the Germans on 1 September 1915, to placate the United States. Sinkings continued intermittently. The loss of the *Sussex* in the spring of 1916 led to Wilson's most trenchant complaint yet, and the resumption of unrestricted submarine warfare in February 1917 pushed Wilson reluctantly into war, which was declared on 2 April. For America, the war became a 'crusade,' and to emphasize the gap between the high-minded American motivation for war and that of the shady Europeans, the United States remained an 'Associated Power,' not a full ally.

The war had a traumatic effect on American society. The tiny American armed forces swelled, through a selective form of conscription, to 4.8 million men and women. Blacks moved to the northern cities to supply the labor for the prosperous war economy

ABOVE: *President Wilson addresses Congress in April 1917, advising the severing of diplomatic relations with Germany.*
LEFT: *An impression by the artist Norman Wilkinson of the sinking of the* Lusitania *by a German U-Boat. Acts such as this pushed the United States into a state of war with Germany.*
RIGHT: *An American civilian undergoes the lottery of conscription. By pulling out a certain number the individual might find himself part of the American armed forces. Altogether some 2,084,000 men embarked for service overseas.*

ABOVE: *The man who brought the United States of America into World War I: President Woodrow Wilson.*
RIGHT: *A rather more imaginative recruitment poster issued by the US Navy. The message was the same as ever: the call for manpower.*
LEFT: *A US poster calling for funds toward the war effort. The German in the poster – complete with bloody bayonet – was based upon the 'rampaging Hun,' first developed by France, Belgium and Britain in 1914.*

and black soldiers serving in France tasted freedom in a society where racial prejudice was much less widespread than at home. Both events were to have future repercussions. Liquor was banned as a wartime measure; this was the origin of the 18th Amendment and Prohibition, which brought so much crime in its wake. The racism present in European attitudes to the enemy raised its ugly head, in the form of rabid anti-Germanism, all the more dangerous in the United States because of the polyglot nature of American society. Finally, election results showed the deep divisions in the country over the issue of the war. Anti-war, Socialist candidates received considerable support in the 1917 Mayoral elections: 34 percent in Chicago, 22 percent in New

York City. The Republicans made sweeping gains in 1918, benefiting from the vote of disillusioned Democrats.

In the years following 1918, Americans were to feel themselves 'cheated' by the results of World War I. They had expended 115,000 lives, and $112 billion, and received nothing in return. Nothing could be further from the truth. The years 1914-18 were the foundation of America's economic and political greatness. This had been achieved at relatively little cost, in comparison with the European sacrifices. And 1917-18 saw the emergence of a future superpower into the world stage. The same period was to witness a similar phenomenon occurring on the other side of the world: in Russia.

LEFT: *Captain Edward Rickenbacker, the top-scoring ace on the American side with 26 confirmed kills to his credit. A natural flier, he amassed his score in the few months between March and November 1918.*

ABOVE: *Edmond Genet was one of the many American pilots who volunteered to serve in the French air force before the USA entered the war. A member of the famed Lafayette Escadrille, he had the unfortunate distinction of being the first American killed in action after the US declaration of war.*

Egypt and Palestine 1914-17

Egypt has been recognized as a valuable strategic prize by men as distant in time as Augustus Caesar and Napoleon. For the British in 1914, Egypt was one of the most important location outside of the home islands. Egypt, in strategic terms, equalled the Suez Canal and the Canal represented the shortest route to India. If the Canal was lost, the British Empire would effectively be cut in half. Not surprisingly, the defense of Egypt was given a high priority by the British. In February 1915 a 20,000-strong Turkish force crossed the Sinai Peninsula and marched on the Canal. They were easily beaten off, but thanks to the timidity of the British commander, General Sir John Maxwell, they were not pursued.

The attention of Britain and Turkey was concentrated on the Dardanelles and Mesopotamia in 1915, and thus the Egypt-Palestine front was inactive. Nevertheless, the British still feared that a large Turkish army might reinvade Egypt. Some troops, evacuated from Gallipoli to Egypt, were retained for the defense of the Canal. An obvious precaution was to advance over the Canal, clear Sinai and establish a defensive line on the Palestinian frontier. This had obvious parallels with the Mesopotamian campaign, but the new commander of the Egyptian Expeditionary Force or EEF, General Sir Archibald Murray (the former CIGS) did not fall into Nixon's trap. Murray organized an efficient logistic chain, which included laying railway lines, constructing a pipeline (carrying water) and building a road of wire netting. Murray defeated a Turkish force at Rumani, about 20 miles from the Canal, on 4 August 1916, and then he advanced. The town of El Arish on the Palestinian border was captured four days before Christmas 1916. The Canal was now guarded by the buffer of the Sinai Peninsula, where Africa joins Asia.

ABOVE RIGHT: *Perhaps the most extraordinary figure of the war, Colonel T E Lawrence, better known as Lawrence of Arabia. His ability to inspire and direct the hostility of the desert Arabs toward the Turks was an amazing feat of leadership.*
RIGHT: *Djemal Pasha (left), commander of the Turkish Fourth Army, with his chief of staff behind the front line in Palestine.*

ABOVE: *British troops march toward Palestine as part of General Sir Archibald Murray's advance against the Turkish positions at Gaza. In the background is a camel train, emphasizing the importance of logistics in this campaign.*
LEFT: *British troops engaged in building a railway track across the Sinai Desert. The line was laid to solve the problem of supplying the fighting troops in Palestine from the rearward bases in Egypt.*

The new British Prime Minister, David Lloyd George, saw that an advance into the Holy Land might be a way of obtaining an easy victory, which would raise spirits on the Home Front after the disasters of 1916. Murray was worried about the small size of his force but loyally crossed the border. The EEF clashed with the Turks at Gaza on 26 March and only narrowly failed to win a great victory: the mounted troops, through a misunderstanding, withdrew when on the verge of success, leaving the infantry unsupported. Foolishly, Murray exaggerated the extent of his achievement, and was ordered to advance to Jerusalem. Although he realized that this was probably beyond his means, and had been denied reinforcements, Murray set out to obey his orders, but was bloodily repulsed at the second Battle of Gaza on 17 April 1917. He was replaced by Sir Edmund Allenby. On the surface, Murray's conduct appears to be similar to Townshend's in Mesopotamia, but his downfall was the result of foolishness rather than deceit, and Second Gaza is not to be compared with Kut as a defeat.

'The Bull,' as Allenby was nicknamed, had been given succinct orders by Lloyd George: take Jerusalem by Christmas. Allenby at once imposed his personality on his campaign. As a cavalryman, he revelled in the open spaces of the Holy Land, especially after his claustrophobic experiences on the Western Front. Feinting toward Gaza, 'The Bull' broke through on 31 October at Beersheba, 25 miles away, and rolled up the Turkish line. He made excellent use of his three mounted divisions (which included a Yeomanry and an ANZAC formation) to cover the march of his seven infantry divisions along the coast. The enemy commander was the peripatetic Falkenhayn, who proved to be as skillful as ever, but with less than 40,000 men at his disposal, he was unable to hinder the EEF's progress until it left the desert and began campaigning in the Judean foothills. Then Allenby faced a stiff battle, conducted at the end of a long supply line, but he pushed on, and on 8 November 1917 Jerusalem fell. On the 11th Allenby became the first Christian conquerer to enter the Holy City since the knights of the First Crusade, 818 years previously.

RIGHT: Irish Troops in the Judaen Hills surprised by a Turkish Bombardment *by Henry Lamb.*

ABOVE: *The successful British commander of the EEF, General Sir Edmund Allenby. Unlike Murray, he was able to provide Lloyd George with victory in this theater of war.*

BELOW: *An officer of the Westminster Dragoons, one of the many Yeomanry regiments which fought in Palestine. In marked contrast to the situation experienced on the Western Front, cavalry found a useful role in this campaign.*

Caporetto

The eleventh and last battle of the Isonzo was the most successful of all the Italian attacks on that sector. Fifty-two divisions and 1700 heavy guns were amassed, and on 18 August Cadorna launched his last offensive, timed to coincide with the British campaign in Flanders (as the tenth battle in March had coincided with the Arras and Nivelle offensives). Capello's Second Army at last made some genuine progress, pushing the Austrians back for six miles across the Bainsizza plateau. Cadorna's plans for a pursuit were interrupted when, at the end of September, he became uneasily aware that a major enemy offensive was being prepared. Not for the first time, Germany was coming to the rescue of its Austrian ally. The German Fourteenth Army, under von Below, had been dispatched to Italy. The Central Powers concentrated 35 divisions opposite the 41 Italian divisions on the Isonzo. On 24 October 1917, they attacked at Caporetto: to their surprise, the Italian Second Army dissolved in front of their eyes into a mob of routed fugitives. That day, the assault forces moved forward as much as 12 miles.

The German success was a tribute to their new 'infiltration' tactics, preceded by a 'hurricane' bombardment and the use of gas. The Second Army's defensive preparations were poor, as Capello (in defiance of Cadorna's instructions) intended to meet the enemy assault with a counterstroke. However, the troops intended to perform this had other ideas and ran away. The collapse of the morale of the Italian Second Army is comparable to the French mutinies which occurred earlier in 1917, although in the Italian case outside agitators played a more minor role. The nation was suffering from war weariness, and in particular the army's morale had suffered from Cadorna's apparently endless series of attritional battles. Many of the basic preconditions for high morale – recreational facilities, good officer-man relationships, reasonable food – were absent, and the news that the Austrians had been reinforced by the Germans depressed spirits even further. A young German officer captured a group of disconsolate Italians; so pleased were they to surrender that they hoisted him onto their shoulders, shouting *Evviva Germania*. This officer was to be involved with the Italian army 25 years later: his name was Erwin Rommel.

ABOVE: *General Otto von Below, commander of the German Fourteenth Army which spearheaded the assault against Italian positions at Caporetto. A highly experienced general, Below made extensive use of infiltration tactics to breach the Italian lines.*
LEFT: *Italian gunners pose for the camera with an assortment of Easter 'greetings' chalked on their shells. At Caporetto, however, Italian artillery did little to stem the tide of the Austro-German advance.*

The Italian Third and Fourth Armies, in contrast to the Second, fell back in a reasonably orderly fashion first to the Tagliamento and then, by 10 November, to the Piave. Here Cadorna had prepared some defensive positions and the Italians held firm. The Caporetto offensive was originally intended to be limited in scope; with the arrival of French and British reinforcements from France imminent, the Central Powers broke off the battle. The casualty figures revealed the extent of the Italian disaster. Only 30,000 were killed or wounded, but 275,000 had become prisoners, and substantial numbers had simply deserted. Had the Austro-Germans possessed an effective instrument of exploitation – cavalry or armored cars – the losses would have been even higher. Surprisingly, the Germans failed to take heed of this lesson, which was to be repeated in the March 1918 offensive. Cadorna, however, was replaced by General Armando Diaz.

The position of the Italian army in December 1917 was far better than anyone would have dared to hope two months earlier. An Austrian offensive in the Trentino (led by Conrad, who had been replaced as Austrian Chief of Staff in January 1917 by Arz von Straussenburg) was contained, and a wave of patriotic feeling strengthened Italian resolve to expel the invader from her territory. At last the Italians had a cause to fight for, and the campaigns of 1918 were to show how quickly the army had recovered from the traumas of 1917.

ABOVE: *Austrian stormtroops practice an attack in preparation for the real thing on 24 October 1917. Although German units made the most spectacular advances, crack Austrian formations also made a vital contribution to the Central Powers' victory at Caporetto.*

LEFT: *The long retreat – Italian troops fall back after Caporetto. The speed and the extent of the Italian collapse came as a surprise to both sides.*

177

The Search for Compromise 1914-17

The Germans failed to break through at Ypres in 1914; the French did not expel the invader from her territory in 1915, and the Russians suffered a serious, but not decisive, defeat in Galicia in the same year. Each of these events would have seemed to offer an opportunity for a compromise peace, but on each occasion – and subsequently – the opportunity for such a peace was allowed to slip away, until it was too late. An examination of the factors preventing a negotiated end to the war reveals much about the nature of the conflict.

The years 1914-18 constituted a period of total war. From the very beginning, the war was seen as a crusade, and it is not easy to compromise with an enemy who has been painted in the blackest of colors. Having raised hundreds of thousands of volunteers for Kitchener's Army, for instance, it would have been difficult to simply tell them to pack up and go home without a fight – something that Sir Edward Grey recognized in telling Colonel House in January 1916 that Britain could not ask France to make peace, because the bulk of the British armies had not yet been committed. It should not be forgotten that there was general enthusiasm for the war at least until mid-1915. When war-weariness did set in around 1916-17, there were two schools of thought. The first wanted a negotiated peace, but the second looked back on the massive investment of blood in the war and argued that a compromise would betray those who had given their lives. John McRae's poem of late 1915 expresses this perfectly:

> Take up our quarrel with the foe:
> To you from failing hands we throw
> The torch; be yours to hold it high.
> If ye break faith with us who die
> We shall not sleep, though poppies grow
> In Flanders Fields.

Springing from this general intransigence was the formulation of war aims that simply allowed no compromise. The assumption of power by men who were dedicated to winning the war at all costs – Hindenburg and Ludendorff in Germany, Clemenceau in France and Lloyd George in Britain – epitomized this trend.

Daddy, what did YOU do in the Great War ?

ABOVE RIGHT: *One of the most famous recruitment posters of the war, a cunningly sophisticated appeal for British young men to join the colors.*
RIGHT: *Lloyd George, the British Prime Minister, visits women war workers. As the first mass war in history, almost the entire population was involved to some degree in the war effort. Politicians considered it essential to exhort civilians working in key industries to improve productivity.*

In January 1916, Colonel House, President Wilson's unofficial but influential envoy, traveled to Europe to sound out the possibility of the United States acting as a mediator. The Western Allies rejected House's proposals – which included the evacuation of Belgium and France, and the return of Alsace-Lorraine to France, in return for German colonial compensation – largely because they believed they could win a decisive victory. This would give them both territorial gains and allow them to destroy 'Prussian Militarism,' the latter a war aim particularly loved of the British, but which, in effect could only be realized by the total destruction of German military power. The debate on German war aims has already been referred to. The German Peace Note of 12 December 1916 reflected both her strong military position and (although these were not stated) her wide-ranging political and economic aspirations. Wilson's Peace Note of one week later met with little favor in the eyes of either side; but Germany was shortly to damn herself in Wilson's eyes, not only because of the U-Boat campaign but also because of the notorious Zimmermann Telegram by which Germany incited Mexico to attack the United States.

ABOVE LEFT: *French premier Georges Clemenceau visits a French aviation camp close to the front line. Nicknamed 'the Tiger' he was tireless in his determination to defeat Germany.*
LEFT: *Members of the Imperial War Cabinet with Lloyd George (seated center).*
BELOW LEFT: *The three German war leaders plan their nation's strategy, from left: Hindenburg, the Kaiser and Ludendorff. As the war progressed power was increasingly invested in Ludendorff; he was to prove inadequate to the task, however.*

As long as Germany held Belgium and parts of industrial France, she was not going to give them up easily, but the Eastern Front seemed to offer more scope for compromise. In mid-1915 Falkenhayn pushed for a negotiated, moderate peace with Russia. The Czar, ignoring the defeat in Galicia, preferred loyally to adhere to the *Entente*, trusting his armies to recover. On his accession in 1916, Emperor Karl tried to negotiate a separate peace for Austria-Hungary, behind the backs of the Germans, but the attempt foundered over the Alsace-Lorraine question and the demands of Italian irredentists.

Various other attempts were made to bring about peace, but three in particular are notable. In June 1917 international Socialist unity, which had proved so hollow in 1914, received a boost when a conference was held at neutral Stockholm. British and French but not German delegates were refused passports to attend. The voice of moderation was even heard in militaristic Germany. On 19 July 1917 the resurgent Reichstag passed the Peace Resolution, which in effect called for a Wilsonian 'peace without annexations.' This was the achievement of Erzberger, the leader of the Center Party. Four months later, Lord Landsdowne, a former British Foreign Secretary, published a letter calling for a negotiated peace. Lansdowne predicted that the old order was being radically changed by the war, and 'its prolongation will spell ruin for the civilized world. . . .' From the left, the center and the right came despairing cries for peace. But the insatiable demands of total war caused these cries to go unheeded.

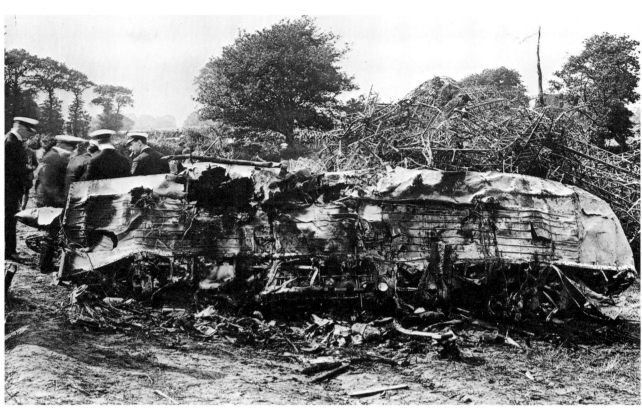

ABOVE LEFT: *A British cartoon ridicules German middle-class attempts at Christmas festivities in the face of the Allied blockade. By the end of 1917 the blockade was causing severe shortages in Germany.*
LEFT: *The war is brought home to the civilian population. British sightseers look at the ruins of a house destroyed by German aircraft.*

BELOW: *German Chancellor von Bethmann-Hollweg addresses the Assembly in the Reichstag, 12 December 1916. Despite his position, Bethmann-Hollweg had little real influence, power being held by the military.*

ABOVE: *The gondola and wreckage of Zeppelin L32 after it had been shot down over Essex, 23 September 1916. For much of the British population the Zeppelin was seen as yet another manifestation of the 'bestial Hun.'*

The Battle of Cambrai

Ten days after the dour attritional battle of Third Ypres was closed down, the British delivered a stunning blow to the Germans at Cambrai, as different in conception and execution from Passchendaele as is possible to envisage. At 0620 hours on 20 November 1917, 1000 guns opened up without a preliminary bombardment, and 381 tanks rumbled across No Man's Land, closely supported by infantry. Surprise was complete; the tanks brushed aside the barbed wire and crossed trench after trench, penetrating three miles into the German positions along a six-mile front. Ahead was open countryside. In London, the church bells were rung to announce a victory – a real victory, not a Loos or Somme. Yet Cambrai was ultimately a failure, not a success. What went wrong?

The Battle of Cambrai had originally been planned as a large-scale raid by the Tank Corps. Brigadier General Hugh Elles, and his chief of staff, one Colonel J F C Fuller, saw that the rolling countryside around Cambrai would be more favorable terrain for the tank than the water-logged area around Ypres. In early August, it was proposed that tanks should be employed en masse as a shock weapon in their own right, rather than as an infantry support vehicle. To this plan Brigadier-General H H Tudor, the commander of 9th (Scottish) Division's artillery, added the surprise of a 'predicted' bombardment, that is, one where ranging shots were not previously fired and the gunners would rely purely on the map; an operation which demands a high degree of skill and demonstrates that the improvement in the Royal Artillery's performance matched that of the infantry. This was to be a 'hurricane' bombardment, essentially a return to the Neuve Chapelle method, although improved upon and updated.

Haig approved the principle of an operation at Cambrai on 13 October, but by then the initial concept had been substantially altered by the Third Army, which was to carry it out. It was now envisaged as a major offensive, which was to breach the Hindenburg Line. This plan was simply not realistic, given the number of divisions available – 19, of which only six would be used in the initial attack. There were few reserves available beyond two cavalry divisions; the recently concluded battle at Ypres and the need to reinforce the Italian Front had the BEF at full stretch, although hundreds of thousands of troops were sitting at home or employed in peripheral theaters.

The attack on 20 November brought spectacular results along the entire line of attack, except on the front of Major General Harper's 51st (Highland) Division. Harper had sent his tanks ahead of the infantry, where, lacking the close mutual support employed on the rest of the front, the attack foundered. The village of Flesquières was held by the Germans, with the result that an important feature, Bourlon Ridge, was not captured. The limitations on the usefulness of 1917 vintage tanks as an instrument of exploitation is shown clearly by the fact that of the 381 tanks that started the battle, only 202 were still running by the end of the day – 114 had broken down, and 65 had been knocked out. Dusk fell shortly after 1600 hours and it was thought to be too dangerous to commit the cavalry or risk the use of yet more tanks in the dark. One squadron of Canadian cavalry, the Fort Garry Horse, did appear, but was unable to make much headway.

The following day, the battle for Bourlon Ridge began in earnest. It was captured after a fierce struggle, but Bourlon Wood remained in German hands. By now, German reserves were flooding into the area. Bourlon Wood was taken on 23 November, partially recaptured by a German counterattack but then regained and held on the following day; but the opportunity for a breakthrough had passed. Instead, the British had to be content with possession of a salient, five miles deep.

The armored punch of 20 November was followed by an equally effective German riposte. At 0830 hours on 30 November, German stormtroopers, supported by a hurricane bombardment and low-flying ground-attack aircraft, attacked the British salient. The 12th and 55th

Divisions collapsed, and a tidal wave of fugitives from the infantry and artillery fled to the rear. For the first time, the new infiltration tactics had been used against the British in a major offensive. Some British units fought well. Curiously, a group of American Civil Engineers became mixed up in the fighting, some months before the bulk of the regular American forces first faced the Germans. Fresh troops, including the Guards Division, 2nd Division and 47th (London) Territorials, three of the steadiest formations on the Western Front advanced and restored the line, but Byng wisely avoided the possibility of creating a second Ypres Salient by withdrawing on the night of 4/5 December. Each side had lost about 45,000 men; the Germans had taken 9000 prisoners, the British 2000 more. Thus Cambrai ended in a frustrating stalemate. But for those who had eyes to see, the battle demonstrated the type of tactics that were to loosen the deadlock along the front and eventually win the war in the New Year.

RIGHT: *In thigh-length waders, reflecting the conditions encountered during the winter of 1917-18, this young soldier shows the dazed and numbed expression of men who had experienced heavy shellfire.*
BELOW LEFT: *A German soldier 'surrenders' for the camera, 20 November 1917. During the battle of Cambrai the British took some 11,000 German prisoners.*
BELOW: *Tank trains stand at Plateau Station awaiting dispatch to forward detraining railheads, 20 November 1917. The tanks were the key to success in the initial Allied advance at Cambrai.*

The Air War in the West 1917-18

The early months of 1917 were a bad time for the Allied air services. In the battle above the Arras offensive of April, the British lost 151 aircraft and 316 aircrew – a rate of attrition which exceeded that of the 'Fokker Scourge' of 1916. Trenchard's policy of aggressive patrolling – which mirrored Haig's determination that his infantry should dominate No Man's Land – bit deep into the reserve of experienced pilots. A vicious circle developed; the average replacement reaching the front was extremely inexperienced, and usually survived less than three weeks before he too became a casualty, to be replaced by another novice, who in turn became a casualty. Thus the RFC found it difficult to maintain a pool of veteran pilots. British pilots gave this period the soubriquet 'Bloody April,' and the blood-red Albatros DIII flown by von Richthofen came to epitomize the German command of the air in the spring of 1917.

There had been a revolution in tactics since the early days of dog fighting. Both sides had realized the value of using large formations of aircraft to dominate the skies, rather than using smaller groups. In June the Germans began to mass together *Jastas* No 4, 6, 10, and 11 to form the fighter wing or *Jagdgeschwader* 1 (JG1). This formation became known as 'Richthofen's Flying Circus' to the Allies, because it traveled up and down the line in a varied collection of vehicles, seeking to achieve command of the air at a specific area of the Front. Even larger formations were sometimes organized on an ad hoc basis, and were called *Jagdgruppen*, or Fighter Groups. In late 1916 the French also began to form larger units. *'Les Cigognes,'* or the 'Storks' (Group de Combat No 12) was formed under Captain Felix Brocard, an exceptional leader who Guynemer, among others, revered. Their ranks included Capitaine René Fonck, who, with 75 'kills,' became the most successful Allied pilot of the war.

ABOVE RIGHT: *Albatros DIII biplanes of Richthoften's Circus. These aircraft were far superior to anything the Allies could field in the spring of 1917, and in the hands of skilled pilots they shot the British out of the skies during 'Bloody April.'*
RIGHT: *A line-up of SE5a scouts, one of the aircraft types that redressed the balance in favor of the Allies. Although lacking the maneuverability of the Sopwith Camel the SE5a was an excellent gun platform.*

ABOVE: *Ernst Udet, one of Germany's leading aces with 62 kills, stands alongside a Fokker DVII. Although this aircraft arrived too late in the war, and in too few numbers, it was considered by both Germans and Allies alike as one of the finest fighter aircraft of the war.*

LEFT: *One of the more flamboyant and skillful of the French aces, Charles Nungesser (45 kills) poses by his Nieuport biplane.*

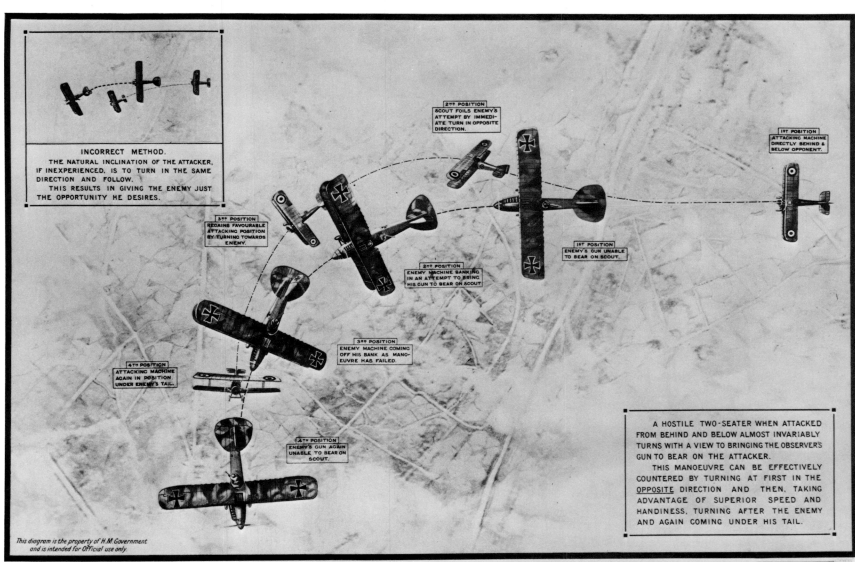

INCORRECT METHOD.
THE NATURAL INCLINATION OF THE ATTACKER,
IF INEXPERIENCED, IS TO TURN IN THE SAME
DIRECTION AND FOLLOW.
THIS RESULTS IN GIVING THE ENEMY JUST
THE OPPORTUNITY HE DESIRES.

2ND POSITION
SCOUT FOILS ENEMY'S
ATTEMPT BY IMMEDI-
ATE TURN IN OPPOSITE
DIRECTION.

1ST POSITION
ATTACKING MACHINE
DIRECTLY BEHIND &
BELOW OPPONENT.

3RD POSITION
REGAINS FAVOURABLE
ATTACKING POSITION
BY TURNING TOWARDS
ENEMY.

1ST POSITION
ENEMY'S GUN UNABLE
TO BEAR ON SCOUT.

2ND POSITION
ENEMY MACHINE BANKING
IN AN ATTEMPT TO BRING
HIS GUN TO BEAR ON SCOUT.

3RD POSITION
ENEMY MACHINE COMING
OFF HIS BANK AS MANO-
EUVRE HAS FAILED.

4TH POSITION
ATTACKING MACHINE
AGAIN IN POSITION
UNDER ENEMY'S TAIL.

4TH POSITION
ENEMY'S GUN AGAIN
UNABLE TO BEAR ON
SCOUT.

A HOSTILE TWO-SEATER WHEN ATTACKED
FROM BEHIND AND BELOW ALMOST INVARIABLY
TURNS WITH A VIEW TO BRINGING THE OBSERVER'S
GUN TO BEAR ON THE ATTACKER.
THIS MANOEUVRE CAN BE EFFECTIVELY
COUNTERED BY TURNING AT FIRST IN THE
OPPOSITE DIRECTION AND THEN, TAKING
ADVANTAGE OF SUPERIOR SPEED AND
HANDINESS, TURNING AFTER THE ENEMY
AND AGAIN COMING UNDER HIS TAIL.

This diagram is the property of H.M. Government
and is intended for Official use only.

OUTMANOEUVRED.

AIR TECHNICAL SERVICES
O.T.S 1686 21·5·18

excellent patrol leaders and aerial tacticians. Patrols of six or more aircraft would fly in formation, offering mutual support. Only when contact was made with enemy aircraft would the formation dissolve into individual combats. By placing the most experienced men in the most vulnerable positions of the formation, novices could be nursed through their first few actions.

Gradually the British recovered from their mauling of April 1917. New aircraft began to appear: the Sopwith Triplane (affectionately nicknamed the 'Tripehound'); the two-seater 'Brisfit' (Bristol Fighter F2A); and, by the summer of 1917, the 'classic' British fighters of the war, the SE5 and the Sopwith Camel, were coming into service. The French began to receive the highly maneuverable Spad XIII. The Germans continued to build excellent airplanes, such as the Pfalz DIIIa, Fokker DrI triplane and Fokker DVII (perhaps the finest fighter of the war), but the Allied numerical superiority enabled them to achieve command of the air by 1918. On occasions, the Germans were able to achieve local air superiority – for instance on the Somme for their March 1918 offensive – but never again was the general Allied domination of the skies seriously put at risk.

The year 1917 saw the beginnings of the widespread use of airplanes in the ground-attack role. In the Third Battle of Ypres the British employed their scouts in low-flying attacks, directly against enemy 'teeth' formations, and interdiction and tactical bombing of reserves and the logistic 'tail.' The Germans too made use of close-support low-level attacks as an integral part of their assault tactics of 1917-18; their use of ground-attack aircraft at Bourlon Wood in December 1917 made a vivid impression on the defending British infantry. During the Spring Offensive of 1918 the RFC were thrown into the battle to halt the Germans by flying low-level sorties – one German officer was actually run over by an SE5a. Like so many aspects of warfare, the last two years of the air war foreshadowed the use of airpower in 1939-45 and in subsequent campaigns. The Battle of Amiens, 8 August 1918, was particularly significant. On that day Allied infantry, tanks and aircraft combined to bring about the 'Black Day' of the German Army.

By the time of Amiens, 740 American aircraft were present on the Western Front. Even before the United States entered the war, individual Americans had served with the RFC, and an entire squadron of American citizens served with the French *'Escadrille Americaine'* (later renamed Escadrille Lafayette). Flying Nieuports and Spads, their finest pilot was probably Raoul Lufbery, who scored 17 victories. After their transfer to US service the US 94th Pursuit Squadron, the greatest American ace of the war emerged: Captain Edward V Rickenbacker, who achieved 26 'kills' in the incredibly short period of four months.

The first 'strategic' bombing raid of the war – a raid which was not in direct support of a ground force – was launched as early as September 1914, when four Royal Naval Air Service (RNAS) aircraft attacked the Zeppelin sheds at Dusseldorf and Cologne. Later that year, similar raids by Avro 504s and Sopwith Tabloids actually succeeded in destroying two airships. However, it was the Germans who began to attack purely civilian targets. In a series of raids on Britain in 1915-16, Zeppelins dropped bombs that killed 556 people. In 1917 airships were replaced by a more efficient 'delivery system' – the Gotha IV bombing aircraft, which was able to carry a 1102-pound bomb-load, and was equipped with a primitive bombsight. On 13 June, 14 Gothas appeared in daylight over central London, and caused 162 deaths and over 400 injuries. All the raiders returned home safely. This was the bloodiest air raid of the war.

German air raids had repercussions out of all proportion to the damage caused. The British, who since 1805 had thought themselves invulnerable to invasion, had been rudely awakened, and were impressed by the implications for the future. The Royal Air Force was formed from the RFC and RNAS on 1 April 1918, and enthusiastically embraced the doctrine of strategic bombing. An Independent Air Force (IAF, the forerunner of Bomber Command) was set up, and from 6 June to 11 November 1918 the IAF dropped 543 tons of bombs in 242 raids over Germany. If the war had continued into 1919, Handley-Page V/1500 heavy bombers would have attacked Berlin. Strategic bombing, in one form or another, has remained central to British strategic thinking ever since.

ABOVE LEFT: *A German Roland CII biplane. By the standards of 1914 the aircraft of 1916-17, such as this Roland, were vastly more sophisticated and were capable of undertaking a variety of roles.*
LEFT: *A poster for British aircrew providing hints and tips for aerial combat.*

ABOVE: *Although the fighter aces gained mass public attention, the main role of the aviation services was to provide aerial reconnaissance for the ground forces. Here, a mosaic of photographs taken over enemy lines is assembled at an RFC office near Arras, 22 February 1918.*

Although individual ace pilots continued to flourish – men such as Verner Voss, who came to prominence during Bloody April and achieved 48 victories – air fighting was increasingly being conducted by formations rather than lone planes. It is significant that many aces, such as Manfred von Richthofen (84 victories), the South African, Captain A W Beauchamp-Proctor VC (54 victories) and Major Raymond Collishaw (62 victories), a Canadian, were above all

187

1918
The Year of
Decision

Chronology 1918-19

1918

March 3	Treaty of Brest-Litovsk
March 21	Operation MICHAEL – German offensive on Somme begins
March 26	Foch appointed Supreme Commander of Allied Armies
April 9	Operation GEORGETTE – German offensive in Flanders begins
April 23	British naval attack on Zeebrugge
May 9	British naval attack on Ostend
May 27	German 'diversionary' offensive on Chemin-des-Dames begins
June 15	Collapse of final Austrian attack in Italy
July 15	Second battle of Marne
July 18	French counterstroke on Marne
August 8	Battle of Amiens begins
August 14	Spa Conference
September 2	Drocourt-Quéant line stormed
September 12	St Mihiel
September 14	Allies attack Bulgaria
September 15	Austrian peace feelers
September 18	Battle of Megiddo begins
September 26	General Allied offensive in West
September 26	Bulgarian Armistice
September 29	Storming of Hindenberg Line
October 3	Prince Max of Baden appointed German Chancellor
October 3	First German Peace note
October 23	Final advance in Mesopotamia
October 24	Italian final offensive begins
October 29	German Fleet mutinies
October 30	Turkish Armistice
November 2	Final Allied push on Western Front
November 3	Austrian Armistice
November 4	German Revolution begins
November 9	Kaiser abdicates; Republic established in Berlin
November 11	British re-enter Mons
November 11	Armistice with Germany
November 21	High Seas Fleet surrenders
1919	
June 28	Treaty of Versailles signed

LEFT: *British soldiers crowd round a brazier alongside the infamous Menin Road outside Ypres. By early 1918 the British army in France was becoming dangerously understrength, so much so that the infantry divisions had to be* *restructured to take the shortfall into account. This shortage of troops in the front line was to be keenly felt when the German Spring Offensive was launched on 21 March 1918.*

The Armies of March

The armies on the Western Front in January 1918 were rather different in character from the armies of earlier years. The French army, for so long the mainstay of the Allied war effort, was now a fragile instrument indeed. Under Pétain's command it was showing signs of recovering from the traumas of 1917, but the *poilu* of 1918 was far removed from the enthusiastic soldier of 1914, or even the veteran of Verdun. A manpower shortage forced the reduction of the total number of divisions from 109 to 100. With the Germans poised to attack in the West, there was a question mark over the ability and even the willingness of the French army to resist.

The British army, too, was a markedly different force from that of 1914. A rough meritocracy had emerged; any suitable man could receive a commission, regardless of his social background. Units contained a high proportion of conscripts, and to find a regular soldier or even a volunteer of 1914 was relatively rare. After the March Offensive, it became rarer still. The BEF on the eve of battle was not wholly inexperienced: Third Ypres had been concluded only four months previously. What was lacking was experience of the defense. This was particularly disturbing because the British had just adopted an unfamiliar version of 'defense in depth.' Thus on the eve of its first major defensive battle since 1915, the BEF was trying to come to terms with a major new tactical concept. Like the French, the British were suffering from a crisis in manpower. This was largely self-inflicted, as a total of 3½ million British soldiers served on fronts other than the main Western one from 1914-18. Many of these sideshows were extremely tangential to the overall aim of the war, that is, the defeat of Germany. A rationalization, an attempt to match resources with commitments could have brought much needed reinforcements to Haig. In addition, there were 600,000 trained men in the British Isles in early 1918, for Lloyd George, unable to prevail in the strategic debate, had deliberately starved Haig of reinforcements. The numbers of the BEF had fallen by about 200,000 in January 1918 to just over 1 million men from 12 months previously. As a result, the infantry component of divisions was reduced from 12 battalions to nine, 141 battalions being broken up to provide reinforcements. This represented a considerable blow to British morale, which was already suffering as a result of Third Ypres, and added to the BEF's tactical difficulties; British tactical doctrine had been based around an establishment of four battalions per brigade, not three as now available.

The German army had passed through the searing experiences of 1916 and 1917 and emerged as a better organized fighting machine. The new doctrines for offensive and defensive warfare have already been outlined, but not their evolution. When Hindenburg and Ludendorff assumed command of OHL in September 1916, they quickly realized that the policy of *Halten was zu heiten ist* (Hold on to whatever can be held) was inappropriate. A period of consultation with low-level staff officers and front-line soldiers followed. Ironically, such a pooling of experience would have been unthinkable in the army of 'democratic' Britain. A small team of relatively junior officers, the most important of which were Oberst (colonel) von Lossberg and Hauptmann (captain) Geyer sifted the evidence and codified it into a new tactical doctrine.

The structure of the army was changed to suit the new tactics. The strength of each infantry division was reduced, but its firepower considerably augmented: it now included 50 trench mortars and 350 heavy machine guns. (The comparable British figures were 36 and 64). The unwieldy divisions of 1914 were reorganized for greater flexibility, and elite units were formed. These included divisional *Scharfschutzen* machine-gun units, and stormtroops. The first *Sturmbataillon* had been formed in 1915, and the principle was gradually extended throughout the army. Storm battalions had a dual function: of leading attacks (or providing counterattack units in elastic defense) and of training other units. Training was the key to the successful use of the

new tactical doctrines. Stormtroopers received better rations and were usually excused trench-holding duties. These were simply shock troops: they had no connections with the SS of the Nazi era.

The creation of elite units tends to reduce the overall quality of the army: but, as a whole, the German army was probably more efficient than the French or British. This was because they allowed (and encouraged) more initiative among NCOs and privates. Unlike the British, who had an average of 20 officers per battalion (over 30 at full strength), the Germans had only seven. Thus tasks that would be undertaken by a subaltern in the British army would be delegated to an NCO or *Offizier Stellvertreter* (officer substitute) in the German.

RIGHT: *A carefully posed photograph showing British Tommies gathered around a camp, swapping soldiers' stories. Although faced with a manpower shortage, the British army on the Western Front went to considerable lengths to rest its troops by pulling them back from the front line at regular intervals.*

BELOW RIGHT: *A German infantry battalion is allowed a short break during its march towards the front. During the winter of 1917-18 the German army instituted a rigorous training program to improve basic skills and introduce the new concept of infiltration tactics.*

LEFT: *General Oscar von Hutier pioneered the new tactical system at the Battle of Riga on the Eastern Front and was appointed to command the Eighteenth Army for the coming offensive.*

BELOW: *British troops undergo the discipline of physical exercise at a base camp.*

The German Spring Offensive

At the beginning of 1918, it was obvious that time was running out for Germany. Unrestricted submarine warfare had failed to bring Britain to its knees, and now American troops were beginning to reach France. Ludendorff decided on a *Kaiserschlacht*, an Imperial Battle, to win the war before the Americans could arrive in enough strength to tip the scales decisively in the Allies' favor. He had high hopes that it would be successful. The Germans could put 194 divisions in the field, reinforced by troops returning from Russia; the British and French had only 156. Moreover, the hurricane bombardment and infiltration tactics had already been successfully used on the Western Front at Cambrai in December.

Ludendorff's target was the British, rather than the French, whom he rightly saw as the weaker force, in morale if not in numbers. If he was therefore right to attack the stronger British is debatable. The venue for Operation MICHAEL (as the offensive was codenamed) was to be the Somme. Three armies, Von der Marwitz's Second, Below's Seventeenth and Hutier's Eighteenth, a total of 43 assault divisions, were to attack Gough's British Fifth Army, break its front and roll up the line to the north. A subsidiary attack on the 14 divisions of Byng's Third Army on Gough's left would be made by a further 19 divisions. The Germans would be superior in heavy guns by a ratio of five to two. The Fifth Army, in particular, was in a parlous state. Gough had to cover a front of 42 miles with only 12 divisions. The defenses (of the new 'flexible' variety) were incomplete, and valuable training time had to be spent on exhausting labor to prepare them. The concept of 'elastic defense' was imperfectly comprehended by the Fifth Army commanders; up to one-third of the infantry was crowded into the Forward Zone, which was intended to be a mere 'crust,' the main action taking place in the Battle Zone. The average soldier neither understood nor liked the new tactics. Morale was low, although not as low as some commentators have claimed, and Haig had few illusions about the condition of the Fifth Army. He had deliberately kept it weak, seeing the Somme as the least important part of his front, and gave Gough explicit orders to retire if necessary.

The battle opened with a classic 'neutralizing' bombardment, planned by Bruchmüller (nicknamed Durchbruch Müller, or 'Breakthrough Müller'). For five hours, the Fifth Army was battered by high explosive and gas shells. At 0935 hours a last frantic five-minute crescendo began, with mortars rejoining the barrage. When the bombardment lifted, the infantry went in. It was 0940 on 21 March 1918. The final act of World War I had begun.

RIGHT: *Colonel Georg Bruchmüller, the mastermind of the artillery preparation. He had come to the fore after the success of the bombardment against Russian positions at Riga.* BELOW: *Rifles slung over their backs, German stormtroops demonstrate their skills in attack.*

RIGHT: *A German 21cm howitzer is hauled toward a forward position as part of the great offensive of 1918. Artillery was to be the key element in the German breakthrough, and over 9000 guns and mortars were deployed in support of the ground forces' assault.*

LEFT: *By 1918 large numbers of troops from Central Europe were fighting on the Western Front. Czech soldiers – wearing French uniforms – wait outside a house during fighting in 1918.*
BELOW: *A British 60-pounder at full recoil. In the last year of the war British artillery tactics had reached a new level of sophistication and, far more than tanks or even the infantry, they were responsible for the final Allied victory.*

The front positions fell almost immediately to the German storm-troopers, who crept up out of the fog before the stunned troops could man the defenses. Parties of British fought stubbornly. The 7th Sherwood Foresters lost 171 killed out of 653 men before they were overwhelmed. A counterattack by 2/4th Royal Berkshires led by Lieutenant Colonel J H Dimmer VC made some headway before Dimmer, who was mounted on a horse, was killed and his demoralized men fled. This was the pattern for the day's resistance; as long as there was firm leadership the British generally fought well. Lieutenant Colonel Elstob led an epic defense of 'Manchester Hill' in 30th Division's sector from 0830 hours until his death at 1630 hours. Then about 120 men of his 16th Manchester (1st Pals) surrendered. Other British troops did not offer much resistance. By evening, 20,000 British prisoners had been taken, and Gough was forced to retire to the Crozat Canal. It was the greatest crisis the Western Allies had faced since 1914.

The Third Army had not been attacked so heavily, but was forced to retire to conform with Gough's movements. The retreat was ghastly. Sergeant Sladden of 1/15th Londons (Civil Service Rifles) of 47th (London) Division, described the retreat to Ginchy: 'The road was congested with an enormous mass of traffic ... horses and men,

utterly weary hoped for a little rest ... at Ginchy. But it seemed that the march would never end, for orders came for the retreat to continue ...' They lost 350 men in eight days. Brigadier General Barnett-Barker, who had commanded 22nd Royal Fusiliers at Delville Wood in 1916, was killed by a stray shell on the road back to Albert on 24 March. Despite this seeming chaos, neither Byng nor Gough had been decisively defeated. They were retreating, but their fronts were more or less intact; the Germans were paying dearly for their lack of cavalry, tanks or armored cars to harass the retreating British. Ludendorff was displeased with the progress achieved. He decided to exploit the operational success of his southernmost army (Hutier's Eighteenth) which had been intended as a subsidiary thrust. Instead of using them as a solid mass to thrust northward against the bulk of the BEF, Ludendorff fanned his armies out: the Eighteenth was to head for Paris to the southwest, the Second to head west to the vital communications center of Amiens, while the Seventeenth would remain on its original course. Thus the 'maintenance of the objective' and 'concentration of force,' two of the cardinal principles of war, were sacrificed by Ludendorff for immediate gain: this situation echoed Moltke's irresolution in 1914.

At the Doullens Conference on 26 March, that elusive goal, a unified command of the Allied forces, was at last reached. Previously, an attempt to establish an Inter-Allied General Reserve had proved abortive. Instead Haig and Pétain had merely promised to reinforce each other if attacked. The Frenchman reneged on his promise. He appears to have thought the British were beaten, and the attack in Picardy a mere diversion, and decided to keep his army intact to cover Paris and to face the main German offensive which he believed would be launched in Champagne. Faced with the stark prospect of defeat, all Haig's objections to Unity of Command disappeared. At Doullens, Foch was appointed to be effective Supreme Commander over both Haig and Pétain.

Ludendorff's priority was now the separation of the British and French armies, and he had managed to prise open a 10-mile gap between them. Again, cavalry would have been invaluable. There was a perceptible improvement in the Allied position following Foch's appointment. French reserves began to arrive on the German southern flank, and British troops moved down from the north. Most importantly, the French army was ordered to stand firm. The Germans had thrust their head into a giant sack; they had not broken the Fifth Army, and showed few signs of being able to do so. Their men were tiring, and ominously, their discipline was beginning to crack.

According to Kronprinz Rupprecht, 27 March was 'the turning point in the great offensive.' That date saw no spectacular victories or defeats, merely little German progress. The impetus of MICHAEL was running down, and it was obvious that the offensive had failed. Operation MARS, begun on 28 March, confirmed this. Thirteen divisions attacked eight of the British Third Army south of Arras. They were beaten off, and that evening Ludendorff called off the battle.

Amiens was to be the new objective. The Germans reached Villers Bretonneux, where, on the last ridge before Amiens, they were stopped by the Australians on 4-5 April. MICHAEL was dead. The British had sustained 163,493 casualties in 16 days – a figure that, as historian John Terraine has noted, makes the rate of loss at Third Ypres seem almost trivial. The French had lost 77,000; the Germans probably in excess of 240,000. Gough was made the British scapegoat. He was *Stellenbosched* (the British equivalent of *limogé*) by Lloyd George and the Fifth Army was renumbered as the Fourth Army. Rawlinson returned from the Supreme War Council to take command.

ABOVE: *John Singer Sargent's painting* Gassed. *These men, like most other gas cases of the 1918 battles, were victims of mustard gas.*
RIGHT: *The Germans made extensive use of gas during their 1918 offensives, and here we see a result of this policy: a line of British soldiers awaits attention at an advanced dressing station. A literal case of the blind leading the blind.*
LEFT: *German soldiers adjust the setting of gas dischargers.*

The Battle of the Lys

Ludendorff hoped to reinvigorate the offensive with a major push in Flanders. It is unclear whether he always intended to attack in the north after the blow had been delivered on the Somme, or whether it was an improvised response to MICHAEL's failure. Operation GEORGETTE (a scaled-down version of the original plan, GEORGE) bore a resemblance to a plan suggested as an alternative to MICHAEL, and consisted of an attack on a narrow front from Armentières to the La Bassée Canal. The immediate objective was the railway junction of Hazebrouck, but Ludendorff probably trusted to luck as to further aims, hoping to capitalize on any success, as he had done on the Somme. The ultimate aim was to crush the BEF.

The first moves of the Battle of the Lys brought some gains for the Germans. The usual devilish orchestra of guns preceded an attack on 9 April by the German Sixth Army. A demoralized Portuguese division (derisively nicknamed the 'Pork and Beans' by the British) routed; on its flanks, the British 55th and 40th divisions stood firm. The Germans advanced into the gap, but two fine Territorial divisions, 50th (Northumberland) and 51st (Highland) sealed the mouth of the salient. Ludendorff was worried that only 3½ miles had been gained but remained faithful to his plan and attacked at Armentières on the following day. IX Corps of the British Second Army, and XV Corps of the First Army were forced to give ground. There were few reserves behind them; most were still in Picardy. On 11 April the situation appeared so grave that the normally unemotional Haig issued an Order of the Day that concluded: 'Every position must be held to the last man. There must be no retirement. With our backs to the wall and believing in the justice of our cause each one must fight on to the end. The safety of our homes and the freedom of mankind alike depend upon the conduct of each one of us at this critical moment.'

The Germans were five miles from Hazebrouck but Foch withheld reinforcements, choosing to build a relief force in Amiens. This was in its way a compliment. Foch probably believed that the battered British divisions were still in a better state to fight a desperate defensive battle than the French. He was right. The British held on all fronts. On 24 April the Germans again attacked in Picardy. Villers-Bretonneux was lost, but recaptured by 4th and 5th Australian Divisions, ably supported by 18th (Eastern) and 58th (2/1st London) divisions. This day saw the first encounter between enemy tanks: four British attacked three German models, which were of inferior quality. One British tank knocked out a German machine.

In Flanders, there was one last spasm of the German offensive. The gains of 1917 on Passchendaele Ridge, so painfully bought with blood, were abandoned to make a more defensible line. The Belgians in the north beat off a German attack but French troops, who had at last been sent by Foch to reinforce Haig, lost Mont Kemmel on 25 April. Some 6500 prisoners, mostly French, were taken by the Germans. Fortunately for the Allies, the Fourth Battle of Ypres followed the same pattern as the first two. The Allies under Plumer held firm. The last German attacks occurred on 27-28 April along a 10-mile front and were repulsed. On 30 April Ludendorff halted the battle.

The achievements of the British army in April were remarkable. Recovering from the calamities of March, it had taken on the main body of the German army and fought it to a standstill. The French, who had performed markedly more efficiently in the later than the earlier stages of the battle, had made a valuable contribution, but it was a British victory. The Australians, RFC (which became the RAF on 1 April), tanks and artillery had likewise played an important part but the real heroes were the ordinary British infantry. It is no reflection on them to say that the German army was past its peak. It was Nivelle all over again; despite partial success, decisive victory had eluded the Germans, and disillusionment set in. With American troops flooding into the country, the Allies could look to the future with confidence.

ABOVE: *A German gun , sited on a canal barge, fires on British positions. By April 1918 the Germans had run out of steam, largely because of the staying power of the British army. Although outnumbered and faced by specially trained German troops, the British line had held and exhausted the German attack.*

ABOVE RIGHT: *British gunners fix the sights of an 8-inch howitzer, one of the most effective artillery pieces available to the British.*
RIGHT: *French cavalrymen move up to the front line to stem the German advance on the Lys, 14 April 1918. Co-operation between the French and British armies was, on the whole, good.*

Chemin des Dames and Château-Thierry

The arrival of the French reinforcements had been a vital element in the British defensive victories of March and April. Ludendorff was, therefore, determined to cripple the French army before returning to settle with the British. On 27 May, a typical Bruchmüller bombardment fell on the French positions on the Chemin des Dames; and the infantry of 17 divisions then smashed through the Allied defenses. The local French commander, Duchêne, had deployed his men well forward instead of in depth, and the attack of von Boehn's Seventh Army fell on three worn-out British divisions (21st, 8th and 50th) sent to the Aisne for a 'rest.' Boehn advanced 10 miles in one day. The road to Paris seemed open. In seven days he had reached Château-Thierry, 56 miles from Paris; the Germans were back on the Marne. The Seventh Army's thrust had only been intended as a diversion, and began to slow; the width of its advance remained very narrow. Thus the time was ripe for a counterstroke. It was spearheaded by the effective reserve of the Allied forces: the US Army.

Already, on 28 May US 1st Division had successfully attacked in a minor action at Cantigny, near Montdidier, and on 1 June elements of US 3rd Division had defended Château-Thierry.

At Belleau Wood on 6 June 1918 the inexperienced US 2nd Division counterattacked Boehn in a manner reminiscent of the British New Army volunteers of 1916. Captain J W Thomason of 5th US Marines remembered the beginning of the attack: 'Platoons were formed in four waves . . . a formation proved in trench warfare. . . . It was a formation unadapted for open warfare, and incredibly vulnerable. It didn't take long to learn better, but there was a price to pay for the learning.' One who paid with his life was a veteran NCO of America's Imperialist wars. Two hours after being reprimanded for eating on the march, 'Sergeant Jerry Finnegan lay dead across a Maxim gun with his bayonet in the body of the gunner.' The real significance of these minor actions was as a pledge for the future. The Germans had almost lost the race to end the war before the Americans arrived in strength.

RIGHT: *François Flameng's painting of US troops attacking German fortifications at St Pierre. The Americans are supported by French Schneider tanks.*

LEFT: *A heroic view of an American attack during the battle of Soissons. Although lacking the experience of their French and British Allies the Americans proved themselves redoubtable fighters, earning the respect of their German opponents.*

ABOVE: *Crouching down, an American bombing party advances forward to launch a raid on a German outpost at Badonviller, March 1918. The sacks they are carrying contain the bombs/grenades for this operation.*

ABOVE: *Troops of the American Expeditionary Force march toward the front line during July 1918.*
RIGHT: *The Kaiser's son, Kronprinz Wilhelm, talks to his troops during a lull in the fighting.*

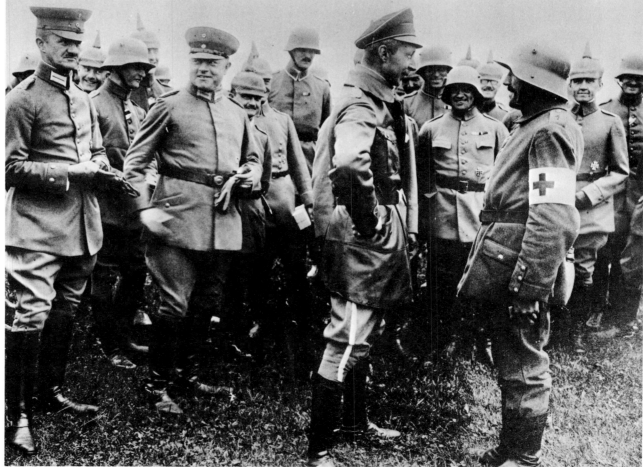

BELOW: *An American Lewis-gun team in action on the Western Front. Despite its tendency to jam if dirt entered the firing mechanism, the Lewis gun was an effective light machine gun, and was highly prized by the Germans who made extensive use of captured examples.*

A second diversionary offensive was begun on the River Matz on 9 June, but it was a failure. A pause then ensued, as both sides gathered their strength. A series of minor operations took place, including a brilliant action at Le Hamel, a co-operative effort between Sir John Monash's Australians and British tanks. Five hundred men of the US 33rd Division, attached to the Australians for training, were ear-marked for the attack, but Pershing was keen to preserve the integrity of his forces and refused permission for them to take part. A furious row erupted between Monash and Rawlinson on one side, and Pershing on the other. Earlier, Rawlinson had condemned Pershing as 'stupid and obstinate,' but to the delight of the men of 33rd Division, he gave way. On 4 July the Australians and Americans attacked with 62 British tanks. Le Hamel was taken in an hour and a half, along with 171 machine guns and 1500 prisoners. Total casualties were low – under 1000. The action was a rehearsal in miniature for the Battle of Amiens one month later. The French were also active. Mangin's Tenth Army recaptured part of the Soissons salient on 28 June. Three days earlier Belleau Wood fell to the Americans. The British, too, were busy. Their 5th and 31st Divisions of the First Army captured all their objectives in the Forest of Nieppe on 28 June. The next major offensive was, however, to be German. It was to be the last time in the war that they held the initiative.

The Second Battle of the Marne

With GEORGETTE in ruins, Ludendorff now switched attention to the French. He still saw the British as the main enemy, and prepared Operation HAGEN, a final offensive in Flanders. Before he began HAGEN he decided to attack the French to pull Allied reserves to the south. Perhaps, in an ironic echo of Haig's perpetual optimism of 1916 and 1917, he also felt that one more blow would be the *coup de grâce* for French morale. On 15 July, the now familiar hurricane bombardment opened on the Marne and 33 Allied divisions of the Army groups of

Maistre and Fayolle were assailed by 52 German divisions of the Third (under Einem), the First (under Mudra), the Seventh (under Boehn) and the Ninth (under Eben) Armies. In contrast to previous attacks, the Germans did not achieve surprise. Gouraud's French Fourth Army neatly turned the tables by opening a bombardment of its own, 30 minutes before the German guns opened fire. This disrupted the infantry which was assembled for the assault. The attack on Gouraud was shattered, in spite of being supported by 20 tanks. West of

Rheims, however, two Italian divisions gave way and had to be hastily reinforced by the British XXII Corps. The Germans here crossed the Marne, leaving the US 3rd Division as an island of resistance. Ludendorff, thinking victory was at hand, ordered the 'battering train' of heavy guns north to prepare for HAGEN but on 16 July the Germans were still trapped in their bridgehead, and French counterattacks were pressing them back.

It was Mangin who masterminded the counterstroke. At 0435 hours on 18 July, the French artillery crashed down onto the German positions, and then Degoutte's Sixth Army moved behind a rolling barrage to strike the western side of the Soissons salient. Then 45 minutes later, Mangin's Tenth Army of 18 divisions surprised the Germans by debouching from woods and gained four miles by midday. By the evening 15,000 prisoners and 400 guns had been taken. A key element in the French victory was the use, en masse in the style of Cambrai, of 346 tanks (mainly the relatively fast Renault light models, capable of

LEFT: *Painted by one of Britain's leading war artists, Eric Kennington's* Gassed and Wounded *dramatically reveals the horrors of the fighting.*
RIGHT: *The heroic image of the German soldier at war. For the most part, the German army fought with great resolution right up until the armistice, but it was overwhelmed by the material superiority of the Allies.*
BELOW RIGHT: *German flamethrowers advance along a trench on the Marne. A fearsome weapon when used against green troops, it was far less effective when faced by experienced soldiers who usually had little trouble in dealing with the exposed and cumbersome flame-thrower teams.*

Helft uns siegen!

zeichnet die Kriegsanleihe

6mph). The use of the oversize, and keen, US 1st and 2nd Divisions as assault troops was also crucial. On the eastern side of the salient, even without the element of surprise, the French made further gains.

Once the initial shock of the Allied attack subsided, the Germans – composed in part of second-rate trench-holding troops – fought well, but the salient was now untenable. On the night of 19/20 July, they pulled back across the Marne. Pétain halted the battle on 6 August; Soissons had been recaptured and the bump in the line ironed out.

The casualties were heavy on both sides. The Germans lost 138,000, in addition to 30,000 prisoners and 800 guns; the Allies about 120,000. The Americans were still taking disproportionately heavy losses, because of their inexperience and active role as assault troops. The Second Battle of the Marne had, like the first, restored the position after a debacle rather than inflicted a decisive defeat. Its importance, above all, lay in the indefinite postponement of HAGEN. The initiative had passed to the Allies for once and for all; until the Armistice, the Germans would dance to the tune of Foch and Haig. A German soldier wrote, at the height of the counterattack on 25 July, in these terms: 'We have been spending uncomfortable days . . . disturbed day and night by bombardment and bombing . . . I do not believe that we shall ever get our hands free again . . . The American Army is there – a million strong. That is too much.'

RIGHT: *US and French ammunition trains move up the front to support the troops holding the German advance. American troops made extensive use of British and French munitions during World War I.*

LEFT: *A British tank captured by the Germans crosses a trench in a counterattack in the fall of 1918. Despite pioneering infiltration tactics the Germans were slow to see the possibilities of the tank as a weapon of breakthrough and exploitation. Although the Germans developed the enormous A-7 tank in 1918 they found captured British tanks more effective.*

LEFT: *German infantrymen manage to negotiate the wreckage of a blown bridge across the Marne/Aisne canal during the fighting in June 1918. While not a complete success this piece of demolition denied the Germans use of the bridge for vehicles and horses.*

RIGHT: An Advanced Dressing Station in France, 1918, *by the British war artist Henry Tonks. The painting consists of a number of scenes at an advanced dressing station, which was the first step for wounded men following emergency treatment at the front and prior to dispatch to the casualty-clearing stations well to the rear. Tonks was particularly well-qualified to undertake this painting as he was not only an established painter but an experienced surgeon as well. Tonks had worked as a doctor on the Marne and in Italy before being appointed as an artist to the Ministry of Information.*

Amiens – The Black Day of the German Army

At 0420 hours on 8 August 1918, the Battle of Amiens began. By the end of the day the Allied forces had inflicted, in the words of a German official history, 'the greatest defeat which the German army had suffered since the beginning of the War.' The blow was delivered by the French First Army and the Canadian, Australian and III Corps of the British Fourth Army. In this battle, the lessons so painfully learned in the past were applied, and the result was a crushing victory. Broadly speaking, the factors that led to victory were: surprise, air power, the scientific use of artillery, and close co-operation between infantry and tanks. The cement that joined these into a cohesive whole was effective radio communications. For the key to victory lay in the meshing of diverse elements into an overall plan; in other words, close inter-arm co-operation.

Haig wanted to use the Canadians to spearhead the assault. They had not fought in any of the battles of the retreat, and were, therefore, reasonably fresh. To have openly moved the Canadians to the Somme would have been to reveal his plan to the enemy; thus two Canadian battalions remained behind in Flanders. Their presence, and more importantly, their signal traffic, fooled the Germans into believing that they were to attack around Mont Kemmel. Moreover, security over the Amiens region was very tight, and almost complete surprise was achieved on the day of the attack. Only one lapse occurred. The perpetually aggressive Australian 5th Division raided the enemy lines on 29 July. The Germans retaliated while British III Corps were taking over the front, and pushed them back. On 8 August III Corps had, therefore, to attack an enemy already alerted.

The operation was begun on a 14-mile front without a preliminary bombardment. Out of the fog emerged 414 tanks, backed by a further 120 supply tanks, catching the Germans by surprise. The infantry of seven divisions advanced close behind the armor, each battalion in four waves. The head gunner of the Fourth Army, Major General Budworth, proved himself the equal of Bruchmüller. His 'predicted' bombardment demoralized the defenders, a state of mind reinforced by the activities of the RAF ground-attack aircraft who played a significant part in the victory. Communication, the bane of exploitation and fire-control in previous years, was greatly improved by the use of

LEFT: *Commander of the Australian Corps Lieutenant General Sir John Monash, one of the most talented generals on the British side.*
BELOW LEFT: *British troops advance in 'artillery formation' over the chalk downlands of the Amiens-Albert battleground.*

ABOVE: *A British gun-carrier tank transports a 6-inch howitzer and its ammunition up a sunken lane during the fighting in August 1918. The gun-carrier tank represented an imaginative solution to the problem of moving heavy artillery over the battlefield.*

BELOW: *Mark V tanks prepare to move forward, equipped with 'cribs' to enable them to cross over wide ditches. By the summer of 1918 the British had realized the strengths and limitations of the tanks and were able to deploy them with maximum effectiveness.*

Continuous Wave (CW) radio sets. The Canadian Independent Force of armored cars and truck-mounted machine guns, for instance, ranged far and wide over the battlefield and was still able to keep in touch with Corps HQ. Aircraft were able to spot centers of resistance and radio back to Corps to inform them. Ground-attack aircraft would then be dispatched or artillery would range in. The system was still fairly primitive. Infantry battalions, aircraft and tanks could not contact each other directly, but this was nevertheless a vast improvement over the situation of 1916.

The attack of the Dominion (or 'Colonial') troops in the center was the most successful. The 2nd and 3rd Australian Divisions led off, and by 0830 hours the two follow-up divisions, 4th and 5th, began to move up to their start line. Unfortunately, 58th (London) Division of III Corps had a more difficult task, and were slower to advance, leaving the Australian left flank exposed. Even so, the bulk of the Australians were on their final objective by 1330 hours, having covered six miles. The Canadians, too, took all their objectives, except on one flank, where the French IV and XXXI Corps lagged behind. The French had only 72 tanks and therefore substituted a 45-minute bombardment, and made slower progress. Currie's Canadians won four VCs that day. A further two were won by members of 13th (Royal Highlanders) Battalion who, in separate incidents, silenced seven machine guns and three howitzers.

The British III Corps had to advance from a more distant start-line than the Colonials, against an alerted enemy, yet still managed to progress two miles. On a local level, some units did achieve a measure of surprise. Colonel Bonds of 10th Essex Regiment, in 18th (Eastern) Division, took the surrender of a German battery, overrun in Gressaire Wood. The first the German commander knew about the attack was 'when he found a dozen rifles leveled at him; his calmness did not entirely leave him . . . "I am your prisoner, Sir," he said, with a show of anxiety.' However, the Germans mounted a counterattack and the 10th Essex suffered 290 casualties in an unsuccessful attempt to take the wood.

The extent of the German defeat is revealed by the usefulness of horsed cavalry that day. The 15th and 19th Hussars (now amalgamated into one regiment) were able to pass through the Canadians and ride for more than a mile through the broken German forces. They then dismounted, and held their ground until the infantry caught up with them. Horsed cavalry, armored cars and 'Whippet' light tanks were able to operate with a freedom absent from the Western Front since 1914. If the German infantry had been of the caliber of even six months before, it is unlikely that the cavalry would have enjoyed much success. Although the co-operation between tanks and horses was not a great success, on the whole the Allied instruments of exploitation were reasonably effective.

In terms of casualties, the Germans lost 15,750 prisoners, almost all taken by the two Dominion corps. In all, the Germans suffered losses of 27,000 men and 400 guns. Allied casualties, by contrast, were light: about 9000 men. That the Canadians lost 4000 men and the Australians only 652 (including 83 fatalities) is a reflection of the differing quality of the opposition these formations faced. If human losses had been light, material losses had not. The German air arm had been reinforced during the day, and the RAF had suffered heavily – 44 aircraft shot down and 53 badly damaged. The tanks, too, had been severely reduced through the effectiveness of German antitank defenses and mechanical breakdowns. At the end of the battle, only 145 were still fit for action; this was reduced to a mere six by the fifth day of battle. Although the usefulness of armor had been demonstrated, the tanks of 1918 were still too unreliable for sustained action.

RIGHT: *Just some of the 15,750 German troops captured by the British Fourth Army in the battle of Amiens. The ease with which so many Germans let themselves be captured was a telling pointer to the future.*
BELOW: *Australian troops stand alongside an A-7 tank, captured during the summer fighting of 1918. Despite its armament of a 5.7cm main gun and six machine guns and a crew of 18 men, the A-7 was a largely unsuccessful tank: too heavy, too unreliable and too unmaneuverable.*

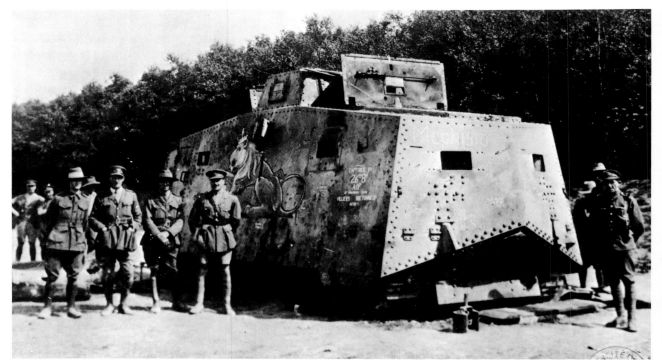

LEFT: *Troops of the New Zealand Division march past a British Whippet or Medium Tank Mk A. Capable of a maximum speed of 8mph the Whippet was intended to act in a cavalry role and be able to exploit any breakthroughs in the enemy line.*
RIGHT: *Mk V tanks at the village of Meaulle, 22 August 1918. Their function was to work with the artillery and infantry to smash a hole through German positions.*

The battle of Amiens hastened the terminal decline in morale in the German army. Reinforcements were abused as 'blacklegs' by soldiers in the line; prisoners were only too happy to surrender. In his memoirs, Ludendorff was brutally honest: 'August 8th was the black day of the German army in the history of the war . . . 8th August made things clear for both army commanders, both for the German and for that of the enemy.' Ludendorff was right. Foch and Haig could now look forward to victory, perhaps even within the year.

In strategy, as well as tactics, Haig and Rawlinson demonstrated how much they had learned. The German spring offensives had begun promisingly, but swiftly run out of impetus. The same fate threatened the Amiens offensive. On 9 and 10 August, progress was disappointing. Haig decided to switch the point of attack north to the Third Army's front. Haig had to argue the point with Foch, who wanted to continue to press home the attack on the Somme. Foch eventually gave way. By opting for the attack by the Third Army, Haig was abandoning the search for a breakthrough in favor of a series of attacks at different points of the line, the aim being to keep up the pressure on an enemy already demonstrating the symptoms of disintegration. This was attrition, of a kind, but a very different type of attrition to the bludgeoning of earlier years.

The September Advance and St Mihiel

The resemblance between the actions of the US Army of 1918 and those of the British New Armies of two years before has already been briefly mentioned. The 30 division US Army of November 1918 was built on a slender cadre of regular officers; only 18,000 of the 200,000-strong officer corps were from the regular army or National Guard. The rest were the product of Officer Training Units or 'Plattsburg Schools,' first established in the United States in 1915 and later in France. Thus the American forces were inexperienced; they brought to the battlefields of Château-Thierry and the Argonne the raw enthusiasm shown at Montauban and Delville Wood in 1916. At first they were, like Kitchener's men, badly equipped. Even after they reached Europe they were largely equipped by the French, for priority was given to shipping out men, not material.

The American divisions were enormous – at 28,000 strong they were three times the size of French divisions. Mere numbers are not everything, and the Americans had even greater assets – freshness, and high morale. To British and French observers, the Doughboys were similar in quality to the ANZACS, in that they were physically impressive and self-confident. To some extent, this was an idealized picture. Not all Doughboys were bronzed Midwest farmboys – perhaps one draftee in five was a foreign-born immigrant – but in battle nearly all American troops performed well. The only black combat unit was 93rd Division, which fought with the French; three out of four regiments of the division were awarded the Croix de Guerre. Shamefully, their performance was ignored by the white military establishment.

ABOVE RIGHT: *General Jack Pershing, commander of the US Army in France. A forceful personality, Pershing was understandably determined to maintain complete control over his troops so that they could operate as an autonomous army, rather than follow the Allied proposal that the army be deployed as separate divisions under overall Franco-British control.*

ABOVE: *Crewed by US artillerymen, a French 75mm field gun fires on German positions within the St Mihiel Salient. The '75' was capable of a very high rate of fire – up to 20 rounds per minute – as this photograph suggests. The elimination of the St Mihiel Salient on 12-13 September 1918 was the first major US action of the war and a great boost to morale.*

LEFT: *Armed with a British Vickers machine gun, US troops fire upon retreating German forces during the last few weeks of the war.*

General John J Pershing, the American Commander in Chief, had a hard fight to assemble an integral American army. The British and French grasped at American units as a drowning man grasps at a lifebelt. While many units were assigned to foreign command – and many British units received an American Medical Officer in 1917-18 – by July 1918 Pershing had enough men to create the First Army of the American Expeditionary Force (AEF). At the Conference of Bombon on 27 July, he was allocated the quiet St Mihiel sector, south of Verdun. Here the preparations could be completed, and, in time, the German salient could be reduced. Beyond St Mihiel lay the fortress of Metz, and beyond that, the valley of the Moselle, a natural highway into the heartland of the Reich.

To the north, events were moving so swiftly that the St Mihiel operation was threatened with redundancy. On 20 August Mangin advanced to the River Oise. The British Third Army attacked Below's Seventeenth Army on the fourth anniversary of Mons (23 August), and advanced two miles. The French Third, and British Fourth and First Armies also attacked in this period. The effect was of a series of hammer blows against the German salient. The results were patchy, but the general thrust of the Allied line was forward, and the Germans were being given no time in which to recover. They withdrew on a wide front on the night of 26-27 August, abandoning the Lys salient opposite the British Second and Fifth Armies (the latter having been re-formed under Birdwood). The twin spearheads of the Allied advance, the Canadian and Australian Corps, once more refused to allow Ludendorff time to catch his breath. The Canadians, part of Horne's First Army, prepared to attack the 'Wotan' position, known to the British as the Drocourt-Quéant Switch Line. They reverted to the set-piece tactics of Vimy Ridge, softening up the strongly held position for 48 hours with artillery. On 2 September they stormed the line. They were supported by the British 4th and 57th divisions, 59 tanks and assorted ground-attack aircraft. They broke through; German morale was now so low that they could not even hold a position as strong as this. Not to be outdone, Sir John Monash's Australians had previously captured Péronne and Mont St Quentin, and routed a German Guard division. And still the Allies advanced.

RIGHT: *Renault light tanks advance up a hill. The US Army made extensive use of these tanks during the final battles of 1918.*

LEFT: *A painting by George Harding entitled* Village of the Dead. *A common scene during the last few months of the war, it depicts US artillerymen moving guns through a ruined French village.*

ABOVE: *US soldiers prepare a Stokes mortar for action. This British-made weapon was a useful trench weapon, capable of firing its mortar bomb up to a distance of 800 yards.*

Haig and Foch asked Pershing to abandon the St Mihiel operation and move his army 60 miles to the other side of the Verdun salient, to co-operate in an Inter-Allied offensive into the Argonne. The limited St Mihiel operation had been superseded by the need to continue to harry the Germans, who, Haig was convinced, were beaten. Pershing agreed to the move but insisted it take place after the St Mihiel operation: he was not to be cheated out of his first independent offensive, and Foch had to be content with that.

Three thousand guns heralded the Battle of St Mihiel. At 0500 hours on 12 September the barrage lifted and Ligget's I Corps and Dickman's IV of the First US Army attacked on two sides of the salient. The battle was a fairly straightforward affair. The Germans were caught in the act of withdrawing and bundled out, losing 15,000 prisoners and 450 guns. American losses were about 7000. Two future heroes of the next war were present. Douglas MacArthur commanded a brigade in the

Rainbow Division, and Colonel George S Patton was commanding a mixed force of French and American tanks. Patton's career nearly came to an abrupt end that day. A shell landed 20 feet away from him, killing 15 men. He was unharmed.

Although America's allies had played a part in Pershing's victory – none of his artillery pieces were of American manufacture, and French II Colonial Corps had played a supporting role in the attack – St Mihiel lifted the self-confidence of the American forces and gave notice of the arrival of a major military power on the continent of Europe. The Allied successes since Amiens had been remarkable. Since 8 August the British advance had averaged 25 miles on a 40-mile front. Losses, again, had been heavy: 190,000 British and about the same for the French, but their morale was nevertheless high, for victory was in sight. The war was not over yet, however. Ahead of them lay the formidable defenses of the Hindenburg Line.

ABOVE: *Canadian troops advance toward the Canal du Nord, 27 September 1918. The Hindenburg Line was breached after a ferocious preliminary bombardment: from noon on 28 September to noon on the following day, 943,847 rounds were fired – the highest British 24-hour total of the war.*

LEFT: *US Army Signallers at work during the battle for St Mihiel. Good communications were essential in large operations of this kind.*

ABOVE: *British troops prepare to move out while behind them Mk V tanks are assembled prior to the crossing of the Hindenburg Line near Bellicourt, September 1918.*

ABOVE: *The artist Colin Gill had enlisted in the Royal Garrison Artillery in 1914, hence the subject matter of his painting* Heavy Artillery *which featured a battery of 9.2-inch howitzers. The patchwork camouflage applied to the guns was intended to make them unrecognizable to enemy aircraft. In 1916 Gill had been seconded to the Royal Engineers as a camouflage officer, thereby gaining familiarity with camouflage.*

The Collapse of Turkey

The battle of Megiddo (or Armageddon) in September 1918 was Allenby's greatest triumph. Yet it can be argued that this phase of the Palestine Campaign should never have been fought; Jerusalem having been captured, the bulk of Allenby's army should have been transferred to the Western Front. However, the War Cabinet still hoped that Germany's 'props' could be 'knocked away,' and thus Allenby was ordered to take the offensive.

Allenby had to delay until September 1918, having sent 60,000 troops to France and having received Indian replacements who needed time to acclimatize. He spent this profitably on an elaborate deception plan to fool Liman von Sanders (the new enemy commander) into believing that an offensive was planned inland. The ruses included the ostentatious movement of troops to the area, the construction of dummy horses and horse-lines and the like. The plan worked brilliantly. When Allenby struck out along the coast, the Turks were taken completely by surprise.

Megiddo was a masterpiece of combined action. A furious bombardment opened on 19 September when two infantry corps (XXI and XX) smashed an opening for the cavalry. The horsemen, accompanied by armored cars, raced through the gap to cut off the Turkish retreat. The RAF strafed and bombed the fleeing Turks, who faced the additional hazard of marauding Arab irregulars. Ten thousand prisoners were taken. Allenby then marched on Damascus and Beirut, which fell on 1 and 2 October respectively. The last action took place near Aleppo, nearly 200 miles beyond Beirut. There, appropriately, it was Mustapha Kemal who gave the British their only bloody nose of the campaign, on 25 October.

Perhaps the most romantic figure of the war was T E Lawrence ('Lawrence of Arabia' or el Urunz to the Arabs) who led a guerrilla force against the Turks in support of the British. The legend created in his books (and a Hollywood film) tells of the enormous success of the guerrillas, who were ultimately to be cheated of their rights by the British and French. The truth is rather more prosaic. The Turks took little notice of Lawrence, who was no more than an annoying gadfly to them. His dream of an Arab kingdom under Emir Feisal, ruled from Damascus, was never seriously entertained by the British and French, who under the Sykes-Picot agreement had decided to divide the region between their colonial empires. Even more damaging to the Arab cause was the Balfour Declaration of November 1917, which gave British support for the idea of a Jewish National Home in Palestine. Lawrence's military and political achievements were meager, but as a propagandist and author he was wildly successful.

BELOW: *A Russian armored car stands guard at a street corner in the Persian city of Teheran. The growing demand for oil and its by-products during the war gave oil-rich Persia a new strategic significance. Britain and Russia exercised virtual control over Persia and developed its oil industry for their needs.*

LEFT: *British troops search surrendering Turkish soldiers captured after the engagement at Tuz Khurmath, 29 April 1918.*
BELOW: *Carrying an Islamic banner, Turkish troops set off to the war. By the summer of 1918, British pressure had virtually brought Turkey to her knees.*

ABOVE: Charge of the 2nd Lancers at El Afuli, Palestine *by Thomas Dugdale. The campaign in Palestine was one of the few theaters of the war where cavalry could be employed in its traditional role. Dugdale's painting recalls an incident in the Valley of Armageddon when the 2nd Lancers surprised a body of Turks in a dawn raid. Despite attempting to fight back, the Turks were routed, as Dugdale recalls: 'The 2nd Lancers each chased a Turk and tent-pegged him as he lay firing.'*
RIGHT: *Enver Pasha, Turkish commander on the Dardanelles Front.*

ABOVE RIGHT: *Armistice celebrations in Baghdad, 1918. Despite overall success the campaign in Mesopotamia was a constant drain on British resources.*
RIGHT: *Wearing full tropical kit British troops march through the streets of Kut following its recapture on 24 December 1916.*

In Mesopotamia, Sir Stanley Maude had been appointed as British commander, and was eventually given instructions to take Baghdad, and thus to revenge Kut. Paying careful attention to logistics, he advanced, and took Kut on Christmas Eve 1916. Baghdad fell in March 1917, after a pause to allow supplies to be brought up. The hot season precluded any further advance until September, and in November Maude died of cholera. His successor, Lieutenant General Marshall, was faced with further action in 1918. Again, the sensible course – to advance no further – was ignored. Instead, troops poured into 'Mespot,' and further objectives, political rather than military, were found for Marshall's army.

The Russian Revolution had given the Central Powers the opportunity to take advantage of the turmoil and seize the oil wells at Baku, on the Caspian Sea and in Persia (modern-day Iran). 'Dunsterforce' was formed under Major General Dunsterville (a boyhood friend of Rudyard Kipling and the model for 'Stalky') and dispatched to Baku. At first it enjoyed little success, but eventually Baku was reoccupied after the Turkish armistice.

In Mesopotamia proper, Marshall took the offensive in September, initially to support Allenby but later simply to seize as much territory as possible before the Turks capitulated. It developed into a race up the Tigris for the oil wells of Mosul. The town was entered after the armistice was signed, against the strict letter of the agreement. From beginning to end, the Mesopotamia campaign had cost the British Empire 92,000 casualties. Of all the peripheral campaigns undertaken by the British this was perhaps the most unnecessary.

The cumulative blows of Megiddo and the Bulgarian collapse forced Turkey to pull out of the war. Appropriately, the armistice was signed on board HMS *Agamemnon*, in Mudros harbor. As a result, the British achieved what had proved impossible in 1915: the occupation of Constantinople by British troops.

The Collapse of Austria-Hungary

Neither side particularly wanted to reopen the fighting on the Italian front in 1918. Both Emperor Karl and his Chief of Staff, Arz, were well aware of the fragile state of the Hapsburg armies, but German pressure forced them into aiding the *Kaiserschlach* by attacking in Italy. Arz originally intended to conduct a limited offensive, but Conrad and Boroevic bullied him into allowing an attack on both the Trentino and Piave fronts on 15 June. It is possible – although, given the state of the Austrian armies, unlikely – that, had the forces been massed on one of these fronts, a decisive success could have been obtained. Instead, there was overall failure. Failure was complete on the Trentino front. A limited advance was made across the Piave, but British aircraft destroyed the Austrian pontoon bridges; in any case, the lack of sufficient reserves would have condemned the attack to ultimate failure. The Austrian army lost 150,000 men and its offensive capability was effectively at an end.

Diaz was as keen as Arz had been to avoid battle; Pétain's 'healing offensives' were not for him. He delayed attacking the Austrians until 24 October, and then the main objective appears to have been to strengthen Italy's hand at a future peace conference, for the events in Bulgaria seemed to spell the end for Austria. Diaz's plan was for the Eighth Army to cross the Piave and drive a wedge between the Austrian forces on that front and on the Trentino. The Eighth Army would be supported on the right by the Tenth Army (commanded by Lord Cavan and including two British divisions, the 7th and 23rd) and on the left by the Twelfth Army (commanded by the French General Graziani and including the French 23rd Division). In the event, it was the supporting divisions which did most of the hard fighting, clearing the far bank and allowing the Eighth to cross.

ABOVE: *General Diaz (left) with General Babington, commander of the 23rd Division, one of the two British divisions in the Anglo-Italian Tenth Army. After the collapse of the Italian Army at Caporetto, British and French Forces had been sent to Italy to steady the situation.*
LEFT: *Two commanders on the Salonika Front – the British General Sir George Milne (right) and the Serbian General Mishitch, January 1917.*

ABOVE: *Czech legionaries fighting with the Italian Army train with flame-throwers, 3 August 1918. The Czechs had little sympathy for the Austro-Hungarian empire and many changed sides to fight against Austria.*
LEFT: *Two Albanian soldiers make use of the shade from an umbrella, Salonika, August 1916. The Allied forces around Salonika contained troops from many nations although France and Serbia made the most important military contributions.*

227

The Austrians had fought well in the center, but by 29 October the Allies were in full cry. The battle, known as Vittorio Veneto, caused the final collapse of the Austrian army. It had been on meager rations – 200 grams of meat a week, for instance – and the disturbances on the Home Front had badly affected its morale. On 16 October the Empire had been belatedly proclaimed a Federal State, and many minority soldiers simply deserted to go home. By 4 November, 500,000 prisoners were taken. The Empire had ceased to exist, and its late soldiers saw no further reason for fighting. The surprising thing was not that the heterogeneous army collapsed, but that it survived for so long against all the odds.

Austria-Hungary had also been threatened on another front: in the Balkans. Since October 1915, an Allied force had been stationed in Macedonia, in the Greek port of Salonika. It was quite unable to aid the Serbs in 1915, but remained in a huge fortified camp in Salonika, largely for reasons of French internal politics. The Germans sneeringly called Salonika their largest prison camp. The force was still there in 1918, having launched ineffectual offensives against the Bulgarians in 1916 and 1917, and having interfered in Greek internal affairs to the extent of deposing the pro-German King and almost starting a civil war – an ironic comment on an alliance allegedly fighting for the self-determination of small nations. At last, on 15 September 1918, the 'gardeners of Salonika' began to justify the expenditure on their rations.

The new commander of the 'Allied Army of the Orient,' Franchet d'Esperey, had a polyglot army of nine Greek, eight French, six Serbian, four British and one Italian divisions to pitch against slightly superior Bulgarian forces, stiffened with a few Germans. His offensive was swift and triumphant. In 15 days, with the vengeful, exiled Serbs in the lead, they advanced 80 miles. The Bulgarian forces offered little resistance. The Bulgarians asked for an armistice, which sent tremors through the Turks, causing them to take the same course on 30 October. Then d'Esperey pushed on, again with the Serbs to the fore, and crossed the Danube into Hungary. The Hungarian successor state, in the throws of revolution, sued for peace. Thus both halves of the old Dual Monarchy had been defeated; the heir to the medieval Holy Roman Empire was no more.

ABOVE: *Part of France's colonial war effort, troops from Indochina stack arms outside Salonika. Along with Britain, France made considerable military use of her colonial peoples.* RIGHT: *Italian troops march up a mountain road in the Val d'Assa during the final offensives of 1918.*

TOP: *One Italian soldier who was to play a significant role in the next world war, Benito Mussolini. Like Hitler, Mussolini made great play of his war service during the interwar period.*

ABOVE: *Weary-looking Austrian troops stand outside a dug-out built into the mountain side. The political disintegration of the Austro-Hungarian Empire led inexorably to the military collapse of its army.*

The Advance to Victory

'*Tout le monde à la bataille!*' This was Foch's battlecry in the fall of 1918. Between 5 and 8 September his plan for the last phase of the war emerged. His 217 divisions were to begin a series of offensives along almost the entire length of the front. In Flanders, an army group under King Albert (12 of his Belgian divisions, six French divisions and Plumer's British Second Army) were to break out of the Ypres area. On the Somme, the British Third, First, and Fourth Armies and the French First Army would strike toward Cambrai and St Quentin. On the Aisne, the French center would attack; while the Meuse-Argonne Sector would see a joint offensive by the French Fourth Army and the US First Army.

The joint attack commenced on 26 September and was a logistical triumph. Some 600,000 troops were conveyed over 50 miles from St Mihiel to the Argonne Forest in under 14 days. Thus the Franco-Americans achieved strategic surprise, for the Germans were expecting a much longer delay after St Mihiel. Unfortunately, the speed of the attack also meant that it had to be undertaken with largely inexperienced troops. On the first day of the attack, Pershing made gains of up to three miles, and then German resistance stiffened. In the Argonne, the AEF came up against the problems the French and British had first experienced back in 1915 – that of inching forward at the cost of heavy casualties. A PFC (Private First Class) of US 1st Division described an attack on 4 October in terms reminiscent of Ypres and Verdun. He managed to approach to within 50 yards of the enemy line unscathed, and was then faced with a 'solid sheet' of machine-gun bullets and shells. The Americans advanced 'wave on wave,' clambering over the corpses of their fellow Doughboys to close with the Germans. In sharp contrast to the move to the area, and to the courage of the ordinary soldier, American staffwork proved grossly deficient in the latter stages of the battle, which, in combination with the difficult terrain, made for a slow rate of progress – five miles in 45 days of fighting, at the cost of 117,000 casualties.

ABOVE: *Prince Max of Baden, who was appointed German Chancellor on 3 October 1918. He headed a coalition government which instigated negotiations with the Allies for an armistice.*
LEFT: *Field Marshal Sir Douglas Haig (center) with some of his top generals at Cambrai, 31 October 1918. The British successes in the summer of 1918 were in part a vindication of Haig's resolute strategy during the preceding years.*

The tragedies of the Argonne were largely the result of inexperience. The two American divisions serving with the 39 British divisions in the central push benefited from the experience of the British commanders. The British had a formidable task: to cross two canals (the Canal du Nord and Canal de St Quentin) and to storm the Hindenburg Line. They were opposed by 41 German divisions, in a poor frame of mind. In the first 48 hours the Canal du Nord was crossed and an advance of six miles was made. This seriously alarmed Ludendorff – who made up his mind that an armistice was essential – but the Hindenburg Line itself still barred the way to the advance of Rawlinson's Fourth Army. Rawlinson, like Haig, was in his element in open warfare. The storming of the Hindenburg Line was a triumph to set alongside the battle on 8 August.

Much attention has, rightly, been focused on the role of the elite Dominion divisions in the 1918 battles. The action on St Quentin Canal allows us to redress the balance. At Bellenglise, a brigade of a hitherto undistinguished Territorial division, the 46th (North Midland), crossed the canal and broke through the first section of the Hindenburg Line. Three Staffordshire battalions (5th and 6th South Staffs, 6th North Staffs) had crossed the canal using lifebelts from Channel steamers, scrambled up the steep banks and surprised the enemy. The Australian-American Corps (under Monash) crossed successfully at the same time, but the glory went to the Staffordshire Territorials. As the brigade historian cheerfully admitted, it was the poor quality of the enemy that was the crucial factor in the battle. Thus far had the once-mighty German army deteriorated. By 4 October the Allies had captured the entire Hindenburg Line.

LEFT: *German troops retreat across the Rhine at Bonn. Although defeated in the field the German army remained a force in being.*

BELOW: *The German delegation arrives to begin armistice negotiations at Compiègne, 10 November 1918. The following day World War I was finally over.*

The Germans recognized how desperate the situation was and belatedly attempted to find a political solution. The Kaiser, with transparent motives, transformed himself overnight into a constitutional monarch. The liberal Prince Max of Baden became Chancellor. On 4 October, the Central Powers sent a peace note to Wilson, agreeing to accept his 14 Points – a set of liberal and idealistic proposals to govern international relations. Still the Allies advanced. King Albert's forces advanced eight miles in three days, from 28 to 30 September, and captured the heights around Ypres and then pushed on to the Schelde. In the center, the BEF was marching over familiar territory: Le Cateau fell on 17 October to Rawlinson's Fourth Army, which included two American divisions. The resistance of the German army was becoming progressively weaker. By 10 November the US First Army (a Second Army had been formed under Bullard on 12 October) was on the outskirts of Sedan. The following day, the Canadians occupied Mons. At 1058 hours on 11 November 1918, Private Price of the Canadian 28th (North West) Battalion was killed. Two minutes later the guns fell silent, and the war was over.

Wilson's response to the Peace Note of 4 October had arrived in Berlin on 9 October. Prince Max was dismayed to find that the terms of the armistice were to be dictated by the Allies, not negotiated. If Pershing's advice had been heeded, the Allies would have demanded unconditional surrender. In the next month, the situation worsened. The German High Seas Fleet had been ordered to sea on 29 October, and the sailors rose in mutiny. This was the signal for the outbreak of revolution in Germany. It was the end. With an insurrection at home, and the army decisively beaten in France and Belgium, the Kaiser fled to Holland. The previous day Germany had become a republic with Fritz Ebert, a socialist, at its head. At 0505 hours on 11 November 1918, the Armistice was signed in the forest of Compiègne and it came into effect at 1100 hours on that day.

RIGHT: *The general declaration of the Armistice led to widespread rejoicing by the civilian population. This London scene shows enthusiastic revellers waving the national flags of the United States and Britain.*
LEFT: *A special edition of the* Evening Standard *proclaims the good news.*

LEFT: *President Wilson reads the Armistice terms to Congress, 11 November 1918. The United States was to emerge from World War I as a major world power, although for the next two decades she largely turned her back on Europe and pursued a policy of isolationism.*

The Haig of 1918 appears to be a very different general from the attritionist of 1916 and 1917. It has been said that if he had assumed command of BEF in December 1917, rather than December 1915, his place as a 'Great Captain' alongside Napoleon and Frederick the Great would be assured. This apparent disparity between Haig of 1918 and that of earlier years is perhaps explained by the nature of the fighting. The battles of 1918 were largely 'open' battles, the type of warfare that Haig had been trained for and understood. The trench warfare of 1915-17 was a form of siege warfare, the natural preserve of the sapper and gunner, rather than an infantryman or cavalryman like Haig. Too often, the techniques of siege warfare were ignored, and the totally inappropriate tactics of 'open' warfare – the attempt to achieve a breakthrough, and so on – were employed. Competent generals like Haig, once given a situation where open warfare was possible, performed creditably enough. The record of the previous years cannot, however, be expunged because of the brilliance of the battles of the second half of 1918.

Three elements may be given the pride of place in the Allied victory. The naval blockade slowly starved Germany and undermined morale. The AEF was extremely important, not so much for its achievements (creditable though they were) as for the prospect, demoralizing for the Germans, of a million more Americans arriving in 1919. The third element was the BEF, and particularly the Dominion contingents. It was the BEF that smashed the German army: it was Haig's victory.

The Aftermath

The exact total of casualties of World War I is unknown. Quite apart from deaths in battle, an influenza epidemic in 1918 took millions of lives. The resistance of the peoples of Europe had been weakened by a wartime diet and the stresses of four years of war. In round figures, the number of military deaths probably amounted to about 13 million. The heaviest sufferer was Russia, whose total casualties (not just fatalities) approached 10 million. The Germans suffered losses of 6½ million, the French 4½ million, and the Austro-Hungarians 7 million. The British Empire, for which the most accurate figures are available, had losses of 3,260,581. Over 2.5 million were from the British Isles. The Turks lost nearly 3 million, the Italians almost 2 million, and the United States 325,876. The killing did not stop on 11 November 1918. A series of small wars continued. Until 1921 Britain fought to retain Ireland; in Eastern Europe the Bolsheviks fought the Poles. A war that was far from small disfigured Russia into the 1920s, as 'White' counter-revolutionaries, assisted by British, French, American and other troops tried to overthrow the fledgling Bolshevik regime. Revolutionary uprisings had broken out across Europe, and machine-gun fire was heard in the streets of Berlin and Budapest.

BELOW: *Left-wing Spartacists hold a barricade during the uprising in Berlin in January 1919. The new government had little real control during the immediate postwar period and both left- and right-wing gangs fought for political control at street level.*

RIGHT: *A German newspaper* Vorwaerts *announces the abdication of the Kaiser, 9 November 1918. The Kaiser fled from Berlin and travelled to permanent exile in Holland.*
FAR RIGHT: *Berlin in revolution – the forces of left and right engage in street fighting alongside the Royal Palace, 10 November 1918.*

2. Extraausgabe Sonnabend, den **9. November 1918.**

Vorwärts

Berliner Volksblatt.

Zentralorgan der sozialdemokratischen Partei Deutschlands.

Der Kaiser hat abgedankt!

Der Reichskanzler hat folgenden Erlaß herausgegeben:

Seine Majestät der Kaiser und König haben sich entschlossen, dem Throne zu entsagen.

Der Reichskanzler bleibt noch so lange im Amte, bis die mit der Abdankung Seiner Majestät, dem Thronverzichte Seiner Kaiserlichen und Königlichen Hoheit des Kronprinzen des Deutschen Reichs und von Preußen und der Einsetzung der Regentschaft verbundenen Fragen geregelt sind. Er beabsichtigt, dem Regenten die Ernennung des Abgeordneten Ebert zum Reichskanzler und die Vorlage eines Gesetzentwurfs wegen der Ausschreibung allgemeiner Wahlen für eine verfassunggebende deutsche Nationalversammlung vorzuschlagen, der es obliegen würde, die künftige Staatsform des deutschen Volk, einschließlich der Volksteile, die ihren Eintritt in die Reichsgrenzen wünschen sollten, endgültig festzustellen.

Berlin, den 9. November 1918. **Der Reichskanzler.**

Prinz Max von Baden.

Es wird nicht geschossen!

Der Reichskanzler hat angeordnet, daß seitens des Militärs von der Waffe kein Gebrauch gemacht werde.

Parteigenossen! Arbeiter! Soldaten!

Soeben sind das Alexanderregiment und die vierten Jäger geschlossen zum Volke übergegangen. Der sozialdemokratische Reichstagsabgeordnete Wels u. a. haben zu den Truppen gesprochen. Offiziere haben sich den Soldaten angeschlossen.

Der sozialdemokratische Arbeiter- und Soldatenrat.

BOTTOM: *Left-wing revolutionaries stand aboard a truck with two machine guns at the ready while guarding the Brandenburger Tor, Berlin. The uprising was later put down with considerable bloodshed.*

ABOVE: *Bolshevik leader V I Lenin (black suit and coat) walks across Red Square with his military leaders. Faced with White counter-revolutionaries and Allied intervention the Bolsheviks were forced to expand the Red Army in order to keep power.*

RIGHT: *Some of the leading figures in the Bolshevik party. On the far left stands Leon Trotsky who led the Red Army during the civil war years, and on the far right is Josef Stalin, who gained power after Lenin's death and progressively assumed the role of an autocratic dictator.*

BELOW: *President Wilson of America and President Poincaré of France (right) at a parade in Paris in 1918. While Wilson argued for a broadly idealistic approach to the postwar settlement, the French and their other allies favored far harsher terms.*

BOTTOM: *World War I was to lead to another world war some 20 years later. The experience of the first great war was to mold its stamp on the leaders of the second. In this photograph of German troops on the Western Front, Corporal Adolf Hitler is on the far left.*

The victorious Allies wreaked their revenge on Germany. The Treaty of Versailles, signed on 28 June 1919, was harsh, although no harsher than the terms imposed on the Bolsheviks by the Germans at Brest-Litovsk. The German army was reduced to 100,000 men, all volunteers. Tanks and aircraft were banned, and the navy was severely limited in size. Territorial annexations were made. Alsace-Lorraine went to France, Eupen and Malmedy to Belgium, and, most controversially, a 'corridor' of land was given to the newly independent state of Poland, which divided East Prussia from the rest of Germany. Reparations were to be paid to the victorious powers. The grievances of Germany were to plant the seeds of World War II.

The impact of the war on the social and political fabric of Europe was immense. Democracy collapsed in Italy in 1922, when Mussolini's Fascists came to power. It survived until 1933 in Germany, when the Weimar Republic was dismantled by Hitler, the victim of economic pressures and its unwelcome birthright, the *diktat* of Versailles. The myth grew in Germany that their army had not been defeated in 1918, it had been 'stabbed in the back' by the 'November Criminals.' Britain and France were swept by pacifism and anti-militarism in the late 1920s and early 1930s; few bothered to nail this lie. Democracy survived in these countries, but neither was the power it had been in 1914. France reacted against the losses of war and adopted a defensive mentality, epitomized by the construction of the Maginot Line to defend her borders. As a corporal, M Maginot had fought at Verdun. Britain's Prime Minister from 1929 to 1935 was Ramsay MacDonald, the pacifist of 1914; this too was symbolic of Britain's inter-war mentality.

The publication of Remarque's *All Quiet on the Western Front* in 1929 was followed by a series of cathartic books on the war by ex-soldiers of all nations. When the Nazis began to make threatening moves in 1935, the war-weary democracies were in no mental state to oppose them. 'Appeasement,' not firmness, was the policy of Britain and France. This was perhaps the greatest tragedy of the 'war to end all wars.' It proved to be merely the first installment of a European civil war that lasted from 1914 to 1945, with a 20-year truce intervening. The Allied war machine, at such fine pitch in 1918, was dismantled. The United States turned her back on Europe. Wilson's brainchild, the League of Nations, was, without American participation, stillborn. The Allies had to begin all over again in 1939-45. By the end of that war, no European power counted for very much. The extra-European powers who had emerged onto the world stage in 1917 were now dominant: the United States and the Soviet Union.

SELECT BIBLIOGRAPHY

Ashworth, T, *Trench Warfare 1914-18*. 1980
Bennett, G, *Naval Battles of the First World War*. 1983
Bidwell, S and Graham, D, *Firepower: British Army Weapons and Theories of War 1904-1945*. 1982
Bond, B, *War and Society in Europe 1870-1970*. 1984
Cruttwell, C R M F, *A History of the Great War, 1914-18*. 1934
Dixon, N, *On the Psychology of Military Incompetence*. 1976
Edmonds, J, *A Short History of World War One*. 1951
Falls, C, *The First World War*. 1960
Fussell, P, *The Great War and Modern Memory*. 1975
Griffith, P, *Forward into Battle*. 1982
Gooch, J, *Armies in Europe* 1980
Keegan, J, *The Face of Battle*. 1975
Marwick, A, *War and Social Change in the Twentieth Century*. 1974
Middlebrook, M, *The First Day on the Somme*. 1971
Simpkins, P, *Air Fighting 1914-18*. 1978
Stone, N, *The Eastern Front 1914-1917*. 1975
Strachan, H, *European Armies and the Conduct of War*. 1982
Terraine, J, *The Smoke and the Fire*. 1980

ACKNOWLEDGMENTS

The author would like to acknowledge the help of the following people: his colleagues, past and present, in the Department of War Studies, Royal Military Academy Sandhurst, and especially Mr Keith Simpson, Dr John Pimlott and Dr Ian Beckett; Mrs Pam Jones, who typed the manuscript, the Librarian and staff of the Central Library at RMA Sandhurst, and the staff of Welwyn Garden City Library, and in particular Miss Vivienne Davis.

The publisher would like to thank all the picture agencies and individuals listed below and particularly The Imperial War Museum, London, who supplied all the illustrations except for the following:

BBC Hulton Picture Library pages: 4-5, 17 (bottom), 44 (bottom), 45 (bottom), 49 (top), 52 (bottom), 64 (both), 102 (bottom), 102-3, 104 (top), 127, 130 (bottom right), 133 (top), 140 (top), 141 (both), 144 (middle), 146 (bottom), 151 (left), 153 (bottom), 161 (top), 171 (bottom), 176 (bottom), 177 (both), 193 (top), 194 (middle), 196 (bottom), 225 (top), 232 (bottom), 233 (bottom)

Bison Picture Library pages: 20 (top), 29 (top), 40-1, 57 (top), 86-7, 109 (top), 113 (top), 142 (top), 171 (top left), 179 (top), 201 (bottom), 216-7, 218 (top)

John Frost Newspapers page: 117 (top)

Archiv Gerstenberg pages: 10, 12 (top), 14 (both), 15, 18 (bottom right), 19 (both), 26 (both), 27, 30 (bottom), 31, 33 (top), 34 (top), 34 (bottom left), 37 (right), 38 (bottom & top left), 39 (bottom), 43 (left), 46-7, 72 (both), 73, 76 (bottom), 77 (both), 81 (top), 84, 85, 88 (both), 104 (bottom left), 106 (top), 110, 126, 128 (top), 129 (bottom), 146 (top), 147 (middle), 157, 161 (bottom right), 165 (top), 166 (both), 167, 170 (right), 180 (top), 205 (top), 229 (top right), 231 (both), 234, 235 (bottom), 236 (both).

Robert Hunt Library pages: 18 (top), 21 (bottom right), 22-3, 25 (top), 28 (bottom), 30 (top), 32 (bottom), 36-7 (top & bottom), 40 (top), 42, 44 (top), 45 (top), 48 (both), 50 (bottom), 51 (top), 53 (top), 56 (top), 60, 62 (bottom), 66 (top), 68 (bottom), 70, 71 (top & bottom right), 75, 80, 87 (top), 89 (bottom), 90-1, 92 (top), 92-3, 96, 104 (bottom right), 107 (bottom), 109 (bottom), 118 (bottom), 121 (top), 123 (top), 124 (bottom), 126 (bottom), 128 (bottom), 129 (top), 130 (bottom left), 131 (bottom), 132 (bottom), 133 (bottom), 135 (top), 144 (both), 145 (both), 147 (bottom), 148, 152, 154, 155 (both), 164 (bottom), 169 (top), 170 (left), 172 (bottom), 176 (bottom), 186 (top), 194 (top), 195 (bottom), 198, 199 (top), 200, 202 (top), 203 (bottom), 206, 207 (both), 210 (top), 212 (top), 214 (top), 214-5, 217 (top), 219 (bottom), 222 (bottom), 223 (bottom), 224 (bottom), 225 (bottom), 227 (bottom), 230 (top)

The Mansell Collection pages: 25 (bottom), 34 (bottom left), 115 (top), 125 (bottom), 168 (both), 179 (bottom)

The Museum of London page: 178 (bottom)

National Army Musuem, London page: 174 (bottom)

Richard Natkiel maps on pages: 39 (both), 46, 69, 93, 96

Peter Newark Historical Pictures page: 83 (bottom right)

Novosti Press Agency pages: 2 (bottom left), 36 (left), 38 (bottom right), 43 (top left), 94 (top), 165 (bottom)

Official US Air Force Photo page: 171 (top right)

TPS pages: 12 (bottom), 144 (bottom)

TPS/Keystone pages: 41 (top), 169 (bottom), 236 (both)

TPS/Three Lions pages 13 (both), 62 (top), 71 (bottom left), 82 (top), 195 (top), 235 (top left)

Ulster Museum page: 103 (bottom)

US National Archives pages: 1, 215 (top), 217 (bottom), 232 (top)

INDEX